GREEN
IS THE
NEW
RED

GREEN
IS THE
NEW
RED

An Insider's Account
of a Social Movement Under Siege

Will Potter

City Lights Books | San Francisco

Library of Congress Cataloging-in-Publication Data

Potter, Will, 1980–
 Green is the new red : an insiders account of a social movement under siege /
Will Potter.
     p. cm.
 Includes bibliographical references.
 ISBN 978-0-87286-538-9
 1. Green movement—United States. 2. Ecoterrorism—United States.
 3. Environmentalists—United States. I. Title.
 GE197.P68 2011
 320.5'80973—dc22
                        2010053209

City Lights Books are published at the City Lights Bookstore,
261 Columbus Avenue, San Francisco, CA 94133.

Visit our website: www.citylights.com

For Madre.
Roses will bloom.

Here comes the future and you can't run from it
If you've got a blacklist I want to be on it
—Billy Bragg

CONTENTS

CHAPTER ONE

Blacklisted

June 3, 2007 For a few seconds at a time, today feels like any other day, maybe even like a vacation, and Daniel McGowan forgets what he knows will happen tomorrow. The wind blows west through Oregon's Willamette National Forest, rustling the dense lower patchwork of vine maple, dogwood and red alder. The rodlike Douglas firs pay no attention to the breeze as they reach over two hundred feet to the sun, just as they have for three hundred, four hundred, five hundred years. If he breathes deeply enough, McGowan might smell tansy in the wind, or perhaps it's camphor; so many wild things have grown over each other and into each other for so long it's hard to tell which. If he breathes deeper still, he might taste the white water of Fall Creek before seeing or hearing it. He breathes in, pulls the wind and creek and forest deep into his lungs, and slowly releases them. Then McGowan remembers that at nine o'clock on Monday morning he'll be wearing his best suit, the black one with three buttons, and he'll be sitting quietly with his hands folded in his lap, staring blankly ahead, while a U.S. District Court judge sentences him to prison as a terrorist.

He steals a few more seconds and fights off thoughts of tomorrow. He tries to forget that his statement to the court needs another practice reading, that his press release needs editing, and that his dad, his sister and his wife, Jenny Synan, will be sitting on rigid

1

pews in the front row of the courtroom, silently crying. Right now McGowan has paused on the trail to Fall Creek, with his nose three inches away from a stegosaurus of an ant walking along a smooth moist stone. He yells to his wife, standing right behind him. "Jenny, check this out!" He is crouching, hands on his knees, mouth open and smiling, tongue poking out the left side. "My niece Lily would be so excited," he says. "Lily loves bugs."

This is one Daniel McGowan, Daniel the Uncle. The Daniel who knows everything Lily loves and doesn't love, all of her favorite stories and favorite jokes and who says, in one excited breath, "Did I tell you what Lily did the other day seriously she is so goddamn adorable I can't even tell you." There may be a thousand more Daniels. How many depends on who you ask. Federal prosecutors say there are Djenni, Dylan Kay, Jamie Moran, Sorrel, Rabid: the aliases he used during his underground life when he destroyed genetically engineered crops and helped commit two arsons as part of the Earth Liberation Front. McGowan earned one of the names after hiking near this same creek years ago, when a friend showed him the edible, heart-shaped leaves of the sorrel herb. McGowan ate the plant by the handful. "It gave me the shits," he says. His mouth is now full of the green foliage, and as he follows the trail he periodically reaches for more, having either forgotten the past or made a concerted effort not to remember.

At least two more Daniels walk through the forest this afternoon, Today's Daniel and Tomorrow's Daniel. Like the others, they curse like sailors, the sons of an Irish New York City cop from Queens. Today's Daniel takes center stage, cracking jokes and performing for his small audience, a handful of somber friends. Most of all he tries desperately to make his wife smile. As if bracing for her husband's terrorism sentencing were not difficult enough, Synan has had sneezing fits, watery eyes and shortness of breath since stepping off the plane yesterday. Burr-ragweed, mugwort, vetch, fireweed, smotherweed, knotweed, smartweed, barnyard grass, cock's-spur grass, false rye grass, quaking grass, panic grass. They may not all be here in the forest right now, but they are somewhere in the wind, finding their way to Synan's nose. Brooklyn has less-than-pristine air, full of taxicab exhaust and godknowswhatelse, but at least concrete doesn't make you sneeze. Not as much, at least. On their first date, back in New York, McGowan brought Synan a bouquet of allergy medicine. "This is nature, Jenny, na-a-a-ture," he says to her now, grinning. Synan looks too exhausted to laugh, but he persists. "Jenny! Jenny!" he shouts, pointing to the trees behind her. "Watch out for pygmies!" She rolls her red eyes.

Today's Daniel must also remember the two-man camera crew that has followed him for six months, trying to film every fundraiser, happy hour and family gathering for a documentary about his case. Their clock is ticking. Once McGowan reports to prison they will have limited opportunities to tape him, even fewer if he reports to a maximum-security facility. McGowan does not want their only footage to be of Defeated Daniel. What message would that send to the FBI? What message would that send to the movement?

McGowan wears a wireless microphone that peeks out of the top of his black T-shirt. The battery pack hooks onto his black shorts, cut well below his knees. He approaches the water. He keeps his game face on, giving the filmmakers the sound bites, monologues and close-ups they need, but never letting them too close. If the mood feels too heavy, he redirects the conversation. He pulls a six-pack of microbrewed beer from a nook made by two rocks in the creek, where friends had placed it to chill. He hoists it triumphantly. "Look, we caught some wild beer!" Sometime in the same act, different scene, McGowan pauses briefly and turns back to the camera crew. "I think we're getting some interference. Do you want me to ask the river to be quiet? Want me to unplug that shit?"

Tomorrow's Daniel is always nearby, though, and now he takes a seat on the river rock. He rails against activist groups like the Rainforest Action Network and Ruckus Society, groups he has volunteered with for years, groups that refused to speak out against the government labeling him a terrorist. McGowan and his attorneys volunteered to write a letter to the court if only the groups would lend their name and credibility. But these national organizations didn't want to publicly support a saboteur. That's understandable, McGowan says, but can't they at least say destroying genetically engineered crops is not the same as flying planes into buildings?

McGowan's friends try to fight off tomorrow. Talk of creeks and water prompts someone to ask if McGowan has ever been to the nude beach off the McKenzie River. "I really love nudie rock," he says. "You throw yourself in and man you just go shooting down this whitewater and you pop up and it's totally amazing." Someone in the group has jumped into the water, and McGowan's friends coax him. Jump! JUMP! Someone says this may be his last opportunity to swim in fresh water for six to eight years. "Maybe you should just throw yourself in," Synan says, "and see where it takes you."

While his friends pop open another round of beers and begin to speculate about what prison life will entail, McGowan breaks away from the group and meanders along the cold creek, letting his skin feel the damp moss. He is between worlds. Having stepped out of the forest, but not yet touched the water, he walks softly, balances carefully, step by step along the edge. A few more steps and he pauses on a large riparian stone. It has been carved into a gentle parabola not by drastic action but by steady, patient pressure. McGowan sits, then folds his arms across his knees as he pulls them to his chest; he turns and stares upstream. Enough sunlight falls through holes in the old-growth forest canopy to make the creek shimmer like broken glass. He could listen to water all day, he has said before. He listens. Listens to the tone, pitch, melody and rhythm of the current. A song playing far too softly to penetrate thick walls of concrete and steel and remorse to reach McGowan, sitting alone, in a prison cell.

He returns to the group, now in the midst of yet another conversation about prison life, prison location, prison sentences, prison behavior and prison food. McGowan's attorneys will request that he report to the Federal Correctional Institution in Fort Dix, New Jersey. It's a low-security facility—not the usual stop for a convicted terrorist, but McGowan has no violent history and thinks the Bureau of Prisons will grant his request. At Fort Dix, Synan and his family could make the hour-and-a-half trip south to visit. After McGowan's sentencing, though, paperwork and protocol could last five or six weeks before prison. His friends worry that instead of spending those weeks free, with Synan, he'll have to report to the Metropolitan Detention Center—"The Abu Ghraib of Brooklyn." Arab men rounded up after 9/11 have accused the guards of beating them, violating them during body cavity searches, parading them naked before female guards and calling them "Muslim bastards." The government later deported the detainees, but admitted they were not terrorists.

As the forest darkens, McGowan announces to the camera that he has decided on his sentencing statement. "I am sorry, Your Honor," he'll say. "I have an overacting part of the brain where badassness is located." He gets a few laughs, but gray dusk approaches, followed by darkness, making it harder and harder to forget tomorrow.

On the way back to Eugene, Oregon, the group stops at a gas station for snacks. A small sign that reads "Solar Power" hangs near pumps that, upon closer inspection, contain reservoirs for fuel connoisseurs: various microbrews of gasoline and bioethanol crafted to reduce emissions and, through domestic production, perhaps reduce unsavory wars for oil. The roof is a dense thatch of greens, yellows, oranges, purples and blues, an organic insulating layer of local flowers that keeps the store cooler in warm times and warmer in cool times. The flowers sink roots into what they must think is Oregon soil, only at some point to meet a rubber water barrier, and underneath that, steel or aluminum or wood, and underneath that, a convenience store gone green.

In similar areas—not quite suburban, not quite rural—gas stations often sell hunks of deer jerky, fresh cured and sitting in a tray on the counter. Coolers along the wall contain Lone Star, the national beer of Texas, and Bud or Miller Lite. Shelves hold toilet paper, more jerky, and motor oil. Behind the counter, nudie magazines and, if you ask the clerk, probably some shotgun shells. This gas station outside of Eugene sells vegan donuts and brownies, sitting in a wicker basket on the counter. Coolers along the wall contain fresh, local, organic greens and cheeses. Shelves hold 100 percent recycled toilet paper, more vegan brownies and peppermint toothpaste not tested on animals. Behind the counter, a full-service espresso bar, and the beans are all organic, fair trade, shade-grown.

"Soy latte?"

"Please," Synan says.

The barista eyes the group, including the two filmmakers who walk in to shoot McGowan perusing organic tortilla chips and salsa. Synan sees an opportunity and tells the woman about her husband's case. The barista says she thinks she heard about that somewhere, and didn't it involve torching some Hummers? Well, Synan says, some things like that have certainly happened, but not in McGowan's case. Oh, the barista says, she really hates those jerks in their Hummers. Synan doesn't miss a beat, urging her to visit SupportDaniel.org and to attend the hearing tomorrow. McGowan will need all the support he can get.

Five years earlier It's nine in the morning. My girlfriend, Kamber, sleeps on the futon, exhausted from a night shift as a sous-chef at the Chicago Diner, a local vegetarian restaurant. Her hands perch on her chest. They always ache from hours of chopping carrots, potatoes and hunks of faux meat. I put on my shoes and say goodbye to the dogs, Mindy and Peter. Mindy is part chihuahua, part dachshund, with one ear pointed and one ear floppy. She's short and sturdy, maybe a bit chubby. Peter looks like a compressed greyhound. He has a runner's legs, sinewy and taut, which I envy. He has a way with the ladies, which I also envy. He always cries when I leave. Just as I place my hand on the doorknob, someone knocks three times.

I turn the knob without looking through the peephole. It must be the landlord. Again. He's gotten into the habit of arriving un-announced with prospective tenants. He says he likes showing our apartment, one of the freshly renovated studios in the seventy-some-thing-year-old building in Lincoln Park, because it's so "clean" and "uncluttered" (meaning we can't afford more than the futon). I think he also likes the way Mindy rolls on her back for him. Even though I'm still groggy, I'm prepared to tear into him, in hushed breaths so not to wake Kamber, and say that if he wants to interrupt us at all hours we need a rent reduction, and not fifty dollars or some non-sense like that. Before I open the door, though, I know it's not Steve the Landlord. The dogs are barking. Mindy and Peter are snarling, and they never snarl, they never growl. I open the door anyway.

God and Darwin work together sometimes, scheming a kind of divine natural selection, predetermining certain people for certain occupations. This is not to say that a seven-foot-two man cannot rise beyond a basketball stereotype or that boys named Devendra must become hippie poet laureates wearing beaded vests and braided beards. It just seems natural. And these guys, with their manicured goatees, navy blue suits, broad shoulders, hard jawlines, wholesome haircuts and eyes looking for a fight—these guys are just naturally FBI agents. I don't even need to see the badges.

I say I'm in a hurry and have to get ready for work, and then I start to close the door, as if they're kids selling third-tier magazines for an alleged school basketball team. The good cop—or I'll call him the good cop, only because he looks less eager to kick my ass—puts his left palm on the gray steel door. I can either come downstairs, he says, or they can visit me at work, the *Chicago Tribune*.

The dogs bark. Panic. I'm not afraid of them, but I am afraid of a spectacle in the newsroom. I say okay. I gently close the door, hoping that Kamber, a few feet away, might sleep through all of this, hoping that, if I'm quiet enough, I can tiptoe my way out of my apartment and out of my skin. I roll up my right pant leg so it won't catch in my bike chain and I pick up my road bike. What's going on, Kamber says. It's the FBI, I say matter-of-factly, just as if it had been Steve the Landlord.

We cram into the freight elevator, Good Cop, Bad Cop, my bicycle and me. I don't know what to do with my eyes. I look at Good Cop and he looks at my bike, peering over his slightly bulging midriff and down at the hubs, bending to see the crank arms and the rear derailleur. He seems like the kind of guy I cross paths with downtown who climbs out of his SUV, with pleated khakis and blue polo, and says something like, "How far do you ride?" And no matter what I reply, three miles or thirty miles, he says, "Oh, that's not bad at all." The elevator grinds to a halt, the latticework steel door creaks open, and we walk through the dark hallway to the alley. It is a gloriously sunny Chicago summer day, but the sunlight cannot overcome the condominium towers of steel and glass, cannot swim through the cracks in the walls, and so I step into an alley shrouded in gray.

In college, I had learned about government programs like COINTELPRO and the tactics the FBI had used to harass and intimidate political activists. False names, phone taps, bugs, infiltration. I had learned from books, from professors and from Law & Order episodes that if approached by the FBI, for any reason, you should never talk. Nothing good can come of it. They are not trying to be your friends, they are not trying to help you. You should simply say, "I don't have anything to say to you. You may contact my lawyer."

Both Good Cop and Bad Cop had heard that line before.

"Look, we just want to talk to you," Good Cop says. "We want you to help us out. We can make all this go away."

I laugh. He becomes angry. I open my mouth, even though I know I shouldn't.

Working long hours on the metro desk at the *Chicago Tribune*, covering shooting after shooting, interposed only by obituaries and more death, turned me into the reporter I had never wanted to become. For months I had felt detached, apathetic and cynical. About a month before the visit from the FBI, I wrote in my journal: "I'm tired of writing meaningless stories, I'm tired of going to sleep at night feeling like I left the world the same way I saw it in the morning." I was haunted by one afternoon at another newspaper, the *Arlington Morning News*, when I was eighteen. At a sleepover, after his pals had tired of roughhousing, playing games and watching television, a twelve-year-old boy decided to show his buddies his father's gun. It was fired. A best friend was killed.

My editor had told me not to come back without the story. It was a poor, North Texas suburban neighborhood, predominantly Mexican immigrants, the kind of place where most folks use pay phones as their home phones. I knocked on doors, found a translator, and interviewed the boy's sobbing mother and glass-eyed friends. One of his friends, who had not even the first soft sprouts of facial hair, stopped me as I walked to my car. He said that that morning, when he stood near the police tape and watched the spectacle, a butterfly landed on his shoulder, slowly raising and lowering and raising its wings, refusing to fly away from the flashing blue-and-whites and punctuating wails. He said his friend had become that butterfly. Didn't I think so? Of course, I said. Couldn't I please put that in my story?

When I returned to the newsroom, I told my editor I had enough for an article. She told me to have fifteen column inches in an hour. After I turned and walked to my desk, I heard her yell to the night editor. "Scratch that. Potter got something. Bump back that other piece and make room for this one. You can slug it 'deadkid.'" Dead kid. Two words that could quickly identify the story in editorial meetings while distancing reporters and editors from any emotional attachment to the boy, any sense of responsibility to his family, and any memory beyond a solid clip on page one.

I had told myself I would never become that kind of reporter. I would not put up that wall, even if, like one copy editor I will never forget, it meant keeping a fifth of Jack Daniels in the file cabinet, even if, like another reporter I knew, it meant snorting cocaine in the bathroom stall. Even if the grief slowly burned away at my stomach lining and my heart.

After only a few months into my stint at the *Tribune*, I had already built a spectacular wall of emotional detachment. It felt as if it were made of broken bottles and concrete chunks, sharp and gray. I would never survive this beat, I thought, unless I found some way to keep a toehold on my humanity. I did not have the gumption for Jack Daniels or cocaine. Instead, a friend, whom I had met at a journalism conference, offered me the email addresses of a few local animal advocacy groups.

I had gone vegetarian in 1998 and vegan six months later. At the University of Texas, I had worked with a few activist groups to campaign against the economic sanctions on Iraq, serve free vegetarian food on campus, and organize a film and lecture series on journalism issues. I did not think it would be appropriate to take a leadership role in any organization while working at the *Tribune*. Newspapers sometimes frown upon their reporters moonlighting with advocacy groups, unless it's something no one would publicly oppose, like promoting the Rev. Dr. Martin Luther King Jr.'s birthday or feeding Sally Struthers's children. But one month prior to the FBI agents knocking on my door, I'd decided to spend an afternoon leafleting.

Kamber and I met six local activists at the A-Zone, or

Autonomous Zone, which was part independent bookstore and part rabble-rouser gathering place. It offered titles on topics including the Zapatistas, herbal medicine and bicycle repair. From there we caravanned to Lake Forest, a suburb north of Chicago and the home of a corporate executive with Marsh Inc., an insurance company for an animal testing lab called Huntingdon Life Sciences. I had learned about Huntingdon while working on a story at the *Texas Observer*. My story mentioned a group called Stop Huntingdon Animal Cruelty, or SHAC, that pressured corporations to sever ties with the lab after multiple undercover investigations exposed animal welfare violations.

The goal of that Sunday afternoon was simply to pass out leaflets in the neighborhood of the Marsh insurance executive. We split up in pairs and hung fliers on brass and brushed-steel doorknobs. The front of the fliers featured one of two photographs, either a monkey or a beagle puppy in a cage. On the back was a short history of the lab and its abuses, and a request that readers urge their neighbor to cease doing business with Huntingdon. The fliers made no suggestion of violence or property destruction, and they made no threats. They spelled out what went on in the lab, how Marsh was connected, and why readers should ask their neighbor to take action.

After about twenty minutes, we had not made much progress. The heavy wooden front doors sat confidently at the end of long, immaculate walkways that looked as if they'd never been trod. This was the type of neighborhood where people pulled their Mercedes or BMW straight into the garage. When we finally reached the executive's cul-de-sac, a security guard stood outside videotaping. Not to be outdone, one of the leafletters—the youngest in the group, at about sixteen—pulled out a camera of his own and began filming the security guard filming him. Later, the guard, Al Cancel, wrote a voluntary statement for the police saying that activists "were now begining [sic] to sarround [sic] me causeing [sic] me to back away so they could not get behind me. Then the one I attempted to speak with directed the other seven in milatary [sic] fashion to film me. . . ." The young activist's video footage showed the security guard on the phone telling police, "They're not doing anything. They're passing out leaflets. You should get over here though."

Squad cars arrived. Police questioned us. More squad cars arrived. The police sat us on the grass, like parents who were about to discipline bickering children but must first decide who did what to whom. They confiscated the leaflets. One cop with aviator sunglasses looked at a leaflet, tilted his head down and peered at us over the gold rim of his sunglasses. The Mercedes, BMW and Lexus SUVs driving by slowed down to a crawl and rubbernecked at the young group surrounded by police. One woman with big hair, a silver sedan and a low-cut tank top lowered her window and leaned out. "Officer! Officer!" She flapped a leaflet at him. "I thought you might need this," she said. "As evidence."

"Thanks, ma'am. We have the situation under control."

A few of the detainees peppered the cops with questions. Why were we being detained? What did we do wrong? If we were putting up fliers for a landscaping service, would we have been stopped? One cop said that this executive's house had been vandalized months before. He said we might have been the ones who did it.

Everyone laughed. I sat cross-legged, picking at the ground between my legs, and I could not help but laugh, too. Why would anyone vandalize someone's home and then return to pass out leaflets?

The cops walked over to Al the Security Guard and talked for a few minutes. When they came back, they said we were being arrested. They would not say what the charge was, and they wouldn't tell us what we had done wrong. We were handcuffed, divided into squad cars, and taken to the police station. Most of the group was in good spirits, because we all assumed the bogus charges would just get thrown out in court. At the station, the officers took mug shots and asked if we had tattoos.

Kim Berardi, wearing a sleeveless shirt exposing a tattoo of a sunflower, with curls of wind twisting around the stem and around her biceps, looked at the officer and, straight-faced, said no. "I draw these on every day," Kim said. "They're washable." The cops and the kids all laughed. Kim looked at me. "Oh man," she said, "Will looks totally pissed. What, are you going to lose your big shot job for leafleting?"

After the FBI agents follow me out of the apartment building and into the alley, Bad Cop starts needling. You were leafleting on a campaign where people have been breaking windows and harassing people, he says. "Just look at the people you were arrested with." He reads names. "Kim Berardi, she has a criminal record taller than she is."

Maybe, I think. She's the shortest woman I know.

"We just want your help," he says. "We need your help finding out more about these people. You could help us."

I should just walk away, I think. There is no reason to be standing here. Nothing good can come of it. He says I have two days to decide. He gives me a scrap of paper with his phone number written on it underneath his name, Chris.

"If we don't hear from you by the first trial date in Lake Forest," he says, "I'll put you on the domestic terrorist list."

Walk away, walk away, walk . . . wait, what? My face feels expressionless, but my eyes must show fear.

"Now I have your attention, huh?"

I can't bite my tongue. Put me on a terrorist list for leafleting? Later, in my journal, I will write as much as I can remember from what he says. "Look," Chris says, "After 9/11 we have a lot more authority now to get things done and get down to business. We can make your life very difficult for you. You work at newspapers? I can make it so you never work at a newspaper again. And Kamber, her scholarships? Say goodbye to them. I can place one call and have all those taken away. Those scholarship committees don't want terrorists as recipients."

I have a Fulbright application pending, and Kamber is preparing for a PhD program in psychology.

Good Cop speaks up. "I can tell you're a good guy," he says. "You have a lot going for you." He says he can tell by the way I dress, where I live. He says he knows my dad cosigned on the apartment, and the FBI knows where he works. "I know you wouldn't have gotten the job at the *Tribune* if you didn't have a lot of promise. You don't want this to mess up your life, kid. We need your help."

I want to walk away, but I am so goddamn angry now I can't. People who write letters, who leaflet, aren't the same people who break the law. "I thought you guys would have figured that out." I crumple his phone number in front of him and toss it in a nearby dumpster. I straddle my bike.

As I pedal off, just before I leave the shadows and reach the sunlight, Chris says: "Have a good day at work at the Metro desk. Say hello to your editor, Susan Keaton. And tell Kamber we'll come see her later."

After I arrive at Tribune Tower, after I report to my editor and settle at my desk with a story assignment—more murder on the South Side—I come undone. My left hand shakes. Strangling the phone so my fingers stop twitching, hunching to look as if I'm interviewing, whispering so colleagues can't hear, I call Kamber. I tell her to deadbolt the door while staying on the phone, to walk past any FBI agents on the way to work, and to think about telling her coworkers in case cops show up asking questions. Don't worry, she says, the guys in the kitchen all hate *la policía*. I scan the newsroom. Do they already know? They know. Right? That Fed, the one who probably manicures his pornstar goatee every morning while listening to Rush Limbaugh, might already be flashing his badge downstairs; his pal, the one who looks like he bought some kind of shrink-wrapped FBI starter kit, with too-short slacks, bad tie, worse haircut, might show up any minute.

He doesn't. But as days go by, I keep thinking that he will. I become the undead. I should be calling sources, I should be writing. I have deadlines looming, but all I can think about is how I am on a domestic terrorist list. I'm convinced my professional life is over. Even worse, I'm convinced these FBI agents will somehow pass the word on to my parents, who will be so disappointed in me, and to my little sister, who'll stop looking up to me. These thoughts burrow somewhere deep in my brain and, no matter how irrational they sound, I begin to see them as truth.

Will the FBI agents make sure I don't receive my Fulbright grant? I want to follow up on a series I wrote for the *Arlington Morning News* about a peace program that brings teens from Northern Ireland to live with host families in the United States. I won a national award from the Society of Professional Journalists for the series, and a slew of professors, editors and teens wrote letters supporting a follow-up project. If I am denied the grant, will it be because of intense competition, or because I'm now on a blacklist? If Kamber is denied full funding for her PhD program, will it be because of budget cuts, or because of an anonymous phone call? If I am denied newspaper jobs I've applied for in Washington, D.C., will it be because of my qualifications, or because I'm now a "terrorist"? Day after day, I go to work, crank out an assignment, come home and sit quietly with the dogs. I don't talk to Kamber, and when I do I snap or scream at her.

During the car ride home from the first, preliminary court date in Lake Forest, Kamber mentions the FBI visit. One of the defendants, Mike Everson, turns to me while driving, and for a few painful moments he does not even speak. He isn't surprised that this has happened, he says, but he doesn't understand why I wouldn't have mentioned such news to the rest of the defendants. I want to explain how I've been consumed by my own fears, but I am barely able to mumble, "Sorry, I know I should have said something." He looks at me with what feels like distrust and contempt.

I am a coward. The history nerd in me cannot help but think

about all the times when the government has targeted political activists. I think about the deportation of Emma Goldman, the murder of the Haymarket martyrs, the bombing of the MOVE home, the attacks on the American Indian Movement and the relentless spying and harassment of Dr. King. I have always hoped, as we all do after reading stories like this, that if I were ever put in a similar position I would not flinch. Instead I feel ashamed, not of something I have said or something I have done—I never consider, even for a moment, becoming an informant—but ashamed that any of this has affected me. Here I sit, a twenty-two-year-old white heterosexual American male, the most privileged of the privileged, turned inside out because of a class C misdemeanor and a knock on the door. Here I sit. Afraid.

I do not know it right now, but this experience will mark the beginning of both a personal and a political journey. After the initial fear subsides, I will become obsessed with finding out *why* I would be targeted as a terrorist for doing nothing more than leafleting. It will lead me to a New Jersey courthouse where activists stand accused of animal enterprise terrorism, to Congress where I'll testify against eco-terrorism legislation, and to a green gas station outside Eugene with Daniel McGowan. I will realize that, although I cannot undo this arrest and I cannot negotiate with those FBI agents, I can choose my role in the script before me.

But today I do not know any of this. Today I only know fear.

With thoughts of Shiner Bock and skinny-dipping in Barton Springs, we decide to move back to Austin. The leafleting case is, as the other defendants suspected it would be, dismissed. Kamber and I pack up our few belongings and prepare for the journey home. I have dreaded moving day, not because of any attachment to Chicago—I've grown to loathe this town—but because I don't want to walk downstairs, through the marble lobby with its Corinthian columns and Victorian couches, and enter Steve the Landlord's office to turn in our keys. He knows. He must know.

The building is old but secure. The FBI agents did not have to kick down any doors when they visited. They flashed badges and were escorted inside. They probably told Steve that Kamber and I were suspected terrorists, and that this was a national security matter that needed urgent attention. Perhaps they showed him my photo, film noir style. Would he even buzz me into his office? Would he ask me to slide the keys under the door, to keep me at a safe distance? Would he refuse to return my security deposit, because there was a "no terrorist" clause in the fine print of the lease?

I open his door and walk up to his desk as he speaks with a couple of prospective tenants. I try to silently slip the keys across the desk, but they jangle like jailer's keys and the sound of metal on wood echoes up into the vaulted ceiling. I turn, exhale and walk away. He calls after me when I'm almost to the doorway. Here it comes, I think.

"Hey Will," he says. I turn to face him. "Give 'em hell."

CHAPTER TWO

War at Home

May 26, 2004 Attorney General John Ashcroft and FBI Director Robert Mueller are holding a press conference at the J. Edgar Hoover building in Washington, D.C. Mueller stands at Ashcroft's right side, hands behind his back. "Credible intelligence from multiple sources indicates that Al Qaeda plans to attempt an attack on the United States in the next few months," Ashcroft says slowly, laboriously. "This disturbing intelligence indicates Al Qaeda's specific intention to hit the United States hard."

The announcement is shocking because it confirms unspoken fears. Two months ago, as thousands of people commuted into Madrid just three days before the general elections, ten bombs full of nails and scraps of metal exploded on Spain's train system and killed one hundred and ninety-one people. Nearly eighteen hundred were injured. The Spanish Judiciary said the terrorist cell that coordinated the attack was inspired by Al Qaeda, but distinct from it. It was the worst attack in Spain since Basque separatists bombed a supermarket in 1987, and the worst attack in Europe since Libyan terrorists bombed Pan American Flight 103 near Lockerbie, Scotland in 1988.

After the Madrid bombings, Spanish cops gave the FBI digital images of fingerprints found on plastic bags containing detonator caps. The FBI announced that the prints belonged to Brandon

Mayfield, an attorney from Oregon. Agents held him for two weeks without charge. In the press and in the courts, he was smeared as a terrorist. Two days ago, the government quietly admitted they got the wrong guy. Ashcroft and Mueller don't mention this, for there is already a new enemy of the hour.

Ashcroft steps away from the podium to gesture to mug shots on easels. The photos and text look like WANTED posters from a post office. These seven are in their late twenties or early thirties, six men and one woman. They are armed and dangerous. "The face of Al Qaeda may be changing," Ashcroft says.

His sound bite probably seems benign to the reporters in the room who have no idea what else the government has planned for the War on Terrorism today.

Stop Huntingdon Animal Cruelty was born in a riot. On April 24th, 1997, World Day for Laboratory Animals, protest organizers arrived at Consort Beagle Breeders near Hereford in England. They had campaigned for a year to close the breeder, which housed about eight hundred dogs—beagles sought for invasive experiments because of their small size, docile temperament and loving nature. The dogs would be sold to laboratories like Huntingdon. The organizers expected a few dozen activists, maybe a hundred. More than five hundred showed up.

The activists used this moment of surprise to swarm the facility. Police in riot gear kept most at bay, but somehow a few activists slipped inside the dog sheds. Muscles tensed. Did they make it? Were they arrested? Should everyone go back to chanting and holding signs? Moments later, two activists in masks appeared on the roof, cradling a beagle. They yelled to the crowd for help.

Riot cops were overwhelmed as people climbed over, and tore down, the razor-wire fence. More police arrived and swarmed the fields like locusts: reserves had been waiting inside the building, and others had been waiting in vans lining the streets. Dr. King once said, "A riot is at bottom the language of the unheard." One could argue that for too long the activists in this crowd—from students to "raging grannies"—had not been heard. Their leafleting, letter-writing, marching and protesting had earned some victories, yes, but not enough. Perhaps they felt they needed a new voice, a new language.

Police clubbed the protesters. They sprayed CS gas, a "crowd control" substance that burns tear ducts and mucus membranes and was famously used by Saddam Hussein against the Kurds. The clubs and gas knocked some protesters to their knees, but the sight of the masked activists with the dog had galvanized the crowd. They kept pushing. After an hour of the beating and pepper-spraying, the masked activists climbed onto an adjacent building and managed to lower the dog to a group of about forty people. Then they immediately ran back to the kennels for another. When word spread through the crowd, the fences came crashing down.

People rolled clothes into bundles under their arms as decoys. Hundreds of police surrounded the crowd, and a helicopter circled the grounds as activists scattered like buckshot across the field toward their cars. Martin Balluch, an animal rights activist from Austria, found himself with a group of about ten protesters all running through the field with the dog, not a fake-bundle-of-jackets dog but the real thing. Police stopped the group and the activists could not escape.

Balluch was in good shape from "sabbing," or hunt sabotage—chasing hunters, and often being chased, through fields and woods with bullhorns and other distractions to scare the animals away. Someone distracted a police officer, and Balluch grabbed the dog and ran. "But a police car spotted me and set a police dog loose on me, who came and bit me and was clinging on to me till police caught up," Balluch said in an interview with *The Abolitionist*. "Some activists came, and we all held on to the dog and built a huge heap of bodies, by then surrounded by ever more coppers. When they were many more than us, they started to attack and arrest one by one, till I was left alone with the dog."

Balluch refused to hand over the dog, so police loaded him, beagle and all, into a squad car and hauled them to the police station. Eventually, police took the beagle away by force. They sent the dog back to the breeder, and most likely it ended up in a laboratory. "But it was also a powerful experience," Balluch said. "To realize that we are strong enough to break through police cordons with hundreds of riot cops, if need be, to liberate one beagle dog."

Three months later—after this riot and after daily protests, all-night vigils, national marches and three covert raids freeing twenty-six beagles—the kennels closed. About two hundred beagles were placed in new homes instead of in laboratory cages.

Activists wasted no time. They picked a new target, Hill Grove farm near Witney, Oxfordshire, and created Save the Hill Grove Cats. Hill Grove sold kittens as young as ten days old to laboratories around the world. About ten thousand cats lived in windowless sheds on the farm. After just eighteen months of campaigning and a groundswell of public opposition, the farm owners acquiesced. About eight hundred cats were placed in new homes, and the only breeder of cats for animal testing in the United Kingdom was closed. Next came Shamrock Farm, Europe's largest supplier of primates to laboratories like Huntingdon. Shamrock was more fortress than farm, with sixteen-foot razor-wire fences, CCTV cameras and trip wires to keep animal rights activists away. Save the Shamrock Monkeys lasted fifteen months, until the lab closed in 2000.

This is how it would work, the activists reasoned: one at a time, brick by brick, wall by wall, until the entire animal testing industry collapsed. They would build off the momentum of Consort, Hill Grove and Shamrock, applying a similar model of relentless protesting and unwavering support for both legal and illegal tactics, both bullhorns and black masks. For their next move, activists decided on a bigger, bolder target, and they formed Stop Huntingdon Animal Cruelty.

Huntingdon Life Sciences had become notorious in the animal rights movement. Five undercover investigations by animal rights groups, journalists and whistleblowers since 1981 had exposed repeated animal welfare violations. Employees had been videotaped punching beagle puppies and dissecting live monkeys. During her six-month investigation of Huntingdon's New Jersey lab in 1996, Michelle Rokke of PETA recorded abuses on video and in her diary. In one entry she wrote, "I saw him pick a dog up off the floor by his front leg and toss him in a cage. . . . When he tried to close the cage door one of the dogs tried to get out. He repeatedly slammed the cage door on the dog's head (a total of four slams) before finally getting the door closed." Huntingdon kills between 71,000 and 180,000 animals annually to test household cleaners, cosmetics, pharmaceuticals, pesticides and food ingredients for companies like Procter & Gamble and Colgate Palmolive.

Huntingdon was significantly larger than previous targets. Its razor-wire fences would be taller, its media campaigns and lawsuits more fierce. The campaign might take eighteen months, it might take years. That's fine, organizers thought. Huntingdon would buckle just the same.

As Ashcroft and Mueller warn that all law enforcement must be kept "operating around the clock" to keep Americans safe, FBI agents are working on another terrorism case. While the government warns the country about seven armed and dangerous twentysomething Al Qaeda terrorists, FBI agents storm the homes of seven unarmed twentysomething animal rights activists.

It's about six in the morning when two dozen FBI agents surround a suburban home in Pinole, California. Pinole is a commuter town, four square miles of cute homes and big box stores.

More politely, it's a "bedroom community" about thirty minutes up I-80 from San Francisco. Less politely, it's dull. It's the kind of town that makes good fodder for frustrated teenagers forming punk rock bands; Billie Joe Armstrong and Michael Dirnt of the band Green Day went to Pinole Valley High School. As the first wave of commuters sip their travel mugs of coffee, turn on NPR and head into traffic, a helicopter circles the house. Then FBI agents, many wearing bulletproof vests, with guns drawn, pound on the front door and threaten to break it down.

Could it be a mistake? The three activists who live here—Jake Conroy, Kevin Kjonaas and Lauren Gazzola—could pass as college students. They seem nice. They always keep to themselves: no parties, no loud music. Every day they walk the dogs, a beagle named Willy and a golden-retriever-looking mix named Buddy, and that is about all the neighbors have noticed. As a helicopter circles the block, as cops in riot gear surround the house, the dogs bark.

Inside the house, Lauren Gazzola, twenty-six, is in her pajamas. Not necessarily because of the early hour, but because she's always in her pajamas. The campaign to close Huntingdon Life Sciences has consumed her life, and the lives of Kjonaas, Conroy and many others. Their house has been ground zero for Stop Huntingdon Animal Cruelty USA, or SHAC. Here they research investors, design fliers, organize protests, print newsletters and publish the website that will be used against them in court.

There's not much point in getting dressed every day, Gazzola often says, when you're just going to sit in front of your computer for eighteen hours, go to bed for a few, then do it all over again. When she's not working day and night on the campaign, she studies for her law school entrance exam. Besides, working on a grassroots animal rights campaign for the last five years has drained her bank account and the accounts of Kjonaas and Conroy too. There is no money for clothes. There is no money for food. The home has been donated, which is good because there is no money for rent.

The incessant, successful campaigning has earned the group quite a few enemies.

Just one week ago, the Senate Judiciary Committee held a hearing called "Animal Rights: Activism vs. Criminality." John E. Lewis, deputy assistant director of counterterrorism for the FBI, testified about the growing threat of underground groups like the Animal Liberation Front (ALF) and Earth Liberation Front (ELF), which have committed more than 1,100 crimes and caused $110 million in damage. Most of the hearing was not about the ALF or ELF, though, it was about SHAC. Witnesses testified about the group's successes and law enforcement's failures. In an ominous statement of what would come in the next few years, Lewis and others argued that terrorism laws must be radically expanded to include the aboveground campaigns of groups like SHAC.

"The FBI's investigation of animal rights extremists and eco-terrorism matters," Lewis said, "is our highest domestic terrorism investigation priority."

Being named the government's top domestic terrorism priority was unsettling, but Gazzola and the others kept organizing. The hearing was just more political posturing, they thought. They were determined not to let it scare them. Gazzola had dealt with the FBI before. They all had. Their homes had been raided, their books, papers and computers taken. They had fought back criminal charges for years, sometimes representing themselves in court, and through it all they had continued undeterred.

But this time—with the helicopters, the guns, the multiple federal agencies—this time feels different.

Ashcroft offers the podium to Mueller, the head of the FBI. Mueller gestures to the mug shots and explains why each individual is a potential terrorist threat.

Adam Gadahn attended training camps in Afghanistan and is a translator for Al Qaeda leaders.

Amer El-Maati "is believed to have discussed hijacking a plane in Canada and flying it into a building in the United States."

Fazul Abdullah Mohammed and Ahmed Khalfan Ghailani both participated in the bombings of U.S. embassies in East Africa in 1998. Two car bombs, detonated simultaneously in Tanzania and Kenya, killed two hundred people and injured more than five thousand. The bombings put Al Qaeda on the map, and put Osama bin Laden on the FBI's ten most wanted list. They are fugitives, he says, and they have the skill to kill again.

Abderraouf Jdey was reportedly selected by Al Qaeda for training to fly more planes into more buildings and kill many more people.

Adnan Shukrijumah could be the ringleader. He has been scouting sites in the United States for a second attack, and he has been in communication with senior Al Qaeda operatives overseas.

Aafia Siddiqui, the lone woman, who has a doctorate in neurological science and has studied at MIT and Brandeis University, is an Al Qaeda "operative and facilitator." She is not linked to any specific terrorist plots, but she is wanted for questioning.

"Now, in reissuing these 'be on the lookouts for,' also known as BOLOs in trade, we want to emphasize the need for vigilance against our terrorist enemies," Mueller says. "Particularly Al Qaeda."

If Ashcroft and Mueller were holding a press conference about the animal rights "terrorists," sharing similar dossiers with reporters, it might look something like this:

Josh Harper is an independent filmmaker. His videos have included footage of activists releasing animals from laboratories and fur farms.

Darius Fullmer has volunteered for a variety of animal rights organizations. He now works as a paramedic.

Andy Stepanian started the first recycle-a-bicycle program in

Long Island and helps distribute donated and "dumpster-dived" food to homeless people with Food Not Bombs.

John McGee . . . well, the government doesn't know much about John McGee. The other six arrestees don't know much about him, either. They've never heard of him, and they think they know everyone who has worked on the campaign. His charges will later be dropped.

Jake Conroy, from the Pinole house, is a graphic designer and an expert on website design and (admittedly) bad zombie movies.

Kevin Kjonaas could be the ringleader. He has been scouting corporations tied to animal testing and has been in communication with animal rights advocates overseas.

Lauren Gazzola, the lone woman, who graduated magna cum laude from New York University, is an aspiring law student. She wants to study Constitutional law.

Ashcroft and Mueller offer few details about the seven Al Qaeda operatives and their plans. Ashcroft says terrorists might find summer events—like the Democratic National Convention in Boston, the Republican National Convention in New York City, and the G-8 Summit in Georgia—"especially attractive." Mueller says he has no reason to believe the Al Qaeda suspects are working together. In short: they may or may not be in the country, they may or may not be working together, they may or may not have any plans for a terrorist attack and if they do, it may or may not be in the United States.

The conventions and G-8 Summit will come and go without a terrorist attack, but in a few years those three events will take on a special significance for the activists arrested today, and for the broader animal rights and environmental movements. Activists will learn that the FBI had paid a student, known only as "Anna," to wear dirty clothes, dye her hair and infiltrate the protest scene. Her journey will start at the G-8 summit. It will include befriending and manipulating young environmental activists, supplying them with bomb-making recipes and bomb-making supplies, funding their travel, and prodding them into action. It will end with Eric McDavid, who grew close to "Anna" and developed romantic feelings for her, sentenced to twenty years in prison as a terrorist. Activists will also learn that a lead organizer of the lawful protests against the Republican National Convention was Daniel McGowan. One of the key figures from the underground had stepped from the shadows into the spotlight. He had taken another name, another life, and while FBI agents were trying to piece together McGowan's past with the clandestine ELF, he was being quoted about the protests in *Rolling Stone* and the *New York Times*.

The reporters are frustrated at the vagueness of Ashcroft's information. "There are inevitably skeptics who say you're overdoing it or you're scaring people or you're just protecting your behind, or what have you," one reporter says to him. "Do you worry about those?"

"No," Ashcroft says.

"You can't overdo it, in other words."

"Well, no. I just don't think my job is to worry about what skeptics say."

The timing of this terrorism warning, leading up to the November presidential elections, seems fishy. If these seven Al Qaeda terrorists warrant a press conference, one reporter asks, why not also raise the threat level? Ashcroft will not answer, deferring the question to Secretary of Homeland Security Tom Ridge.

Ridge, meanwhile, makes the rounds on news programs and says there is no reason to raise the threat level. "We need Americans to just go about living their lives," he says on CBS's Early Show.

"America's job is to enjoy living in this great country," he says on CNN, "and go out and have some fun."

A few days after the SHAC arrests and Al Qaeda press conference, I call Josh Harper, one of the arrestees. We've been friends for about three years, ever since we met when he was on a speaking tour that included Houston and Dallas; a student group I volunteered with in college, Students Against Cruelty to Animals, brought him to Austin for an informal event. I helped organize another speaking event for him in 2002, about the increasing militancy in the animal rights movement and his experience as an independent filmmaker.

Harper coproduced the "Breaking Free" video series about the ALF, and he was involved in the first sabotage of a whale hunt in U.S. waters. He and codefendant Jake Conroy steered small, inflatable boats to place themselves between the whalers, some armed with shotguns, and the whales. Harper threw marine signal flares in front of the whalers to disrupt the killing. For that, and for his involvement in the campaign to close Huntingdon, he has been labeled by people like Rush Limbaugh a "domestic terrorist."

Harper often has a shaved head and wears thick Buddy Holly glasses. On his left forearm is a tattoo of a cartoon bunny demurely holding a monkey wrench the size of its body behind its back, a tongue-in-cheek reference to his support for "monkey wrenching," or economic sabotage, in the name of animal rights and the environment. The bunny could be Harper: quiet, unassuming, self-deprecating, but unable to keep a low profile.

When I last saw him, in Seattle, we spent an afternoon playing Tony Hawk Pro Skater on Play Station. My virtual skating skills rival the awkwardness of my real-world skating skills, and Harper would take breaks from trash talking to show me an old seven-inch punk record or tell a story about a matriarchal tribe in Africa. He has a way of making those topical jumps seem natural. As he speaks he draws connections between seemingly disparate news stories, a reflection of his background with diverse social movements. His mother worked at a factory, and when he was thirteen he joined her in a hunger strike in solidarity with farm workers. He soon began protesting neo-Nazi recruiting events and from there became interested in animal rights. He has an autistic sister, and he says that one day he recognized that the way in which people justified their disrespectful behavior toward her—a difference in her cognitive capacity—was how people justified their behavior toward animals.

Today, on the phone, Harper brushes aside the arrest, saying the charges will probably be dropped in court, eventually, like all the others. The more important news, he says, is that when the FBI agents raided his Seattle apartment, they took note of his movie collection. *Bloodsport, Lion Heart, Double Impact, Universal Soldier, Hard Target, Time Cop, Nowhere to Run, Kickboxer, Death Warrant.* There might have been more. "Whoa," Harper recalls one FBI agent saying. "That's a lot of Van Damme."

I laugh, but I'm embarrassed. I joke that Harper should have used it as a bonding moment, an opportunity to use Jean-Claude Van Damme, "The Muscles from Brussels," to open critical lines of communication between FBI agents and animal rights activists. But I'm ashamed that, even though Harper had his home raided and could spend much of his adult life in prison as a terrorist, he seems to be facing all of this with better spirits, and more courage, than I have.

I am scared. For Harper, Conroy, Fullmer, Stepanian, McGee, Kjonaas and Gazzola. And for myself. I'm too embarrassed to admit such a thing to Harper, but when I learned about the arrests I first worried about the defendants and then quickly, selfishly, worried about myself. I had been arrested leafleting on this same campaign, and those FBI agents from Chicago had threatened to put me on a terrorist list because of it. After returning to Texas, I had moved to Washington, D.C., to cover Congress at the *Chronicle of Higher Education*, then freelanced full time and finally ended up ghostwriting opinion columns for public figures at the American Civil Liberties Union. Sitting in my office at the ACLU, surrounded by piles of documents about the Patriot Act, sneak-and-peek searches, illegal wiretapping and all manner of national security sins, I could feel the fear trying to claw its way up my spine and back into my mind. Were more arrests coming? Would FBI agents show up at the ACLU? Would they finally make good on the threats?

Harper is one of the few people I could talk to about this, but now is not the time. Despite the action-movie style FBI home raids and arrests, he's in good spirits. Right now, nobody knows the scope of the investigation. Nobody knows that more than a hundred FBI agents were involved in the case, or that more government wiretaps were used for this case than any other domestic terrorism investigation.

Harper tells me he's relieved that he and the other defendants were released on a personal-recognizance bond pending trial, but he worries about the impression he made in court. He jokes that the courtroom artist's sketch makes him look slack-jawed and mentally handicapped. Plus, he says, he stood before the judge wearing a T-shirt with a photo of four American Indians with guns. The surrounding text read, "Homeland Security: Fighting Terrorism Since 1492."

In the background I hear the buzz of a sitcom laugh track. His voice softens as if he's talking to himself. "I don't want to be associated with terrorism," Harper says to me. "I fucking hate that when you run my name in a search engine I'm associated with Timothy McVeigh."

I read him the headline from the Department of Justice news release, expecting him to poke fun at the government's public relations efforts. "Militant Animal Rights Group, Seven Members Indicted for National Campaign to Terrorize Company and Its Employees." He doesn't laugh.

I hesitate. I want to press him with questions, and I also want to console him in whatever way I can. It's a tension I've felt throughout my career, a tension only exacerbated by our friendship, and a tension that I sense will become even more strained and taut in months to come. I try to walk some invisible line between reporter and friend. I tell him about the statement by U.S. Attorney Christopher J. Christie: "This is not activism. This is a group of lawless thugs attacking innocent men, women and children."

The indictment does not mention anything like this, and it does not mention mailing anthrax-laced letters, strapping bombs to chests, hijacking airplanes, or anything resembling terrorism. I ask Harper to explain what the government alleges that he actually *did*. He says he still doesn't know. All he knows is that this is an unprecedented use of a terrorism law that attorneys know little about.

The last thing Harper says to me—just before he's interrupted by a phone call from his girlfriend—is that he received an email from his grandmother. She asked him if he is a terrorist.

June 1, 2005 One year after the roundup of the SHAC activists, it's a muggy Wednesday in June and I'm heading up from D.C. to New Jersey—the home of Huntingdon—for their trial. I'm reporting on the case for *Legal Affairs,* but I'm also attending to show support for the defendants. I am dreading my entry into the courtroom and the moment when I will have to decide, in a simple yet significant gesture, if I'll sit in the press section, with the other reporters, or on the benches with friends and family of the defendants. The humidity is suffocating and a storm hangs in the air, ready to pour. As the train crosses the Delaware River, I don't hear any announcement from the conductor to let passengers know we've arrived in Trenton. A neon sign speaks for itself.

"TRENTON MAKES, THE WORLD TAKES" runs in neon letters across the Lower Trenton Toll Supported Bridge, which spans the river. The letters average nine and half feet tall by six and a half feet wide, and weigh about three hundred pounds each. The phrase's glass tubing can be finicky. Sometimes an E or an A will burn out. Sometimes an entire word. But today the neon is lit up, and Trenton shines. The only thing separating the gray Delaware River from the gray horizon of office buildings and the flat gray sky is a neon sign glowing red.

The city has maintained that proclamation since 1911, when the Chamber of Commerce held a contest for a slogan that would remind the thousands of passengers on the Pennsylvania Railroad's Main Line that Trenton was the center of the manufacturing industry. Steel. Pottery. Plaster. Anvils. Mattresses. Bricks. Rubber. Linoleum. Trenton made more tires than any other city. Trenton made the steel rope that held up massive suspension bridges, and Trenton made the world's largest bathtub for the massive President William Howard Taft. A man named S. Roy Heath won that contest, and $25, for "The World Takes, Trenton Makes." However, the slogan needed some editing. Who could put the world before Trenton?

Trenton made, but over the years the world stopped taking. During the sixties, seventies and eighties, Trenton's manufacturing base eroded. In 1924, about one out of every two jobs in the county came from manufacturing. Now it is about one out of every twenty-five. Some manufacturing plants still hum. But the economic backbone of Trenton is now the state government and the pharmaceutical industry. Trenton now depends on making laws and drugs.

I arrive more than two hours early for court, and I'm not the first. Outside the federal courthouse, the defendants and about forty supporters line the street with banners and bullhorns. A dozen police officers surround the demonstrators with tear-gas guns, rifles and a dog at the ready.

The protesters are mostly young women. They don't look terribly threatening, with their court clothes from thrift stores and signs made by hand. The cops say they know better. "This group has a history," one tells me. "We want to be prepared." He holds a pepper-spray cannon so large he needs both hands.

To the people walking past the demonstration, it may appear to be a disproportionately heavy-handed response. To the pharmaceutical industry, the threat is real. Pfizer, Wyeth, Johnson & Johnson, Merck, Sandoz, GlaxoSmithKline, Chiron, Covance, and 245 other pharmaceutical and cosmetic companies call New Jersey home, according to a directory maintained by Rutgers University. They are the heavy hitters in "the medicine chest of the nation," as former Governor Christine Whitman called her state.

"What automobiles are to Michigan and oil [is] to Texas, the pharmaceutical and medical device industry is to New Jersey," said William H. Tremayne, president of the Health Care Institute of New Jersey, an industry group. Some state leaders fear the nation's medicine chest going the way of Motor City. The pharmaceutical job market is shrinking by 3 or 4 percent in New Jersey, while it increases by forty percent or more elsewhere. Nevada and Pennsylvania, among other states, are trying to siphon off some of New Jersey's financial flow. *CEO Magazine*'s "Best and Worst State Report" for 2005 will rank New Jersey's economy near rock bottom at forty-sixth. Business leaders feel the state must act swiftly to secure its position as the pharmaceutical capital of the world. The neon writing is on the wall.

Here, in New Jersey, is a new front in the War on Terrorism. This is where Huntingdon Life Sciences is based. This is where animal rights activists launched a historic campaign that rattled the industry to its core. And here, in Trenton, is where six of those activists will stand trial, on terrorism charges, for attempting to shut down a lab that's crucial to one of the last things New Jersey makes.

CHAPTER THREE

The Green Menace

1983–Present The French film *Les Amants* tells the story of Jeanne Tournier, the bourgeois wife of a newspaper owner who, dissatisfied with her life, frequently visits Paris to see her polo-playing lover. On the way back from a rendezvous, her car breaks down and she catches a ride with a charming young archaeologist named Bernard. Through a Shakespearean chain of events, Jeanne finds herself with her husband, her lover and this new man, all staying in the same country house, eating at the same dinner table. Ultimately the heroine turns her back on her husband and her polo-playing lover and embraces Bernard in some of the most controversial love scenes in the history of cinema. After a screening at the Heights Art Theatre in Cleveland Heights, Ohio, on November 13, 1959, local police raided the theater, confiscated the film and arrested the theater owner. He was convicted on two counts of possessing and exhibiting an obscene film, but fought the case up to the Supreme Court and won. In a concurring opinion for the six-to-two decision, Justice Potter Stewart famously said of obscenity: "I shall not today attempt further to define the kinds of material I understand to be embraced within that shorthand description; and perhaps I could never succeed in intelligibly doing so. But I know it when I see it. . . ."

The film intrigued France yet appalled Ohio not because two different versions of it were shown, but because different worldviews shaped how it was perceived. American audiences found the sex scenes obscene in part because they had not seen anything like them. More important, the scenes challenged widely held cultural and political views about the appropriate role of women. Jeanne Tournier was no June Cleaver: she was a married woman who embraced her sexuality even if it meant needing a lover and another man in addition to her husband. By contemporary standards, both in the United States and France, the sex scenes would not raise an eyebrow and neither would the film's plot. Social values vary between cultures and evolve over time, and as values change so do definitions of art and obscenity.

In my search for a standard definition of terrorism I found myself feeling much like Justice Stewart. Between the poles of "I know what terrorism is when I see it"—9/11 is terrorism, the Oklahoma City bombing is terrorism—and "I know what is *not* terrorism when I see it"—bank robbery is not terrorism, drug dealing is not terrorism—is a large swath of gray.

Although Justice Stewart has been applauded for his candor, subsequent courts have, nevertheless, continued in the quest for a definition of obscenity. Too much hinges on the word to leave it undefined, and thus defined by the whims of those in power. With the word terrorism, much more is at stake. If defined too narrowly, the word has no flexibility, and thus no function, in confronting the evolving threats posed by terrorist groups. If defined too broadly, the word is a political hammer against the enemy of the hour. Is it possible to intelligibly define terrorism in a way that values both freedom and security? And can this shorthand description ever be independent of the eyes of those perceiving it?

In their seminal work, *Political Terrorism: A Research Guide*, first published in 1984, Alex Schmid and Albert Jongman identified 109 definitions of terrorism. They divided them into twenty-two categories, dissected them, studied the pieces, created tables about common elements, and spent more than one hundred pages discussing their meanings. Even after completing this volume, then revising it, the authors said they still had not found an adequate definition. Another expert in the field, Walter Laqueur, has all but given up similar attempts. "Ten years of debates on typologies and definitions," he says, "have not enhanced our knowledge of the subject to a significant degree."

They are not alone. The United Nations has struggled for decades and still has no single, clear definition of terrorism. The U.S. State Department acknowledges that no definition has gained universal acceptance. Even within the U.S. government, different agencies have their own definitions.

The State Department says "'terrorism' means premeditated, politically motivated violence perpetrated against noncombatant targets by subnational groups or clandestine agents, usually intended to influence an audience." It's one of the most widely accepted definitions, but it is far from ubiquitous. The Department of Homeland Security also includes attacks on infrastructure. The FBI's definition is even broader, defining terrorism as "the unlawful use of force or violence against persons or property to intimidate or coerce a Government, the civilian population, or any segment thereof, in furtherance of political or social objectives." And in 2001, the Patriot Act ushered in a sweeping new definition of terrorism, one that encompassed any activities "dangerous to human life" if they are intended to "influence the policy of a government by intimidation or coercion." That language is so vague that civil disobedience fits the criteria.

If that's not confusing enough, definitions of terrorism also vary state by state. Since September 11, 2001, states have clamored to join the War on Terrorism. Ohio turned a slew of crimes into terrorism if intended to "affect the conduct of any government." Illinois and Louisiana included "substantial damage" to livestock in their definitions. Some states opted to decline written terrorism guidelines altogether, leaving the issue to law enforcement's discretion. "There is no one definition we use," a Maine Department of Public Safety spokesman told the *Oakland Tribune*. "I think you know it when you see it. . . ."

If definitions of terrorism lack continuity between countries, within countries, and even between agencies within the federal government, it is unlikely that any definition offered here will satisfy everyone. It certainly would be easiest to leave the term undefined—President George W. Bush used the word thirty-three times in his address to both chambers of Congress after 9/11, and never once defined it—an omission implying that the true meaning is obvious, that no meaning exists other than the one used in that moment and in that context. However, leaving the term undefined cedes far too much power to whoever is speaking, whether the speaker is the president of the United States or a journalist writing a book on eco-terrorism.

To speak honestly about terrorism, we must define it. And in the absence of a widely accepted definition, we must at least have a shared understanding, a skeleton of ideas to give the word form and help us move forward. Although there is no universal definition, common elements consistently appear in state, federal and international uses of the term by people from a variety of backgrounds and political ideologies. By identifying these shared principles, rather than limiting the discussion to the definition provided by one agency or government among many, we can look at the concept more holistically and truthfully. To that end, we discover that most definitions of terrorism share the following three principles:

1) Terrorism is associated with the unlawful use of violence, or threats of violence, by non-state agents.
2) Terrorism is intended to instill widespread fear in a civilian population beyond those targeted.
3) Terrorism is used to force a change in government policy.

The first principle—that terrorism is associated with the unlawful use of violence, or threats of violence, by non-state agents—seems straightforward. Terrorism, perhaps above all else, is associated with violence.

But what is violence? Is it force? Harm? Must that harm be physical? What about psychological and emotional distress? Can humans be violent toward objects that feel no pain and have no thoughts?

The most critical explanations of a concept generally come not from its supporters but from its detractors, so to define violence I turned to those who have dedicated their lives to opposing it. Foremost among them is Gene Sharp. His three-volume work *The Politics of Nonviolent Action* remains one of the defining texts in the field.

Sharp plots a spectrum of activities that are possible in any struggle for social change. At one extreme is "nonviolent resistance and direct action," or the type of conduct most often associated with Gandhi and Dr. King. His list of 178 nonviolent methods includes guerrilla theater, sit-ins and strikes along with more confrontational actions like overloading administrative systems and taunting public officials. Property destruction is not included in this list, but neither is it included in the other extreme of political dissent—violence. Sharp defines violence as "physical violence against persons to inflict injury or death . . . not as a term of moral or political opinion."

Acts of sabotage reside somewhere in the middle of this spectrum of resistance, excluded from definitions of violence and of nonviolence but not free from them. Sabotage is not violence, Sharp makes clear, but it is more closely related to violent than nonviolent action.

There are certainly instances in which property destruction alone can, in fact, be violent and even terroristic. Steve Vanderheiden, a professor of philosophy and political science at the University of Minnesota, makes a compelling case for expanding conceptualizations of terrorism to include attacks on well-chosen inanimate objects that result in violence against people. "Destruction of a basic human need like shelter or sources of potable water amounts to an indirect physical attack upon persons (insofar as it places persons at serious risk of illness or death by deprivation)," he wrote. The power of such attacks is that they could make people not just fear for their property—or fear economic hardship and instability, which is frequently a consequence of property destruction—but fear for their very lives.

In distinguishing sabotage from violence, my intention is not to downplay the severity of property crimes. It is to say, though, that definitions of terrorism—both in policy and in public opinion—are inherently tied to violence, and violence—both in the history of the word, and in the minds of most people—is associated with physical violence against human beings, not inanimate objects. To conflate the two is to disregard what must be a truism of humanity, that lives are immeasurably more valuable than property, their destruction infinitely more costly.

"I am aware that there are many who wince at a distinction between property and persons—who hold both sacrosanct," wrote Dr. King. "My views are not so rigid. A life is sacred. Property is intended to serve life, and no matter how much we surround it with rights and respect, it has no personal being. It is part of the earth man walks on; it is not man."

The latter part of the first principle is that regardless of the definition of violence, it is never terrorism if committed by the government. By using qualifying words like "non-state," "clandestine" and "nonmilitary," all governments define themselves out of the debate and establish a monopoly on violence. In *The City of God*, St. Augustine describes Alexander the Great questioning a captured pirate, asking him how he dares to "molest the sea." "How dare you molest the whole world?" the pirate replies. "Because I do it with a little ship only, I am called a thief; you, doing it with a great navy, are called an emperor."

An unspoken tenet of any terrorism definition is that it does not apply to the systemic violence of people in positions of power against the powerless. It only applies when the flow of violence is redirected upstream, against government. A bomb detonated by a guerrilla, killing dozens of civilians, is an act of terrorism. A bomb dropped by a military airplane, killing tens of thousands, is foreign policy.

The second principle is that terrorism is intended to instill widespread fear in a civilian population beyond those targeted. Terrorists do not aim for military outposts, as in so-called legitimate warfare. They aim for surrogate targets, innocent people, through which they can leverage the weight of fear on countless more. As Michael Walzer wrote in his landmark text *Just and Unjust Wars*, terrorism "breaks across moral limits beyond which no further limitation seems possible."

For example: An Al Qaeda cell sends a suicide bomber into an open-air market. The bomber detonates the device in the middle of the market, killing himself and twenty civilians. The purpose of the bombing is not to punish those in the market, nor is it to stop shoppers from carrying out their plans. The intention is to select a highly visible, symbolic target in order to send a message to a much wider audience.

The power of this violence is the fear it creates, and that fear is dependent on the perceived randomness of the attack. It makes everyday people afraid that they, too, could become victims. The shrapnel of fear can reach further than any bomb. It sends a chill through the rest of society, and this fear, if part of a continued campaign of terror, can destabilize political institutions.

———

The third principle is that terrorism is used to force a change in government policy. This gets to the heart of the inherently political nature of terrorism definitions. It separates crimes committed out of avarice and revenge from those committed because of political ideals.

Some have argued that terrorism is not limited to crimes targeting government conduct, and that all crimes motivated by politics are terroristic. I have drawn from more conservative positions for a few reasons. Discussion of terrorism is consistently shaped by military targets versus nonmilitary targets, state agents versus non-state agents, government conduct versus antigovernment conduct. Government is always central to the debate.

More important, we must keep in mind the impact of a terrorist attack. Random violence is used to instill widespread fear, and that fear is leveraged to push the terrorists' agenda. The question, then, is who would be moved by this leverage? Would it be private individuals and organizations? Or would it be the government, which is responsible for public safety? Terrorist attacks are about influencing government conduct because it is the government that must respond to protect the public and ease fears.

By making this argument I am, of course, falling into a trap created by any terrorism definition. Rather than focus solely on whether a crime was committed, and who committed it, classifying the crime as terrorism also requires that we decipher its intent.

If an anti-abortion activist murders an abortion doctor, is the intent to stop the actions of that specific doctor or to instill fear in the entire medical community? At what point do crimes like this become a campaign of terrorism?

Similar questions are at the heart of the campaign against animal rights and environmental activists, and the way the courts answer them will push the limits of how terrorism is defined.

There is a final element to any definition of terrorism, present in every conceptualization of the term but never spoken. Even if a crime meets all of the above criteria, even if it harms innocent people and instills widespread fear and is carried out by non-state agents and is intended to influence government conduct, that is not enough. Unstated, but understood, is that terrorism must be carried out by those with whom "we" disagree. Terrorism is not violence for political purposes, it is violence for political purposes that "we" oppose. The question "Who are 'we'?" is never posed.

Nevertheless, some political scientists spend entire volumes spelling out elaborate criteria for what is and is not terrorism. They are the Rube Goldbergs of law, creating schemes of bells and slides and hurley whirlys with the hopes that, if all precisely aligned, they will trigger a terrorism label to fall down on the target. Such productions miss the more straightforward point that terrorism can never be defined independent of the group doing the defining.

To speak honestly about any definition of terrorism we must first be willing to acknowledge the true purpose of the term: to demonize the other. In the 1940s, a rallying cry of Italian fascists was "O con noi o contro di noi"—"You are either with us or against us." Or, as Colonel Korn warns Yossarian in *Catch-22*, "You're either *for* us or against your country. It's as simple as that." When George W. Bush addressed a joint session of Congress on September 20, 2001, he continued a long history of invoking stark political dichotomies in times of crisis. "Every nation, in every region, now has a decision to make," he said. "Either you are with us, or you are with the terrorists."

Perhaps the most important question to be asked in any discussion of terrorism is "Who is 'us'?" A definition of terrorism is predicated on the speaker, and the speaker's intentions. President John F. Kennedy said in 1962, "Those who make peaceful revolution impossible make violent revolution inevitable." Sometimes people who foment violent revolution are terrorists, and sometimes they are freedom fighters. It all depends on those in power.

Nelson Mandela joined the African National Congress in 1944 to campaign against the South African government's apartheid policies. As the government's response grew increasingly violent, and after Mandela stood trial for treason and was acquitted, he argued in 1961 that the African National Congress should set up a military wing. He formed Umkhonto we Sizwe, or Spear of the Nation, and went abroad to study guerrilla warfare and military tactics. In the 1970s and '80s, the country's ruling white minority labeled the African National Congress a terrorist organization, and so did the United States. Mandela was later elected president of South Africa. In 1993, he received the Nobel Peace Prize.

We know these dates. The 1983 bombing of the U.S. Embassy in Beirut, the 1993 bombing of the World Trade Center, the 1995 bombing of the Oklahoma City federal building, the 1996 bombing of Centennial Olympic Park, and the deadliest act of terrorism on U.S. soil, September 11, 2001. These dates and the others in the FBI's terrorism timeline hit viscerally. We remember photos of firefighters carrying infants from the rubble of the Murrah Federal Building. We know where we stood when the twin towers fell.

Few people remember April 16, 1987. Sandwiched between some of the darkest, bloodiest days on the FBI's timeline of bloody days is the ALF arson of a building under construction at the University of California, Davis, which caused $5.1 million in damage, destroying the animal diagnostics laboratory and twenty vehicles. The ALF said it was "to retaliate in the name of thousands of animals tortured each year in campus labs." Unlike other terrorist attacks on the FBI's timeline, the Davis arson killed no one injured no one, and targeted no one.

Yet the animal rights and environmental movements top the government's terrorism lists. "The number one domestic terrorism threat," says John Lewis, an FBI deputy assistant director and lead official in charge of domestic terrorism, "is the eco-terrorism, animal rights movement." Lewis told a Senate committee in 2005 that "there is nothing else going on in this country, over the last several years, that is racking up the high number of violent crimes and terrorist actions, arsons, etc., that this particular area of domestic terrorism has caused." He told the *Wall Street Journal*, "There's been no other movement that has brought as much violence and destruction and vandalism."

Demetrius "Van" Crocker, a former member of the neo-Nazi National Socialist Movement, was found guilty in 2006 of attempting to purchase sarin nerve gas and C-4 explosives as part of a plan to blow up government buildings with a "dirty bomb." An impure form of sarin was released in the Tokyo subway system by the Aum Shinrikyo cult in 2005, killing twelve people and injuring thousands. Crocker had also made a version of Zyklon B, the gas used in Nazi concentration camps.

A hero of anti-abortion extremists, Clayton Waagner, proclaimed he was on a mission from God to murder clinic employees. He stole cars, stockpiled weapons, gathered home addresses, broke out of prison when he was arrested and, when recaptured, admitted mailing more than 550 letters in the aftermath of the 9/11 attacks that contained white powder and notes that read, "You have been exposed to anthrax. We are going to kill all of you." Waagner was associated with the Army of God, and in 2003 he was found guilty of more than fifty federal charges including threatening to use a weapon of mass destruction.

William J. Krar, a white supremacist from Texas, pleaded guilty in 2003 to possessing a weapon of mass destruction. Police found a sodium-cyanide bomb powerful enough to kill everyone in a 30,000-square-foot building—thousands of people—along with nine machine guns, more than sixty pipe bombs, remote-control explosive devices and some 100,000 rounds of ammunition.

The FBI consistently downplays, and even omits, crimes like these when discussing terrorism. Instead of acknowledging them, the bureau says that in the three years following 9/11, every act of domestic terrorism, except for one, was the work of animal rights and environmental activists. In that time period alone, the National Abortion Federation tracked hundreds of attacks by anti-abortion extremists: twenty-four assaults, eight arsons, seven attempted bombings/arsons, 240 acts of vandalism, forty-eight bomb threats, twenty-four anthrax threats, and twenty-four death threats. From 1977 to 2009, anti-abortion activists committed eight murders. None of these crimes are recorded by the FBI as acts of domestic terrorism.

Eric Rudolph, another Army of God follower, *is* included by the FBI. Rudolph bombed Olympic Park in Atlanta, along with an abortion clinic and a gay night club. He killed two people and injured hundreds in what he says was a campaign against abortion and homosexuality. But the FBI treats Rudolph as an aberration rather than a symptom of a broader movement, saying that he exemplifies "the FBI's 'lone offender' category of terrorist for those who engage in terrorist activities free from organizational guidance." The FBI labels Rudolph a bad seed, rather than examining the fruit that produced him.

The FBI is not alone in holding and stating these priorities. The Department of Homeland Security, too, lists the ALF and ELF on its roster of national security threats, while often ignoring right-wing extremists. Justin Rood at *Congressional Quarterly* uncovered a homeland security document titled "Integrated Planning Guidance, Fiscal Years 2005–2011" that includes an internal list of terrorist threats, topped by the ALF and ELF. Omitted are anti-abortion, militia, white supremacist, constitutionalist, tax protester and other far-right groups.

If a few right-wing incidents did not make the government's lists, that might be explainable. After all, there is no universally accepted definition of terrorism. At some point, though, there have to be incidents that are not up for debate. The deadliest terrorist attack in the United States prior to 9/11, the bombing of the Murrah Federal Building in Oklahoma City, should be one such incident. Timothy McVeigh timed the bombing to coincide with the second anniversary of federal agents raiding the Branch Davidian compound in Waco, Texas, and also said the attack was retaliation for the standoff between federal agents and a white separatist family in Ruby Ridge, Idaho. James Powers, Homeland Security Director of Pennsylvania—a state with a harsh "eco-terrorism" law on the books—told reporters that McVeigh "is not a terrorist, just very angry with the U.S. government. . . . Whether a person is a terrorist or a criminal is irrelevant to me."

How is it that destroying property is terrorism, while murdering people is not? One explanation is that this is all purely political. The government treats attacks on corporate property more seriously than violence against doctors and minorities not because of the nature of the crime but because of the politics of the crime. The government's domestic terrorism operations are more about protecting profits than protecting people.

The other explanation is that we are missing something, something that elevates the animal rights and environmental movements above groups that have repeatedly demonstrated a willingness to murder. Is there of a history of bloodshed on their part?

Activists consistently claim that, after decades of legal and illegal activity in the United States, the animal rights and environmental movements have not harmed anyone. The ALF and ELF have codes of conduct emphasizing three things: to inflict economic damage (through taking animals or destroying property), to educate the public, and to "take all necessary precautions against harming life," both human and nonhuman. It makes for great sound bites, and it contrasts sharply with the crimes of right-wing extremists. But is it true?

To find out, I turned to the organizations most responsible for labeling activists as "eco-terrorists." If anyone should be willing to expose such crimes, it should be them. Just as activists have an incentive to ignore or downplay violence, these groups have an incentive to display it. A history of violence would certainly bolster their case.

The Foundation for Biomedical Research says it is the only group in the world that tracks the crimes of eco-terrorists. It has produced the "Top 20 List of Illegal Actions by Animal and Eco-Terrorists 1996–2006," ranking in order of severity the most significant crimes committed during the most active time period of the radical animal rights and environmental movements:

1. Arson at a housing development in San Diego.
   Injuries: 0
2. Bombing at the Chiron Corporation in California.
   Injuries: 0
3. Bombing at the Shaklee corporation in California.
   Injuries: 0

And on it goes. The list of top eco-terrorism crimes from one of the top adversaries of these movements does not include a single injury or death. In 1999, a group calling itself the "Justice Department" allegedly mailed eighty-one envelopes containing razor blades to scientists who experiment on primates. No one was injured. The only act of violence on the list took place in England when Brian Cass, the managing director of Huntingdon Life Sciences, was attacked by masked individuals with pickax handles outside his home. Cass was hospitalized with cracked ribs and a three-inch gash on his head. The attack was an anomaly in the British animal rights movement, and the Foundation for Biomedical Research treats it that way. Nothing like it has happened in the United States, and the attack is listed as an afterthought on the Top 20 list, with an asterisk at number twenty-one.

Did the Foundation for Biomedical Research miss something? According to a report by the Southern Poverty Law Center, animal rights and environmental activists have carried out "literally thousands of violent criminal acts in recent decades—arguably more than those from any other radical sector, left or right." The report lists ninety-five crimes from 1984 to 2002, including multiple "pie-ings." A pie-ing is exactly what the name implies. Think Larry, Moe and Curly imbued with the revolutionary spirit of the Situationist International. A group calling itself the Biotic Baking Brigade threw a banana cream pie at a Sierra Club staff member "to protest the Club's support of land exchanges between the government and timber companies" and later pied University of Wisconsin geneticist Neil First in protest of genetic engineering. PETA pied Procter & Gamble executive John Pepper to protest animal testing and in a separate incident lobbed one at U.S. Agriculture Secretary Dan Glickman. It is not clear from the report if these are the first uses of dessert products by terrorists.

Over the years, claims of physical violence by environmentalists have been exposed as complete fabrications. One of the most famous involved tree spiking, hammering heavy nails into trees marked for clear-cutting and then warning lumber companies that proceeding with the cut would threaten their equipment and employees. The tactic caused divisions within Earth First because of the possibility for injury. Playing off these concerns, politicians and industry groups claimed that a mill worker had been injured when a saw blade hit a tree spike.

The true story was this: The victim, George Alexander, worked in a Louisiana-Pacific sawmill in northern California as an off-bearer, someone makes the first cuts to old-growth logs as they arrive from the forest using an enormous band saw with a ten-inch-thick blade. He had been complaining about dangerous working conditions, including cracks in the saws, when in May of 1987 his blade hit a metal spike and shattered. Shards struck him in the face and throat. Alexander had to file a lawsuit against Louisiana-Pacific because it would not cover his medical expenses. Meanwhile, the company offered a $20,000 reward for information leading to the arrest of environmentalists. Years later, FBI files revealed that the Sheriff Department's primary suspect was not an activist but a disgruntled local who had admitted spiking in order to keep timber companies off his land.

In another case, two prominent Earth Firsters named Judi Bari and Darryl Cherney were in Oakland protesting clear-cutting on May 24, 1990. They had been on the road organizing Redwood Summer, a campaign to save old-growth forests inspired by the Freedom Summer of the civil rights movement. Bari had already received dozens of death threats for her campaigning. The two were in Bari's Subaru station wagon when a pipe bomb exploded underneath her, injuring Cherney and nearly killing her. Hours later, while Bari was still in Oakland's Highland Hospital, local police arrested them and said they had knowingly transported the bomb—that they were responsible for their own bombing.

Bari and Cherney were smeared as violent extremists in the press, but police dropped those charges weeks later. The activists sued the police and the FBI, alleging false arrest, slander and conspiracy. In the opening statement of a two-month trial the prosecutor compared Bari and Cherney to domestic terrorists. The activists claimed that the government had refused to follow any of the leads they had to the actual perpetrators in order to smear them. In 2004, the federal government agreed to pay $2 million to settle the civil suit, and the city of Oakland agreed to a separate $2 million payment. It remains unknown who planted the bomb.

After scouring countless documents in my search for acts of violence by animal rights activists, I finally found something. But the incident never appears in terrorism reports, databases, websites, congressional testimonies or press releases. It is the one attempted murder in the history of these movements, yet it is the one incident that the FBI and industry groups would rather not discuss.

Shortly after midnight on November 11, 1988, Fran Trutt exited the passenger side of a rented Chevy pickup and approached the headquarters of U.S. Surgical, the nation's largest supplier of surgical staplers. The company used about one thousand dogs each year in training doctors to use the product, stapling dogs and then killing them. Trutt placed a package in some bushes about ten feet from where CEO Leon Hirsch would park his car the next morning. Inside the package, a foot-long radio-controlled pipe bomb had been wrapped in roofing nails. Maybe Trutt still had doubts as she hid the package and then turned back to her waiting driver. By the time she reached the truck, though, it was too late for second thoughts.

Fran Trutt had been set up. When she returned to the truck, police moved in. U.S. Surgical, the press and most animal rights groups would soon condemn her as a violent extremist and a terrorist. But over the coming months it would be revealed that the plot, the only act of attempted murder in the history of the U.S. animal rights movement, had not been an organic occurrence. The money for the bomb, the truck, the logistics, the encouragement—U.S. Surgical and a "counterterrorism" firm called Perceptions International had orchestrated it all.

Perceptions International was created by Jan Reber, a self-styled "terrorism" expert who had experience demonizing animal rights groups; he also published a newsletter called the Animal Rights Reporter, a dossier on the activities of animal activists crafted for the animal research industry. His firm paid Mary Lou Sapone to infiltrate protest groups and prod members into using illegal tactics. Most activists rejected her unsettling comments, but she was able to befriend Fran Trutt. Later, the firm also paid Marc Mead $500 a week to become friends with Trutt and to give her money to procure a bomb; Mead admitted that the president of Perceptions

International went so far as to tell him when to bring Trutt and the bomb to the U.S. Surgical office.

With evidence of his covert plans mounting, Hirsch finally acknowledged using paid informants. He told the Associated Press that animal rights "terrorists" had left him no choice. "Many of them are very dangerous organizations," he said. "They don't believe in right and wrong as most people in society do." Trutt maintained the she never intended to kill Hirsch; she intended to explode the bomb as he walked into the building. Yet the media circus and aggressive prosecution wore her down, and she signed a plea agreement. In an unusual move, Assistant U.S. Attorney Leslie Caldwell wrote a letter to the U.S. District Judge questioning the handling of the case by Connecticut police and the wiretaps they played in court. "Like a sports highlight film made for the benefit of home team fans, the tape contains many of Trutt's most menacing and outrageous remarks," she wrote. "However, it omits the operatives' goading, encouragement and offers of money."

Fran Trutt was coerced and manipulated, but she bears responsibility for her actions. And although arsons by the ALF and ELF have not harmed anyone, fire is unpredictable and unwieldy. A lack of casualties certainly should not downplay the severity of some crimes. However, to label these movements the top domestic terrorism threat suggests that they earned the title through what most people associate with terrorism—violence.

Instead, they earned the title through a carefully manufactured campaign by their opponents.

The environmental movement is young, an adolescent in the family of social movements, but it was born running. Before it reached a critical mass and became identified as a movement, there were philosophical precursors—John Muir's essays, Aldo Leopold's *A Sand County Almanac*, David Brower's leadership of the Sierra Club— that had influenced public and political opinion. In his history of the American environmental movement, *A Fierce Green Fire*, Philip Shabecoff says such influential leaders had made environmentalism in the United States "a powder keg ready to explode." With the publication of *Silent Spring* in 1962, says Shabecoff, "Rachel Carson lit the fuse."

Carson's poetic call to action is widely credited with igniting the modern environmental movement, which is true, but less well known is how soon after this birth the movement radicalized. By the first Earth Day in 1970, anonymous individuals were making headlines by targeting polluters. Illinois's "The Fox" and Florida's "Eco-Commando Force" developed a cult following. They were environmental vigilantes taking on the big, bad corporations, and people loved them. By 1971, Environmental Action held a national contest soliciting tips on "ecotage." The tips were compiled in a book and featured in national media.

The Fox was merely a lone avenger, though, and *Ecotage* was treated as a collection of pranks. In 1975, Edward Abbey tapped into these sentiments and emboldened them with his novel *The Monkey Wrench Gang*. George Hayduke and the other characters were no hippies—as they sabotaged bulldozers and pulled survey stakes they ate meat, mocked liberals, and left a trail of beer cans in their wake. Abbey's work inspired a quickly maturing environmental movement and threw some dynamite on Rachel Carson's fire. As he later wrote, "Sentiment without action is the ruin of the soul." *The Monkey Wrench Gang* influenced Dave Foreman, Mike Roselle and Howie Wolke as they founded Earth First in 1980. At about this time, Greenpeace gained international attention for its nonviolent direct action, and Paul Watson's Sea Shepherd Conservation Society began ramming whaling vessels.

The animal rights movement radicalized as well. In England, hunt saboteurs had been using direct action to thwart hunters since the 1800s. They placed their bodies between the animals and the hunters' guns, and scared away prey by blowing horns and spreading false scents. In 1972, some of the saboteurs formed a new group called the Band of Mercy, named after youth clubs created by the Royal Society for the Prevention of Cruelty to Animals. They escalated tactics and widened the scope of their targets until two members were arrested for raids at Oxford Laboratory Animal Colonies in Bicester. Dubbed the Bicester Two, Cliff Goodman and Ronnie Lee were called heroes in the press and by members of Parliament. They were released after twelve months. Goodman, who had become a government informant, distanced himself from illegal tactics. Lee gathered the remaining Band of Mercy members and formed a new group interested less in mercy than in revolution. They named it the Animal Liberation Front.

Charting a history of a clandestine group is like painting the portrait of a ghost, and there are different accounts of the ALF's emergence in the United States. In *Free the Animals,* PETA's Ingrid Newkirk tells the story of a former police officer named "Valerie" who flew to England, met Lee, attended a clandestine training camp, and returned to form the first American ALF cell in 1982. Other accounts are less paramilitary. The first animal liberation in the United States seems to have been the release of two dolphins from a Hawaiian research facility in 1977 by "The Undersea Railroad." The first crime claimed by the ALF occurred two years later, when activists dressed as lab workers stole animals from the New York University Medical Center. Throughout the eighties, ALF cells orchestrated elaborate lab invasions. As part of a 1984 raid at the University of Pennsylvania's Head Injury Clinic, activists stole thirty videotapes showing experimenters laughing and playing loud music as they slammed baboons' heads with a hydraulic device. After historic raids at the City of Hope National Medical Center, University of California at Riverside, and University of Oregon, groups like PETA used photographs, video footage and documents obtained by underground activists to wage aboveground campaigns.

The mainstreaming of animal and environmental concerns,

combined with tiers of lawful and unlawful groups, was undeniably a threat to the corporations targeted. They needed to displace activists from their moral high ground. A key development in orchestrating this fall from grace was the decision to wield the power of language. "Whoever defines the issue controls the debate," says Timothy Cummings, a clinical professor and poultry veterinarian at Mississippi State University. Instead of saying "bled to death," Cummings advises farmers to say "exsanguinated"; rather than "killer," say "knife operator." For those who break the law in the name of animal rights or the environment, industry groups would change the language from "monkey wrencher," "saboteur," or just plain "criminal" to the much more powerful "terrorist." Ron Arnold of the Center for the Defense of Free Enterprise claims that in a 1983 *Reason* article he invented the term "eco-terrorism," which he defines as "a crime committed to save nature." He and others would redefine the debate so that the real criminals were not the corporations destroying the environment but those trying to stop them.

Government officials slowly incorporated the term into their lexicon and changed how they spoke of sabotage. After a 1987 arson at the University of California at Davis, the FBI labeled an animal rights crime "domestic terrorism" for the first time. The next year, Senator James McClure introduced the term eco-terrorist into the Congressional record (oddly enough, by comparing the tactics of drug lords to those of environmentalists). In 1990, animal experimentation groups held a press conference before a national "March for the Animals" in Washington; Health and Human Services Secretary Louis Sullivan condemned "so-called animal activists who are, in fact, nothing more than animal rights terrorists."

Despite these linguistic victories, eco-terrorism was not a top government priority. Ron Arnold's organization and the anti-environmental "Wise Use" movement operated on society's fringes; the eco-terror meme remained loosely confined to this niche of free-market true believers, and sympathetic media portrayals continued through the late eighties. The top newspapers in the country published feature articles that considered the merits of direct action. FBI Director Louis Freeh told European newspapers in 1998 that crimes by the ALF, ELF and Earth First were not even on his radar screen.

This began to change when politicians got involved in the issue. On June 9, 1998, the U.S. House subcommittee on crime held a hearing called "Acts of Ecoterrorism by Radical Environmental Organizations." Frank Riggs, a representative from California, testified that his district office was "assaulted by a group of environmental terrorists." Activists had been pressuring Riggs to protect Headwaters, the last large unprotected redwood forest, from clear-cutting by Pacific Lumber Company. Riggs said Earth Firsters wheeled a redwood stump on a dolly into his office. They emptied four garbage bags of sawdust, pine needles and leaves around the stump while four activists—three young women and a sixteen-year-old girl—sat and joined arms around it in metal "lock-boxes," handmade contraptions designed to extend the spectacle of civil disobedience.

Police video footage showed an officer asking protesters to unlock their arms. The women refused. One by one, police applied something to their eyes. "What you were given was a little bit of pepper spray with a Q-tip," an officer said on tape. "What we're going to give now is an actual spray." Police then held their eyelids open and sprayed the chemical. This was not an isolated occurrence. Earth First videotaped three incidents in Riggs's district of police swabbing pepper spray into the eyes of immobilized protesters. Amnesty International called the police behavior "tantamount to torture." Riggs, recipient of more money from the logging industry than any other member of the House, defended the assaults. None of this was mentioned during the Congressional hearing as witness after witness warned of violence by environmentalists.

Ron Arnold testified and called for new legislation. A staff member in Riggs's district office called civil disobedience "hate crimes." Earth First infiltrator Barry Clausen said, "This group advocates anarchy, revolution and terrorism to the youth of our country." Comments made in this hearing, no matter how mendacious, became the fodder of press releases, news stories and political statements as official Congressional evidence of a growing national threat.

The Congressional hearing was prescient on one point. The radical environmental movement was changing. As members of Congress called the civil disobedience tactics of Earth First terrorism, another group was preparing to go much further. The Earth Liberation Front had been active in the United Kingdom since 1992. It debuted in the United States on October 14, 1996, by gluing locks and spray-painting "ELF" at multiple McDonald's restaurants in Oregon. Later that month, "elves" burned a forest service pickup at the Ranger District Headquarters in Detroit, Oregon, and then set fire to the U.S. Forest Service Oakridge Ranger Station, causing over $5 million in damage.

The emergence of the ELF in the United States caused divisions within Earth First, not just because of tactics but because the new, anarchist-influenced movement butted against the cowboy machismo often associated with traditional Earth Firsters. The ELF, here and abroad, positioned itself less as an environmental group than as a resistance movement, incorporating critiques of capitalism, nationalism, gender and animal liberation. A 1997 anonymous communiqué titled "Beltane" set out some of ELF's influences, from the ALF to the Zapatistas, and said, "We are the burning rage of this dying planet."

On October 19, 1998, the ELF burned down multiple buildings at the Vail ski resort. A communiqué said the expansion of Vail Inc. into two thousand acres of wilderness in the Rocky Mountains threatened one of the last habitats for lynx. The arson did not harm anyone physically, but it caused nearly $26 million in damage. The crime undeniably had an impact on FBI Director Louis Freeh, prompting a change of heart on his domestic terrorism priorities.

The ELF was suddenly on his radar screen. Freeh testified before a Senate subcommittee soon after that "the most recognizable single-issue terrorists at the present time are those involved in the violent animal-rights, anti-abortion and environmental-protection movements."

By 2000, the FBI reassigned one of the Joint Terrorism Task Forces to investigate ELF arsons in Long Island, New York. The task force had previously investigated the bombings of U.S. embassies in Africa and the first bombing of the World Trade Center.

Then came September 11th.

Before the smoke had even cleared, anti-environmentalists began exploiting the tragedy. On September 12th, Representative Greg Walden, a Republican from Oregon, said the ELF posed a threat "no less heinous than what we saw occur yesterday here in Washington and in New York." The next month, the *Washington Times* called for war against the "eco-al-Qaeda." Kimberley Strassel of the *Wall Street Journal* heralded a new political climate for neutralizing activists as "eco-terrorists." "The indulgent world in which these groups had operated collapsed on Sept. 11," she wrote.

Industry groups hired PR firms to insert eco-terrorism into the national security dialogue. Similar plans had long been considered. In 1991, for example, the Clorox Corporation hired Ketchum Public Relations to develop a crisis management plan; among Ketchum's recommended tactics was a "Stop Environmental Terrorism" media campaign. After 9/11, this type of strategy became more feasible. Just one month after the attacks, the crisis communication firm Nichols-Dezenhall registered StopEcoViolence.com. The website would become the home of a nonprofit by the same name. Stop Eco Violence billed itself as a grassroots movement, but it was far from it. The group's executive director, Kelly Stoner, previously worked in public relations for Louisiana-Pacific, a company long targeted by environmentalists for the logging of old-growth redwood forests.

Guided by Nichols-Dezenhall, the front group offered itself as an expert source for media outlets including the Associated Press and the *New York Times*. Reporters treated this PR scheme as an organic creation, sometimes even referring to it as a "watchdog group."

Warnings of eco-terrorism saturated mainstream media. Travis Wagner, a professor of environmental science and policy at the University of Southern Maine, has studied how national newspapers portray ecotage. Examining top-tier newspaper articles from 1984 through 2006, he found that terrorism rhetoric appeared throughout the timeline, but its frequency increased dramatically after September 11th and has continued climbing since then. Wagner notes that this increase in ecotage-related stories accompanied a *decline* in actual crimes. According to the North American ALF Press Office—not one to downplay ALF and ELF attacks—crimes decreased by 47 percent after 9/11. As warnings of eco-terrorism made headlines, the threat itself waned.

A niche industry of crisis management firms has joined the fray by producing reports that identify "threats" to business, including activist groups. In this industry built upon fear, corporations pay firms to identify threats to their profits, which leads to more campaigns to address these threats, which leads to more reports, and on it goes. The financial motivation to identify threats results in some interesting reports. For instance, the Society of Toxicology paid a private firm, Information Network Associates, to create a threat analysis in preparation for the group's annual meeting, ToxExpo. One section of the report profiled Seattle activists, including what schools they attended and whom they were dating: "There is a distinct possibility that animal rights activists will use this conference as an opportunity to stage demonstrations or protests, distribute literature, and otherwise promote their animal rights agenda," the threat analysis concluded. "The threat level associated with this event is considered MODERATE."

Another confidential report by the Inkerman Group outlined

the effects of terrorism legislation on activists. As part of that discussion, it identified key developments in the radical environmental movement. Among them: stickers. "Towards the end of 2000, a new form of eco-terrorism emerged in the US against Sports Utility Vehicles (SUVs)," the report says. "Activists, some reportedly part of the ELF, decided to demonstrate against the environmentally-unfriendly vehicles by placing homemade stickers on them . . . with messages such as 'I'm Changing the Climate. Ask Me How.'" For corporate executives who know nothing of the animal rights and environmental movements, reports that label protests a threat and relate bumper stickers to terrorism reinforce a fear of activists.

Law enforcement's institutionalization of "eco-terrorism" followed a nearly identical trajectory, slowly building and then spiking. In the wake of September 11th, government agencies were eager to be part of terrorism investigations, just as reporters were eager to break a new terrorism story. Law enforcement shifted focus from traditional criminals to suspected terrorists, and in 2004 the number of secret surveillance warrants in terrorism cases eclipsed the number of criminal wiretaps for the first time. This institutional pressure was so intense that it led to recurring turf wars between the FBI and the Bureau of Alcohol, Tobacco and Firearms (ATF). Government reorganization after 9/11 had brought the two under the same roof, and the ATF sought an expanded role in domestic terrorism cases. As a result, both agencies often showed up at the same crimes, at the same time, and fought each other for authority.

As former FBI agent, whistleblower and *Time* "Person of the Year" Colleen Rowley told me, in the eighties it was the war on drugs. In the nineties, gangs. Since September 11, the path to career advancement in law enforcement is paved with terrorism investigations. The only question is "Who to investigate?" When government terrorism documents ignore right-wing groups, it makes clear what is not a government priority. When the FBI and Department of Homeland Security domestic terrorism documents list animal rights and environmental activists, it makes clear what is.

At some point over the years, the eco-terror language went viral, replicating by spreading from host to host. The FBI now warns corporations, Lions Clubs, chambers of commerce and student groups about eco-terrorism. John Lewis has traveled to warn the Farm Animal Council of Saskatchewan, Canada, about eco-terrorism spreading north. The U.S. Department of Agriculture has distributed a security survey to laboratories and asked recipients if they have been the victim of attacks by "domestic special interest terrorists" such as PETA.

Unrelated groups like the Anti-Defamation League have cashed in on the new terrorism threat by offering their services to the FBI and local police for "domestic extremism" trainings; the New York City Police Department made one of the ADL's eco-terrorism courses mandatory for all sergeants and lieutenants. At this point, it is impossible to decipher who is creating the threat and who is responding to it. Fear feeds fear, and the specter continues to grow.

Ultimately, the rise of this Green Scare was no conspiracy. It does not seem to be the result of any secret planning document drafted jointly by industry and the FBI. The shift was gradual, slowly merging the rhetoric of industry groups with that of politicians and law enforcement. Eventually, what was once a fringe argument became official government policy.

In 2003, Ron Arnold who claims to have pioneered the use of "eco-terrorism," was hired as an expert consultant by the University of Arkansas Terrorism Research Center. The project was funded by a grant from the National Institute of Justice, the research arm of the Justice Department. Arnold—who has told the *New York Times*, "We want to destroy environmentalists by taking away their money and their members"—was paid by the government to advise law enforcement on the terrorist threat he helped fabricate.

CHAPTER FOUR

Naming Names

January 20, 2006 Osama bin Laden has broken his silence. He's been quiet for more than a year, long enough for some to speculate about his death. In an audiotape released to the press yesterday, he said Al Qaeda is planning its next attack. Military officials, homeland security, and the CIA all responded by saying the tape is evidence of the continued threat posed by Al Qaeda, but in a surprising move, bin Laden opened the possibility of a truce. In his recording, he made his plea directly to the American people and said, "Our situation is getting better while yours is getting worse."

Today, CNN interrupts its international coverage for the government's announcement of a major victory in the War on Terrorism. Eleven environmental and animal rights activists have been indicted for crimes in the name of the ELF and ALF. From 1995 through 2001, the government says terrorists targeted lumber companies, trucking companies, an SUV dealership, a meat-packing company, a horse slaughterhouse, U.S. Forest Service ranger stations, U.S. Bureau of Land Management wild horse corrals, genetic-engineering research facilities, an electric tower, a police station and a ski resort. They caused, by FBI estimates, more than $40 million in property damage.

Eight activists have been arrested: Chelsea Gerlach, Daniel McGowan, Stan Meyerhoff, Jonathan Paul, Suzanne Savoie, Kendall

Tankersley, Darren Thurston and Kevin Tubbs. Three more are considered fugitives: Joseph Dibee, Josephine Overaker and Rebecca Rubin. There will be soon be more arrests—Nathan Block, Jennifer Kolar, Lacey Phillabaum, Briana Waters and Joyanna Zacher—and the announcement of another fugitive, Justin Solondz. An unindicted co-conspirator, William Rodgers was arrested in December and then found dead in his jail cell.

The sixty-five-count indictment has been a long time in the making. The FBI, the ATF and local officials in Oregon, Washington, Wyoming, California and Colorado have been working together for nearly a decade. The investigation became more serious in 2004 when the FBI's Portland field office consolidated seven independent investigations and named the program "Operation Backfire."

Up to this point, law enforcement has been woefully inadequate in combating underground groups. The first person arrested for an ELF crime, Frank Ambrose, had his charges dropped. The government did not convict any saboteurs until early 2001, after an ELF cell set fire to new suburban homes on Long Island in protest of urban sprawl. This first victory against the number one domestic terrorism threat was the conviction of three seventeen-year-old high school students.

Attorney General Alberto Gonzales and FBI Director Robert Mueller are holding this press conference in Washington to make clear that this case is not about vandalism or arson. It is about terrorism. They use the word early, and they use it often. It appears in the headlines of government's press releases, and is mentioned ten times in their brief comments. "Terrorism is terrorism," Mueller says, "no matter what the motive."

When the panelists open the press conference to questions, reporters don't have much interest in the environmentalists. After all, every one of the crimes is more than four years old, and only one occurred after 9/11. Reporters are more interested in yesterday's tape. The first question asked by the press: "How seriously should Americans take the threat from Osama bin Laden?"

I am visiting Seattle and Portland with my friend Kim Berardi, with whom I was arrested three years prior in Chicago, when we see the press conference on television. News reports have little information about the defendants, but I immediately recognize the crimes.

I was involved in the animal rights and environmental movements in Austin when many of the actions took place. Friends and I would read the communiqués in the *Earth First Journal* or *No Compromise.* They targeted SUVs before Al Gore made climate change a mainstream issue, and they targeted genetically engineered crops before "organic" meant anything to consumers. Even more radical than the issues, though, were the tactics. The emergence of the ELF, and its embrace of arson, made monkey wrenching seem moderate. The crimes were flashpoints in the movement, prompting condemnation by national groups and divisions within Earth First. Many activists, myself included, were eager to read every news article, zine and website posting about the crimes. Nobody knew what it all meant for the future of the movements, but one thing was sure—everything was changing.

Two of these crimes in particular had already become folkloric. The first was the 1997 arson at Cavel West horse slaughterhouse in Redmond, Oregon. The U.S. government had been rounding up thousands of wild horses on public lands and offering them for adoption, as part of a program intended to protect them. An investigation by the Associated Press revealed that Bureau of Land Management employees were profiting from selling the horses to slaughterhouses, where they were butchered and shipped to Europe for human consumption. About 90 percent of the young, healthy horses corralled by the government ended up as pieces of meat. The ALF used "vegan jello," a mixture of glycerine tar soap, gasoline and diesel fuel, to burn down Cavel West. The communiqué said the arson "would bring to a screeching halt what countless protests and letter writing campaigns could never stop." It caused about $1 million in damage. The slaughterhouse never reopened.

More infamous was the 1998 arson at Vail ski resort in Colorado. Vail was so big it did not even seem feasible. In his book *Powder Burn*, journalist Daniel Glick speculated whether the development company might have been involved, as part of an insurance scheme. Some local activists suggested the arson was a government job, because it disrupted their lawful campaigns to preserve lynx habitat. The fact that activists somehow climbed a mountain, in the snow, with buckets of fuel and supplies, escaped and remained undetected gave the crime a mystique. One photograph of the arson became an iconic image of the radical environmental movement. In it a lone tree stood in the foreground, the snow and sky glowed electric blue, and Vail burned a biblical burn.

Of the defendants, only one stands out to me. Jonathan Paul has long been considered a hero of the animal rights movement. He cofounded Hunt Saboteurs with Rod Coronado and placed himself between bighorn sheep and hunters' rifles. He investigated fur farms across the country, led a campaign against shark hunting near Santa Cruz, and, along with SHAC defendants Jake Conroy and Josh Harper, steered inflatable boats between whales and Makah hunters. Paul had leadership roles in some of the most influential and controversial campaigns of the animal rights movement.

In 1992, he was subpoenaed by a federal grand jury investigating an ALF lab raid. Grand juries were, and still are, secretive proceedings where witnesses have few rights. Threats of jail time are used to pressure activists to speak about their political beliefs and political associations. Paul went to jail for five months for refusing to testify. His twin sisters Alexandra, who starred on *Baywatch*, and Caroline, a San Francisco firefighter, campaigned for his release wearing "Free Jonathan Paul" T-shirts in *People* magazine.

While Paul was making a name for himself with his aboveground campaigns, he also had an underground life. He formed the Western Wildlife Unit of the ALF with Rod Coronado. He drove the getaway car at UC Davis—the first ALF arson in the United States. In other raids, he helped steal dogs, cats, monkeys and mice from labs. At the Bureau of Land Management's corrals in Litchfield, California, he used a hand saw to cut a section out of a large wooden fence through which wild horses ran free.

Few other activists have had such a pivotal role in the growth of the ALF in the United States. Jonathan Paul has escaped conviction for two decades, and now the government only has evidence to charge him with one crime—the arson that put Cavel West slaughterhouse out of business.

Berardi and I watch a Seattle TV station display mug shots of the arrestees. Except for Paul, I do not recognize any names or faces, but Berardi does. Some of the defendants were prominent aboveground activists who had been involved in animal rights, forest defense and other protest groups for years. Something seems odd to her about one of the photos. She says she recognizes the face of Daniel McGowan, because they had met a few times through mutual activist friends when she lived in New York City. But she had known him by another name.

The FBI had not accomplished this on their own. After years of investigating the ALF and ELF, the trail had gone cold until the FBI's first break walked right in the front door. In 2001, on the same day the ELF set fire to SUVs at Romania Chevrolet, a Eugene activist named Heather Coburn called the police to report her truck stolen. She named her roommate, Jacob Ferguson, a suspect in the theft. (She later found the truck down the block.) A few days later another activist walked into the same police station and requested the police reports for the Romania arson and the truck theft. Through these events and some additional surveillance, police suspected a link between Ferguson and the fire—although none actually existed. Prosecutors served him with two grand jury subpoenas. They kept Ferguson, a heroin addict, under constant pressure for months. In 2004, prosecutors threatened to charge him with the arson. In response, he offered the government more than they had ever expected.

He told them about more than a dozen ALF and ELF crimes and named others involved. Ferguson eventually admitted his role in at least twenty-two arsons and acts of vandalism, far more than were committed by any of those he implicated. In addition, he agreed to wear a wire as he tracked down defendants across the country, recording eighty-eight hours of conversation in about forty meetings. He teased out bits of information from the others, including McGowan, that he could trade to the government for leniency. When FBI agents made arrests based on his information, Ferguson sometimes accompanied them.

After each arrest, cops made clear that the defendants were up against multiple federal agencies working in tandem with state and local law enforcement. They said that that the only hope for salvation, the only way to avoid life in prison as a terrorist, was to name names. According to government statistics, those threats are accurate. About 95 percent of all federal criminal defendants plead guilty, and of those who fight their charges in court, nine out of ten are convicted.

This is how the net grew. Rather than rely on investigation and evidence, the government used the power of fear. On the same day of the first arrests, several other activists were subpoenaed to testify before a federal grand jury in Eugene. A local activist and nursing student named Jeff Hogg refused to testify about his political beliefs and associations, and he'll spend six months in prison for not naming names.

One by one, the defendants turned on each other, some before their fingerprint ink had even dried. Within hours of his arrest,

Stan Meyerhoff had agreed to cooperate and provide information on the others. He implicated his own fiancée, Lacey Phillabaum. Jennifer Kolar met with FBI agents to offer names, including that of her ex-boyfriend, Jonathan Paul, and then went back two weeks later to offer more. Kevin Tubbs and Suzanne Savoie both pointed to McGowan. Chelsea Gerlach not only cooperated but embarked on a personal campaign to convince the other defendants, including her boyfriend, Darren Thurston, to snitch.

"This is the ultimate betrayal, delivered straight into the hands of my enemies," wrote William Rodgers from jail. Rodgers, known to friends as Avalon, suffocated himself with a plastic bag in his cell. In his suicide note, he wrote: "Certain human cultures have been waging war against the Earth for millennia. I chose to fight on the side of bears, mountain lions, skunks, bats, saguaros, cliff rose and all things wild. I am just the most recent casualty in that war. But tonight I have made a jail break—I am returning home, to the Earth, to the place of my origins."

Through all of this, even after the government press conference, Daniel McGowan, Jonathan Paul, Nathan Block and Joyanna Zacher have refused to talk. Their principled stand will likely have serious consequences. Cooperators will testify against them at trial, as stipulated in their plea agreements, and prosecutors promise to show no leniency. If they want to avoid life in prison they must either divulge new names, beyond the information provided by the others, or come up with a creative solution.

Around the time of McGowan's arrest, the *New York Times* reported that President Bush had secretly authorized the National Security Agency to spy on Americans, without warrants, as part of terrorism investigations. The revelations set off a debate about the balance between national security and civil liberties, between safety and freedom. Months later, *USA Today* reported that the NSA had been gathering the phone records of tens of millions of Americans with the cooperation of the nation's largest telecommunications providers, including AT&T, BellSouth and Verizon. Whistleblower Mark Klein, a former AT&T technician, said that the company had built "secret rooms" in major cities, allowing the NSA to splice directly into its circuits.

These news reports exposed a sea change that had been developing for some time. The romanticized, old model of police work—hunting down leads, burning shoe leather, knocking on doors—was being replaced by a new "full-pipe" model—vacuuming up mounds of information and attempting to filter out the few terroristic particles.

The domestic spying programs, however shocking, were not new. During the Cold War, the NSA ran nearly identical programs. From 1945 to 1975, the NSA's operation SHAMROCK monitored the telegraph communications of U.S. citizens; the three major carriers passed messages directly to the NSA. From 1969 to 1973, the NSA's operation MINARET maintained watch lists of Americans; included on the lists were the names of civil rights and antiwar activists provided by the FBI.

Within the FBI, the Counter Intelligence Program, or COINTELPRO, began as a plot to obstruct the Communist Party USA. The tactics spread to other groups including Students for a Democratic Society, the Southern Christian Leadership Conference, NAACP, American Indian Movement, and American Friends Service Committee. According to FBI Director J. Edgar Hoover, COINTELPRO aimed to "expose, disrupt, misdirect, discredit, or otherwise neutralize" these movements and leaders, using any means at their disposal. He advised agents targeting the Black Panther Party that the purpose of the operation was disruption, thus "it is immaterial whether facts exist to substantiate the charge." Hoover and the FBI developed a particular obsession with Dr. King, gathering thousands of pages of surveillance on him alone. William Sullivan, who headed the domestic intelligence division of the FBI, attempted to connect Dr. King to the Communist Party. In a memo to Hoover, Sullivan advised that in order to accomplish this "it may be unrealistic to limit ourselves as we have been doing to legalistic proofs or definitely conclusive evidence."

Congressional investigations in the 1970s exposed these and other rogue operations. The Church Committee reports resulted in safeguards such as the 1978 Foreign Intelligence Surveillance Act. The law set protocol for NSA spying on U.S citizens, including establishing a secret court for the obtaining of national security warrants. Since then, the United States has ostensibly had a two-tiered surveillance infrastructure. The NSA is given wider latitude in its operations because its targets are foreign spies and governments. Domestic operations are generally the purview of the FBI. The NSA can only monitor communications of Americans if they are believed to be "agents of a foreign power" and if a warrant is obtained through the Foreign Intelligence Surveillance Court. In a quarter century of operation, this court has rejected only four requests for warrants. The Bush administration, however, said such safeguards were too restrictive.

Thus the government has been engaged in what could be seen as illegal activity in the use of the NSA for domestic spying. If those tactics were part of the Operation Backfire investigation that led to the charges against the defendants, perhaps this provides an opening in their case.

Attorneys for the non-cooperating defendants decide to use these revelations to go on the offensive. On March 24, 2006, they serve prosecutors with a request for all materials obtained through the Foreign Intelligence Surveillance Act (FISA) or the NSA. This case would have been a prime target for illegal surveillance. FBI officials have told Congress that the ALF and ELF are top domestic terrorist threats, and antiterrorism resources were used to investigate these crimes. Discovery materials provided by the government have shown that McGowan had been spied on for his lawful, aboveground activism long before he became a suspect in this case. He was monitored because of his correspondence with prisoners and his organizing against the Republican National Convention.

The Bush administration claims that the NSA has only spied on Americans with ties to foreign terrorist groups like Al Qaeda. Even if this is true, it wouldn't preclude spying on these defendants. FBI Deputy Director Lewis testified before Congress that domestic and international terrorism investigations draw from the same resources and that Joint Terrorism Task Forces have a "strong liaison with foreign law enforcement agencies." In a preliminary court hearing, the assistant U.S. attorney said, "These conspiracy members have affiliations throughout the world with ALF and ELF, like-minded sympathizers."

So what is the extent of the government's warrantless surveillance? Are tools designed to spy on foreign terrorism threats being used illegally to spy on environmentalists? And if so, who else is being watched?

During the anticommunist hysteria of the Red Scare, some of the worst abuses occurred at the local level. Beginning during the 1920s, major cities established Red Squads, specialized police surveillance units that targeted communists, socialists and anarchists. One of the most notorious Red Squads was in Chicago, with roots that stretched back to the 1886 Haymarket Riot, when anarchists were framed and then executed. The Red Squads spied, wiretapped and used other dirty tricks to compile dossiers on citizens and groups. They grew in popularity and power during the 1930s, continued into the second wave of the Red Scare, and by the 1960s evolved into broader counter-subversive units. Courts reined in the Chicago Red Squad in the 1980s, but Mayor Richard Daley successfully campaigned to dissolve these restrictions, arguing that they hampered terrorism investigations.

While the scope of the NSA's current surveillance is unknown, multiple other federal, state and local agencies have embraced a post-9/11 Red Squad model. President Bush has called local police the "front line of defeating terror." The FBI operates one hundred Joint Terrorism Task Forces, which bring together dozens of law enforcement agencies to share information and coordinate terrorism investigations. The task forces have essentially deputized about one thousand local cops as terrorism investigators. At the same time, a steady stream of money has flowed from the federal government to state and local "fusion centers" with few strings attached. The Department of Homeland Security provided about $1.6 billion through its grant programs in 2006. To qualify for this and other federal funding, states must create lists of the "potential threat elements" they face. *U.S. News & World Report* obtained nine state homeland security plans, and the lists varied wildly. In Texas, for example, state officials identified 2,052 potential threats, including environmental groups. Like the Red Squads, these local counterterrorism operations—both in coordination with the FBI and independently—have demonstrated a lack of oversight, training and safeguards against abuse.

One of the best-known examples of terrorism surveillance was featured in Michael Moore's *Fahrenheit 9/11*. Members of Peace Fresno were shocked to open the newspaper and see a photo of Aaron Stokes, a local antiwar activist, identified as Aaron Kilner, a deputy with the Fresno County Sheriff Department's Anti-Terrorism unit. Moore depicted the infiltration as a case of bumbling counterterrorism cops who mistakenly targeted peaceniks holding potlucks, but in doing so he missed the mark. Many more towns have their own Aaron Stokeses. This surveillance is no error, no silly mistake. It is systemic.

The FBI acknowledged in December of 2005 that it had been targeting two of the most recognized names in the animal rights and environmental movements, People for the Ethical Treatment of Animals and Greenpeace. Industry front groups like the Center for

Consumer Freedom have long claimed that PETA, in particular, has ties to the ALF and ELF. The FBI developed confidential informants within these organizations, such as interns and employees, and even infiltrated the groups in order to monitor protest activity. The spying went nowhere, and no charges were ever filed.

In Colorado, local police, at the FBI's request, gathered the names and license plate numbers of activists protesting a 2002 lumber industry meeting.

In Florida, the Joint Terrorism Task Force monitored the delivery of elephants to the Lowry Park Zoo, on the lookout for "PETA/ ecoterrorist types."

In California, the FBI spied on an environmentalist commune after attacks on a nearby Hummer dealership. FBI Director Robert Mueller personally briefed President Bush about the case.

In Massachusetts, FBI agents tailed one animal rights activist too closely between protests and rear-ended his car. He received a check for $1,600 to cover his expenses.

In Pennsylvania, FBI agents monitored the Thomas Merton Center for Peace and Justice, a community space for more than twenty-five organizations. FBI documents describe the Pittsburgh center as "a left-wing organization advocating, among many political causes, pacifism."

Minnesota, Iowa, Maine. Antiwar groups, civil rights groups, veterans' groups. Homeland Security, FBI, Department of Defense. Mix and match the details and the story is always the same.

The nation's first local department of homeland security was established just weeks after 9/11 outside of Atlanta, using $12 million in federal funds. In December 2003, Caitlin Childs and Christopher Freeman were distributing leaflets about vegetarianism outside of a HoneyBaked Ham store in DeKalb County when they noticed men in street clothes photographing them. They wrote down the make, model and license plate number of their car. After the protest, the two men followed the activists, eventually pulled up behind them and, without identifying themselves, ordered Childs and Freeman to exit their vehicle. When they refused to hand over their notes, they were arrested; the unidentified men were homeland security detectives. The ACLU filed a lawsuit arguing that the search and arrest violated the activists' Fourth Amendment rights. Six years later, the vegans prevailed. The piece of paper was never returned, though, because homeland security argued it could identify the car—which was being used in other investigations.

I have spoken with dozens of activists who recount similar scenes, albeit with less positive resolutions. The men in dark SUVs are not always homeland security. Sometimes they are FBI or, increasingly, corporate security firms. This cottage industry employs current and former military and police officers to surveil political activists for high-profile corporate clients. Stephens Inc. hired a firm called Global Options to spy on activists protesting the company's ties to Huntingdon Life Sciences; the firm monitored activists at home, at work, and even at a vegan picnic. Burger King has hired Diplomatic Tactical Services to spy on the Student/Farmworker Alliance, a group of college students working to improve the wages and lives of immigrant workers in Florida.

James Ridgeway of *Mother Jones* has chronicled the exploits of a private company called Beckett Brown International. BBI regularly dumpster-dived at the offices of Greenpeace and other environmental groups, then recycled information to public relations firms such as Ketchum and Nichols-Dezenhall, who represented corporations targeted by environmental activists. In 1998, BBI retained Mary Lou Sapone to help infiltrate a Louisiana environmental group. Sapone could draw upon her previous experience with Perceptions International, when she had been hired to infiltrate animal rights groups and coerce activist Fran Trutt into an attempted bombing.

Spying at the ham store and sleuthing in Greenpeace dumpsters may sound like Keystone Kops, but this is no skit. It is a reflection of institutional changes in the operations of local police and their surrogates. Since September 11th, there has been political and financial pressure for local law enforcement to 1) identify new threats and 2) produce new intelligence on those threats. As historian Ellen Schrecker has written of the Red Squads, "Members had an ideological and occupational stake in countersubversion and the suppression of dissent." These stakes are starkly on display in the proliferation of state programs dubbed "fusion centers." Fusion centers collect data from multiple agencies and jurisdictions; by 2009, there were seventy-two of them receiving about $254 million in federal homeland security funds. The constant pressure to identify threats has resulted in "intelligence" of questionable value.

A terrorism threat assessment by the Virginia fusion center includes detailed descriptions of animal rights and environmental activism. "Animal rights extremist presence has been reported in Henrico, Norfolk, Richmond, and Smithfield," the report says. "The majority of animal rights groups' activities have consisted of nonviolent protest demonstrations and public speaking events." The threat of animal rights terrorism in the state is low, but local Earth First groups have engaged in civil disobedience, protests and university outreach, thus "eco-terrorists remain a considerable threat to Virginia."

Another fusion center is the California Anti-Terrorism Information Center. In 2003, the agency was exposed for building dossiers on "extremists" and distributing Terrorism Advisories on groups including Earth First, the Ruckus Society, SHAC, Sea Shepherd and PETA. One terrorism advisory warned of an "eco terrorist" lecture and public symposium at Fresno State University.

In 2008, a similar program was exposed in Maryland. State police classified at least fifty-three nonviolent political activists, along with protest groups, as "terrorists" in state and federal intelligence databases. The information was gathered by an undercover state trooper who infiltrated dozens of meetings and lawful protests.

The files maintained on activists followed a similar structure, listing a "primary crime" as terrorism and a "secondary crime" as a slew of social issues. For instance, Josh Tulkin, deputy director of Chesapeake Climate Action Network, had his crime listed as "terrorism—environmental extremists."

State police superintendent Thomas E. Hutchins authorized the program. He will tell Maryland legislators: "I don't believe the First Amendment is any guarantee to those who wish to disrupt the government." He will characterize the activists targeted as "fringe people." These fringe people include animal rights activists, environmentalists, antiwar activists, a former Democratic congressional candidate, an individual who is "involved in puppet making and allows anarchists to utilize her property for meetings," and Dominican nuns.

Maryland's files were shared with a half-dozen federal agencies. Among them, the agency that is at the center of the motion to reveal warrantless surveillance against the Operation Backfire defendants—the NSA.

On August 22nd, after months of government stalling, Judge Ann Aiken holds a hearing on the NSA motion. Prosecutors argue that they have turned over all of the discovery materials in the case, including seventy-two CDs and 28,000 pages of documents. They say no information "in the possession" of the prosecution was obtained illegally. If they ever received materials obtained through warrantless surveillance, they say they had no way of knowing and no security clearance to find out. Attorney Stephen Peifer tells Aiken, "I've been working on this case for ten years, and the term FISA has never come up."

"To you," Aiken replies. In another case, assistant U.S. attorneys were unaware of NSA spying until the government accidentally disclosed it to defense attorneys for the Al-Haramain Islamic Foundation. Information obtained through warrantless surveillance could have been filtered into the Operation Backfire investigation unbeknownst to prosecutors.

There is only one way to know for sure. In a major victory for the defense, Aiken rules that the government must disclose whether the NSA spied on the defendants.

The ruling does not bode well for the prosecution. A group of constitutional scholars, law professors and former government officials has sent a letter to Congress saying that, although not all details of the spying program have been revealed, it "appears on its face to violate existing law." The Congressional Research Service, the nonpartisan investigative arm of Congress, has issued a report with similar conclusions. In at least five other lawsuits, courts have forced the government to disclose whether NSA surveillance played any role in the case; on the morning McGowan's attorney filed the motion, another court ruled that NSA surveillance violated the First Amendment, Fourth Amendment, and the Foreign Intelligence Surveillance Act. "It was never the intent of the Framers to give the president such unfettered control," Judge Anna Diggs Taylor wrote in *ACLU v. NSA*, "particularly where his actions blatantly disregard the parameters clearly enumerated in the Bill of Rights." If NSA surveillance is disclosed in this case, it will likely be ruled unconstitutional. And if it is ruled unconstitutional, then all of the Operation Backfire cases could be dismissed.

But the government could lose more than these cases. The Bush administration has fought hard to keep its spy programs secret. When the Justice Department's Office of Professional Responsibility began examining the role of government lawyers in the program, President Bush denied security clearances to investigators and shut them down. In an interview with the *El Paso Times*, National Intelligence Director Mike McConnell stated that to even question government spying threatens American lives. "So you're saying that the reporting and the debate in Congress means that some Americans are going to die?," the interviewer said, repeating McConnell's statement. "That's what I mean," he replied. "Because we have made it so public. We used to do these things very differently, but for whatever reason, you know, it's a democratic process and sunshine's a good thing."

If prosecutors hand over new information about the Terrorist Surveillance Program, it could prove suspicions that the government's spying has extended far beyond Al Qaeda. It could lead to Congressional hearings, much like ones that dissolved SHAMROCK, MINARET, and COINTELPRO. Exposing NSA spying on the animal rights and environmental movements could dismantle the entire domestic spying apparatus, and the Bush administration along with it.

Two months later, Daniel McGowan's attorney, Amanda Lee, quietly withdraws the NSA motion. Neither she nor Assistant U.S. Attorney Kirk Engdall will offer an explanation other than that it is "by reason of agreement with the government." A week later, on November 9th, Daniel McGowan, Jonathan Paul, Nathan Block and Joyanna Zacher change their pleas to guilty. The pleas are part of an unusual non-cooperating plea agreement in which they will admit their guilt but not name names.

Neither the government nor defense attorneys will confirm a direct relationship between the withdrawal of the motion and the guilty pleas. But it is clear that both parties had a remarkable change of heart on positions they previously refused to compromise.

From the start prosecutors had said there were two options: snitch and receive a reduced sentence, or go to trial and risk life in prison. McGowan and his attorneys had organized the "non-cooperating defendants" and pushed for a special plea deal, but prosecutors said it was not open for discussion. While this agreement impedes investigation into other ELF crimes, the government avoids a national security investigation.

The defendants had been just as steadfast, saying they would never accept a plea deal. Had they maintained this position, and had the NSA motion revealed illegal surveillance, their cases might have been thrown out. However, those are significant variables with so much at stake. This way, the defendants relinquish any hope of absolution, but they secure reduced sentences.

The defendants' decision comes with an additional, political sacrifice. For McGowan, who always seems to be thinking about the bigger activist picture, the deal means forfeiting a rare opportunity to expose systemic government corruption. On some activist websites and message boards there are comments questioning the decision to cede the upper hand in a national political scandal. The anonymous individuals leaving comments, however, are not facing life in prison.

During a court hearing to change pleas, McGowan is the only defendant to speak. "This plea agreement is very important to me," he says, "because it allows me to accept full responsibility for my actions and at the same time remain true to my strongly held beliefs." As tears form in his eyes, McGowan says his past does not fit his vision of a better world.

"I hope that you will see that my actions were not those of a terrorist," he says, "but of a concerned young person who was deeply troubled by the destruction of Oregon's beautiful old-growth forests and the dangers of genetically modified trees."

After the defendants had pleaded guilty, stories of how they committed some of the most destructive crimes in the history of the environmental movement took form. Some elements of the plot are still hidden, redacted or sealed in court documents, and some characters are on the run—or yet to be revealed. The accounts have varied wildly, depending on the narrator.

The government's account is like a spy novel or gritty true-crime drama. In it the defendants called themselves "The Family." They cut their teeth at the Cascadia Free State and World Trade Organization riots in Seattle. Some grew and distributed marijuana to finance their crimes. They methodically honed their craft, targeting anyone who did anything they opposed. It was only a matter of time before they redirected their rage from property to people.

The narrative told by the cooperating defendants is less true grit, more romance and coming-of-age tale. It is the story of idealists with the right intentions but the wrong path. Stan Meyerhoff says he was young and naïve, easily led underground. Chelsea Gerlach says she was under the "Svengali-like" spell of an older activist, William Rodgers, who took advantage of her teenage crush. Darren Thurston participated in an arson in hopes of rekindling a relationship with Gerlach. Jennifer Kolar, who has a master's in astrophysics and was working toward a PhD in oceanography, was lured into the ELF through a romantic relationship with Jonathan Paul; she later abandoned academia to move closer to her new flame, co-conspirator Joe Dibee. In these accounts, the cooperators' judgment was clouded by love and lust and rage, of which there was plenty.

A third version, told by the non-cooperating defendants, exists somewhere alongside the others, less a parable than a chapter in a longer history of the environmental movement. There was no Family. Some of the defendants did not even know each other. McGowan never met Jonathan Paul until five months after his arrest. The defendants had grown increasingly frustrated with legal defeats and heavy-handed crackdowns on nonviolent protest. Today they have their regrets, but at the time the escalation of tactics was a calm, rational progression from symbolism to direct action.

In each version of the story, some details overlap. Defendants communicated through a shared web-based email account. They typed "draft" messages and stored them online but never hit send. They coded these emails using a series of numbers that corresponded to pages and words in a chosen book. This is how they informed each other of meetings that came to be called the Book Club, a series of five covert gatherings where defendants briefed each other on picking locks, encrypting email and creating timed incendiary devices.

In preparation for a crime they methodically tested and re-tested their tools. Some were as simple as wooden matches rubber-banded to an incense stick and then stuck in a fuel-soaked sponge. Others needed assembly in DNA-free "clean rooms." One model used an alarm clock, a lamp filament and a 9-volt battery: when the timer went off it completed a circuit, which heated the lamp filament, which lit a book of matches, which turned a bucket of fuel into a bucket of fire.

They experimented with both the high-tech and the low-bud-get. During reconnaissance for the arson of the Litchfield wild horse corrals, Thurston tested Dibee's night-vision scope. For the Boise Cascade arson on December 25, 1999, Overaker and Gerlach trans-ported buckets of fuel in boxes wrapped like Christmas presents.

The defendants created fake IDs and registered cars in false names. They communicated on two-way radios with pseudonyms like Country Girl, Country Boy, Bob, Dog, Jack, Seattle, Sorrel, Sheba, Sabina, Rabid, Maria, India, Exile and Avalon. After a crime, they washed backpacks in soap and water and wiped down tools with alcohol. They tossed clothing in random dumpsters, or dug holes in the woods in which they destroyed them with muriatic acid. Some evidence, like a roof rack, was simply returned to the store.

No matter which names they used, or how sophisticated their techniques became, the crimes involved human beings with human flaws. They made many mistakes along the way. Some were forgiv-able, as when Jonathan Paul brought Jennifer Kolar to Cavel West without having cleared it with others first. Or when Rebecca Rubin opened the gates too early at the wild horse corral in Rock Springs, and in the confusion of dust and hooves the action had to be aborted. Other errors could have ended it all, as when Ferguson used a ciga-rette lighter to ignite the incense timing device at an Arcata trucking company. He fumbled, and then his fuel-soaked gloves caught fire.

The stress of underground life intensified personal dramas. Dibee had worked with Paul on anti-whaling campaigns, and the two had a falling out. They loathed each other. One night, Dibee and Meyerhoff drove from Seattle to rural Southern Oregon with a police scanner and semi-automatic hand gun, intending to murder Paul. They got lost, and a police officer questioned them in a parking lot. They decided to call it a night and go home.

McGowan is a natural raconteur on all things except his past. Normally he cannot stay quiet. He goes and flows and will hand you a new scientific study as he talks and walks through the New York City subway, skirting the arsons at Superior Lumber and Jefferson Poplar to talk about that animal rights conference when everything changed, and boy did it change, because, as he found out, his mouth can be his downfall. It's hard to unravel the yarn within the yarn, the personal and emotional trajectory that sent his life bounding from one story to the next. When pressed he amicably continues talking, but his storytelling transforms imperceptibly, perhaps unintentionally, from an unrestrained, unending flow to a pensive staccato.

Sometimes hypodermic needles floated in the water off Rockaway Beach, McGowan says; other days the city would call out surfers to test their hair for pollution. Algae blooms and medical waste would shut down some of his favorite surfing and swimming spots, and he learned at an early age that communities with few resources end up with the most pollution.

After graduating from SUNY-Buffalo, he went to work for environmental nonprofits in Manhattan. He cared about the environment, as a concept, but his exposure to the natural world was always, first and foremost, as a New Yorker. He learned about issues at the Wetlands Activism Collective or independent bookstores on the Lower East Side. He campaigned to preserve national forests here and in South America without having ever set foot in one on either continent. It did not take long for him to feel uncomfortable defending the environment from a cubicle. He wanted firsthand experience.

In the late 1990s, activists in California and the Pacific Northwest had earned a reputation for no-compromise environmental campaigning. In the Headwaters Forest of northern California, Julia Butterfly Hill lived in an ancient redwood tree for 738 days to protect it from loggers. At Warner Creek and Fall Creek in Oregon's Willamette National Forest, activists created "free states" and defended them using tree sits, road blockades and new forms of civil disobedience like "sleeping dragon" lock-boxes. Environmentalists went West not looking for gold or land like the settlers before them, but seeking out this culture of resistance.

In 1998, McGowan packed his bags and headed to San Francisco. From there he intended to travel three hundred miles north, join the Headwaters Forest Campaign and save redwoods. But while McGowan was on a train somewhere in the middle of the country something terrible happened. In a forest of steep old growth, a logger made threatening comments to forest activists. A video of the scene showed the logger saying if the activists did not move he would "make sure I got a tree coming this way." Then he did just that. One of the activists, David "Gypsy" Chain, was crushed and killed. The local district attorney refused to press charges against the logger. When McGowan arrived in California, the Headwaters campaign was in a state of flux.

This detour led McGowan to explore others issues and tactics in the Bay Area. He had already worked on a variety of campaigns, but something about genetic engineering particularly moved him. In part it was the audacity of men playing gods, attempting to alter the very foundations of life—decisions that, once made, cannot be undone. National environmental groups had done little to elevate the profile of the issue, so he decided to help things along. In the fall of 1998, at the signing ceremony of a research contract between the University of California at Berkeley and biotech giant Novartis, McGowan hit the CEO, Douglas Watson, with a whipped-cream-covered vegan pumpkin pie.

The "Biotic Baking Brigade" made national headlines with their pastry jihad. The group also served Monsanto CEO Robert Shapiro, Maxxam CEO Charles Hurwitz and other corporate upper crust. It was fun and exciting, so McGowan spent some more time in the kitchen, but the media sometimes lost sight of the issues in the melee. Even the messiest meringue, perfectly tossed, couldn't stop scientists from creating new species. It was becoming increasingly clear to McGowan that he needed to take more direct action.

While in San Francisco he met Suzanne Savoie, who shared his passion for the environment and opposition to genetic engineering. They later became romantically involved. Soon after her arrest, she told the government everything—not just about the Operation Backfire cases but about ten or more other crimes she and McGowan committed together. Over the years he had gradually increased in confidence and experience. He used scythes to destroy genetically engineered crops in California as part of the "Lodi Loppers," and pulled genetically engineered corn crops out of the ground as part of "Reclaim the Seeds." Later, he helped sabotage a biotech lab in Rhinelander, Wisconsin, and uprooted creeping bent grass, genetically engineered for golf courses, as part of the "Anarchist Golfing Association." McGowan is not necessarily proud of those crimes and others, he says. They were not always strategic or sophisticated, but they were patination that prepared him for the Earth Liberation Front.

He left San Francisco for Seattle and the 1999 World Trade Organization protests, and then in 2000 made his way down to Eugene to work for the *Earth First Journal*, a cornerstone of the movement that had been McGowan's New York portal into radical environmental politics. Post-WTO, Eugene had been labeled the epicenter of anarchism; the phrase "Eugene anarchists" became so common in news reports one might have thought it was the name of the town football team, perhaps with black jerseys and a Molotovwielding mascot. Eugene was the town of John Zerzan, author and anarcho-celebrity, and it was the staging area for forest defense campaigns. As soon as he arrived in Oregon, McGowan says, he knew he would never be the same.

He had never seen anything like it. Trees like skyscrapers, forest canopy blocking out the sky. Seeing those old-growth forests marked for clear-cutting only solidified his renunciation of mainstream environmental groups and embrace of direct action. He immersed himself in Eugene's environmental and anarchist movements, and through both found others who had also been radicalized. In September 2000, he attended his first meeting of the Book Club in a motel room in Santa Cruz and gave a presentation about genetic engineering. By December, he was taking part in reconnaissance for a plan that would draw national attention to the issue, and to the ELF.

Sometime before two in the morning on January 2, 2001, Kevin Tubbs drove McGowan, Ferguson, Meyerhoff and Savoie toward Glendale, Oregon, in a van filled with timing devices and fuel. Superior Lumber Company used helicopters to clear-cut old-growth forests on public lands. It had been engaged in legal battles over the environmental impact of its operations. The company was controversial, but it was also symbolic of typical logging operations in the region, and that's why it was targeted.

Meyerhoff had prepared the devices in advance, and McGowan had done reconnaissance for several days. When they pulled up to the property, Savoie headed to a telephone booth on the south side of the building. McGowan went to the north side, hid behind bushes, clutched a radio and watched for trouble. Ferguson set one incendiary device underneath a window on the back of the building. Meyerhoff set the other. With the fires lit, they radioed Tubbs, who picked them up, one by one, and drove through the dark to a rest area where they split into two cars. They ghosted back I-5 to Eugene, listening to their scanners as flames rose behind them. The blaze caused more than $1 million in damage, reducing half the company to ashes.

McGowan spent the night in Eugene and the next day traveled to Portland with Savoie to prepare the communiqué. It called Superior Lumber a "typical earth raper contributing to the ecological destruction of the Northwest." After speaking with him for even a few moments, it's easy to see why McGowan was involved in the preparation of this communiqué and others. He is articulate and well read, but on some issues he becomes fervid. He does not shy away from words like fascism, patriarchy, ecocide. His voice has the timbre of a communiqué, whether he is in the forests of Oregon or the streets of New York City.

A few months later, he is shown the communiqué for a crime he had not aided and did not support. Block, Meyerhoff, Tubbs and Zacher set fire to SUVs at the Romania Chevrolet Truck Center in Eugene, causing about $959,000 in damage. They chose Romania because it had previously been targeted by Jeff "Free" Luers and Craig "Critter" Marshall, who burned three SUVs to make a statement about global warming in 2000. The fire caused about $40,000 in damage and the trucks were later resold. Luers and Marshall had been arrested and were facing trial at the time of "Romania II." McGowan tried to convince the others to remove any mention of his friend Luers from the communiqué, because it could provoke the judge and lead to a harsher sentence. They refused. In the communiqué for their crime, they said: "The techno-industrial state thinks it can stop the growing resistance by jailing some of us, but they cannot jail the spirit of those who know another world is possible. The fire that burns within Free and Critter burns within all of us and cannot be extinguished by locking them up."

McGowan was furious, but he continued working with those who refused to heed his warning.

———

By May 21, 2001, McGowan was ready for a much more substantial role. Savoie drove him, Block, Zacher and Meyerhoff from Zacher's home in Olympia, Washington, an hour and forty-five minutes south to Jefferson Poplar Farm. The farm sits on about seven thousand isolated acres five miles north of Clatskanie, Oregon. It was selected for its production of hybrid poplar/cottonwood trees used in paper manufacture.

McGowan purchased some of the supplies, including plastic containers, some radios and a book to decipher scanner codes. He had also been involved in the production of the timing devices, which at this point had progressed to a professional operation involving layers of plastic gloves and Tyvek hooded plastic suits.

Savoie dropped off the group at the farm and then pulled away, turned off the headlights and monitored the scanner. Zacher looked out while Block carried five-gallon buckets of fuel. Meyerhoff began placing them, one underneath a window and the other near the office steps. McGowan carried fuel containers and placed them at the office and garage, then ran to the barn, shadows sewn to his heels. He moved from truck to truck, running fuel-soaked pieces of cloth "trailers" between them to create what would become a grid of flames. Meyerhoff set the timing devices, McGowan spray-painted "ELF" at the scene, and they radioed Savoie for pickup.

As they drove back to Olympia, tossing their clothes in suburban dumpsters, the fire consumed two buildings, eighteen vehicles, and a trailer. It caused about $1 million in damage, a significant blow on its own, but its impact was magnified by a parallel crime 150 miles away. For the first time, two ELF cells simultaneously targeted the same issue at the same time.

For the second half of the "double whammy," as they called it, another cell in Seattle set fire to the University of Washington Horticulture Center and caused about $3.3 million in damage. Using digital timers, roadside flares and plastic containers of gasoline, they destroyed Merrill Hall, and with it laboratories, library materials, and the office of Professor Toby Bradshaw. The communiqué called Bradshaw's work with hybrid poplars "reckless 'science'" to increase the profits of paper companies. Bradshaw said he used traditional means of cross-breeding, not genetic engineering, and he compared environmentalists burning research to Hitler's SS burning books.

As he had before, McGowan helped prepare the communiqué for his group's portion of the coordinated arsons and sent it anonymously to Craig Rosebraugh of the ELF Press Office. "We torched Jefferson Poplar because hybrid poplars are an ecological nightmare threatening native biodiversity in the ecosystem," the message said. "Our forests are being liquidated and replaced with monocultured tree farms so greedy, earth raping corporations can make more money."

Something changed within McGowan that night on the farm, soaked in gasoline and wrapped in vapors. He says he realized the power, and risks, of his actions. A more stark realization came the next month, when his friend Luers was sentenced to twenty-two years and eight months in prison for burning three SUVs. The unprecedented sentence made international news. Within the radical environmental movement, the sentence was a rallying cry and also a fracturing moment. The retaliatory ELF arson and accompanying communiqué clearly had an impact on Judge Lyle Velure. McGowan says the combination of these events—the firsthand experience with fire, the firsthand experience with its repercussions—changed him.

He needed to get out. He went to Canada to cool down and spend time with friends working with the indigenous Nuxalk Nation on environmental issues. As prosecutors tell it, McGowan fled because he knew that grand juries were investigating his crimes. Feeling partially responsible for the draconian sentence, McGowan assumed a leadership role in Luers's prison support committee and continued that labor-intensive and emotionally draining work until his own arrest. He returned to Eugene in 2002, but it was not the same. He knew he was done with the ELF.

He headed home to New York City for his sister Lisa's thirty-fifth birthday, back to the concrete and noise and gray. There he met Jenny, and if there had been any doubts about abandoning his underground life, she erased them.

McGowan moved back to the city, replacing black masks and incendiary devices with public campaigns like the Really, Really Free Market. His new friends knew him as Jamie Moran. The international press learned that name, too, as McGowan became a spokesperson for groups organizing against the 2004 Republican National Convention. The transition from McGowan to Moran was never complete, though. He was aboveground and lawful, but still sympathetic to the underground. He was quoted in *Rolling Stone* saying, "I'd like to see all Republican events—teas, backslapping lunches—disrupted. I'd like to see corporations involved in the Iraq reconstruction get targeted, anything from occupation to property destruction."

One day McGowan found an old copy of the zine made by William Rodgers, "Setting Fires With Electrical Timers: An Earth Liberation Front Guide." It was previously posted on the ELF Press Office website, but with the closure of the press office the site had become a spam page for Cialis and Viagra. Rodgers's zine was "too technical and scary," McGowan said. But he still made clean copies and mailed them to activist distributors, hoping to place them in new hands.

On April 1, 2005, his old friend Jake Ferguson tracked him down at the Grassroots Animal Rights Conference at New York University. Others had been reluctant to talk to Ferguson about their past lives; Jonathan Paul refused to reminisce, and Ferguson walked away with a blank tape. McGowan was much more talkative. He told Ferguson he was concerned about people opening their mouths, but he thought that for the most part everyone was "solid."

"I was kind of running out of air," he was recorded saying. "I felt like, sooner or later I was going to trip up really hard. And you know, I don't want to fuckin' . . . I didn't want to end up in jail, man."

On December 5, 2005, McGowan was sitting at his desk in the office of Women's Law, a Brooklyn nonprofit that helps victims of domestic violence and sexual assault. He had been preparing the organization's holiday cards and was taking a break to respond to emails. A colleague's dog, part pit bull, lounged on the floor nearby as he typed. Work had piled up, but he was eager to leave the office, take care of some errands and meet Jenny. Then the dog barked.

McGowan looked up and saw a colleague walking toward him, followed by three men. They were FBI agents from Portland and New York, along with a Eugene member of the Joint Terrorism Task Force. Before they said a word, he knew.

"Are you Daniel McGowan?" they asked as they quickly closed the gap between the door and his desk. He knew he was in trouble, but had no idea to what extent. They moved faster. "You're under arrest," they said, "and you're going back to Oregon."

The handcuffs clicked and they left as quickly as they had arrived. "I felt like they were trying to get me out before anyone noticed," McGowan said later. "I basically was getting snatched, and I was concerned nobody would know where I was. When I was walked out I just yelled, 'Call Jenny, call Jenny.'"

Days passed. Another prisoner told him that one of his codefendants killed himself. The guards put McGowan on suicide watch, which meant no books, papers, phone calls, visits or blankets. Was it a trick? Was it pressure to make him cooperate? McGowan refused to believe anything that anyone said. He was cold, dehydrated and alone. The government continued the pressure.

"Are you prepared to go to prison for life? You should really think about this."

"If you don't cooperate with us, it will only get worse."

"When you're convicted, you'll be housed in the terror wing, you know."

McGowan bounced between facilities, and at one point was housed with Ahmed Abdel Sattar, convicted of providing material support to terrorists. Sattar saw McGowan distraught as he read a *New York Times* article about his case. He helped McGowan by bringing him pens, pencils and spy novels. Although stories of government agents chasing down terrorists are not McGowan's usual literary fare, these books were about some other terrorism case, and not his own, so they became an escape.

Meanwhile, his friends and family began organizing a national support campaign. The day after his arrest, friends met at a diner across the street from the courthouse to think strategically about how to help. They decided to publish a website, set up an email list, and contact all of the individuals and activist groups that McGowan had supported over the years. They would make T-shirts and stickers, pitch media interviews and organize protests and bake sales. They would run this group like a public relations campaign.

Jenny and his friends were still in shock, not just from the arrest but also from the revelation that McGowan had led dual lives. Yet they had no time for paralysis. It didn't matter to them if he was called Daniel McGowan or Jamie Moran, Sorrel or Rabid. With his arrest, all of those identities coalesced. Only one identity remains, the one listed in every court document that says *United States v. McGowan*, the one about to feel the full weight of the U.S. government pressing down upon him.

CHAPTER FIVE

Red-baiting

February 23, 2006 "And if the righteousness of the cause in your belief is right, you don't care what tactics they take to achieve that?"

"I do care what tactics are taken, sir."

"When you give those speeches, you're not speaking the way you are today, are you?"

"At times I am," Josh Harper says to the prosecutor and the jury. The government has rested its case against Stop Huntingdon Animal Cruelty, and Harper is the defense's first witness. "At times I am not. Generally speaking, I am more fiery than I am right now."

"Because you're trying to incite people?"

"Because I'm nervous right now."

The government is questioning Harper about a speech he gave to three hundred animal rights activists in October 2001, a key component in their case against him. It was prescient that he began that speech by welcoming the FBI agents in the room. He was not certain that there were any of them present that day in Little Rock, Arkansas, but he knew the campaign to close Huntingdon Life Sciences had attracted the attention of people in high places.

SHAC had awakened and enraged the grassroots animal rights movement like a field of dry grass brought to life by flame. What began in England had spread quickly around the world, and after just a few years, the campaign burned so intensely that the lab shifted operations to New Jersey, where laws concealed shareholder identities. Huntingdon came to the United States hoping to hide.

The campaign drew heavily from the American anti-apartheid movement of the 1980s, which led to the dismantling of racial segregation programs in South Africa by targeting one thing which—unlike protests or letters or phone calls—no government can ignore: money. Anti-apartheid activists focused their demands not on the South African government but on universities, businesses and nations with economic ties to the country.

SHAC set out to make Huntingdon the South Africa of the corporate world. Activists incorporated anti-apartheid tactics and expanded on them. They identified banks, suppliers, customers and employees—anyone with any financial ties to the lab, from Fortune 500 companies down to toilet paper suppliers. They focused on businesses with no vested interest in animal experimentation, either philosophically or economically; Huntingdon needed them, but they did not need Huntingdon.

The war room was a website. Through interactive maps, one click could open a state list of every business with ties to Huntingdon. Another click opened a page of contact information, not generic 1-800 numbers but direct office phone numbers, home phone numbers, cell phone numbers, work addresses, home addresses, fax numbers, email addresses and, in some cases, physical descriptions, church memberships, country club affiliations and more. "The Earth is not dying," the folk singer Utah Phillips once said, "it is being killed. And the people who are killing it have names and addresses." SHAC activists found those names and addresses, and published them on their website.

Local activists used this information to take the campaign straight to the executives and employees who held the most sway over Huntingdon. Like the anti-apartheid movement, SHAC prided itself on following the money, but animal rights activists went further. They sought to make the anonymous business decisions of corporations personal. Instead of screaming at twenty-story office buildings, activists protested where they knew they would be heard. Homes, conferences, job fairs, vacations—they created a spectacle everywhere. They dubbed Huntingdon's general manager "Blockhead" and protested outside his home with a twelve-foot banner that said "Blockhead Caulfield, puppy killing scumbag." When one CEO became a member of the exclusive Augusta National Golf Club, SHAC organized a national call-in to complain. Protesters showed up at the clubhouse.

This was only part of the campaign, a word SHAC carefully used with a lowercase *c*. While aboveground activists took to the streets, the phones and executives' homes, there were underground, anonymous activists playing their own role. They set off stink bombs and smoke bombs, they smashed windows, hacked computers, superglued ATMs, stole credit cards, made threatening phone calls and paint-stripped cars. They snuck into a job fair at Rutgers and stole the files of Huntingdon applicants—and then told them their prospective employer kills puppies. One executive awoke to find a boulder on his car. A Huntingdon director received a subscription to a magazine called *Revolver*; it was in her son's name.

On their own, tactics like these are nothing new. All social movements have both legal and illegal elements, and in other movements the extremists have done much more than throw paint. At about the time Mohandas Gandhi was on his nonviolent march against the British salt tax, the Bengal Volunteers were storming prisons and murdering police. Such disparate tactics typically exist in different worlds, with each camp harshly critical of the other, and that same demarcation exists in the animal rights movement. Nearly all national organizations have publicly condemned illegal tactics and groups like the ALF. At best, they have remained silent. SHAC set itself apart by vocally, unapologetically supporting the underground.

Every action in the name of the campaign went up on the news section of the website. Protest recaps were published alongside anonymous communiqués such as one that described the sinking of a Bank of New York executive's fishing boat. Underground activists lowered his Stars and Stripes, raised the Jolly Roger, sank the boat and signed the communiqué "Pirates for Animal Liberation. . . . HLS thar she blows!" A few days later about thirty people protested outside his house, as they had on multiple occasions, except this time they wore pirate hats.

As Judy Gumbo Albert, a founding member of the Yippies, said of the 1971 Weather Underground bombing of the Capitol building, "We didn't do it, but we dug it." SHAC posted disclaimers on the website saying the group did not engage in illegal activity, but supported those who did. The group published a philosophical defense of direct action alongside a photo of an overturned car. At one animal rights conference I attended, the SHAC booth had Animal Liberation Front air fresheners ("Animal liberation never smelled so sweet") and matchbooks with Huntingdon's address printed inside. SHAC did not sail through the night with the pirates, but they proudly flew the same flag.

It worked. Citibank, Merrill Lynch, Charles Schwab and dozens of other corporate powerhouses decided they would not deal with Huntingdon if it meant dealing with SHAC. Huntingdon's stock plummeted from $30 per share in 1997, before the campaign began, to 25 cents per share in 2000. SHAC grew bolder. In November 2000 Kevin Kjonaas, one of the defendants in the 2006 trial, called the investment firm Stephens Inc. and said he wanted a personal meeting. This was the power SHAC knew it had acquired.

As a gesture of goodwill, Kjonaas agreed to take down StephensKills.com, a parody website with photos of mutilated puppies alongside the Stephens logo. A Stephens representative and a lawyer met Kjonaas on neutral ground at a law office in New York City in January 2001. At the two-hour meeting, Kjonaas presented brochures and photos of what happens to animals at Huntingdon. Activists had already been calling and emailing Stephens offices, urging them to divest. Do it, Kjonaas said, and SHAC would end its campaign. Refuse, and things would get worse.

Stephens balked. A few days later, news broke that the Royal Bank of Scotland had pulled out as Huntingdon's senior lender, and Stephens saved the lab from foreclosure with an emergency $33 million loan. Stephens became the primary financier of Huntingdon, and in turn, Stephens became the primary target of SHAC. The group published personal information, printed leaflets, organized phone and email blockades, and told supporters, as they had for so many other corporate targets, "hit 'em hard."

STRATFOR, a "global intelligence" company that creates custom reports for corporations and governments, explained the campaign model well. There are three legs to the SHAC campaign: illegal activists (the smallest group), legal activists (with signs and bullhorns) and passive sympathizers (opposed to animal cruelty, but not sure how to help). "Since there is no formal membership," STRATFOR's report says, "the numbers are in no way fixed—anyone can wake up tomorrow, read about SHAC on the Internet, and engage in an activity that night that propels them directly into the first tier."

This was the subject of Harper's speech in Little Rock, as hundreds gathered for a weekend of protests at the homes and offices of Stephens executives. Harper had lived in town for several months prior, submitting paperwork, talking to city council members and meeting with police. His speech made it clear, though, that his work was only one form of social change. He told activists that no matter how they choose to fight Huntingdon, legally or illegally, they should not condemn those who choose other methods. All of it would bring Huntingdon closer to financial collapse.

As he spoke—looking out at hundreds of activists, film crews, mustachioed undercover cops, and men from Global Options, a private security firm—one thing could not have been more clear: his words mattered.

In the nine trial days before Harper took the witness stand, prosecutors built their case against the SHAC defendants. Corporate executives detailed what they had experienced because of their business relationship with Huntingdon. Prosecutors had them read aloud page after page of printouts from the SHAC public website, including action alerts, protest write-ups and anonymous communiqués. Although none of the defendants were accused of any of the crimes posted on the site, the government hoped to convince the jury that by identifying targets, posting personal information and unabashedly supporting illegal actions, they were part of a conspiracy.

Historically, conspiracy charges have been used against political activists when the government cannot make anything else stick. The Chicago Seven, for instance, were on trial for conspiracy to riot and disrupt the 1968 Democratic National Convention in Chicago. In 1968 Dr. Benjamin Spock, the baby doctor, was convicted of conspiracy to "counsel, aid, and abet resistance" to the draft because he spoke out against the war. Evidence used against him included public speeches and news footage. The alleged SHAC conspiracy was even more amorphous, conflating not just words and actions, but a national organization and an entire underground movement.

Now, all defendants have been charged with conspiracy to violate the Animal Enterprise Protection Act. For Darius Fullmer and Andy Stepanian, it is their only charge. Fullmer sent emails about protests and helped research corporate targets online. Stepanian took part in protests, and one witness testified that he instructed protesters where to stand in order to comply with police.

Harper faces an additional charge because of two speeches in which he advocated email blockades, electronic civil disobedience and black faxing. Black faxing means sending a completely black piece of paper—sometimes with "Divest" or "Close HLS" in small white letters—to businesses associated with the lab. Continuous faxing clogs company phone lines and drains ink cartridges. The government says that Harper's speeches promoted these tactics and therefore make him part of a conspiracy to harass using a telecommunications device. Conroy, Gazzola and Kjonaas are also charged with this, in large part because the SHAC website promoted electronic civil disobedience.

The non-conspiracy charges being levied against the defendants are no less nebulous. The government argues that the posting of personal information on the SHAC website, combined with protests at individuals' homes, phone calls, emails and the crimes of underground activists, instilled a reasonable fear of bodily harm in three Marsh insurance executives. For this, Conroy, Gazzola and Kjonaas have been charged with conspiracy to stalk and three counts of interstate stalking, charges typically filed against abusive ex-lovers or deranged admirers, not political activists organizing a national campaign. All charges against John McGee are dropped, and the remaining six defendants plus the organization SHAC, which is also on trial, have become known as the SHAC 7.

Evidence presented by the government to support these charges included journals, address books, "to do" lists from their homes, Google search records, stickers from Harper's room, a notebook with a "Support the ALF" sticker, binders full of letters from corporations pledging to sever ties, emails from among the approximately 10,000 that were surveilled and phone calls from among the 8,300 that were monitored. A member of the Joint Terrorism Task Force testified about a job application found during a raid of the SHAC house in New Jersey; Lauren Gazzola, applying for a job at Angelica Kitchen, an organic, vegan restaurant in New York City, had listed as prior work experience "campaign coordinator" for SHAC.

The government seized nine computers from the SHAC house and paid an electronic forensic company $180,000 to scour every file, including those that had been deleted. On most computers was a program called PGP, or Pretty Good Privacy. It is actually really good privacy. The program uses complicated algorithms and electronic key pairs. A public key "signs" emails, and a private key unlocks them. PGP is accessible enough for anyone with basic computer skills and sophisticated enough for Fortune 500 companies. The government depicted PGP as a tool used by those who have something to hide; defense attorneys say that by this logic, the only people who draw their curtains are those about to break the law. The forensic firm ran special software nonstop for days attempting to decode emails, to no avail.

Instead, it was the defendants' non-encrypted communications—the speeches, home protests, websites and emails on public listservs—that comprised the government's case. SHAC's campaign of terror was so brazen, prosecutors said, that they even posted a list of Top 20 Terror Tactics to incite their followers to violence. Firebombing cars, flooding homes, mailing death threats, stealing documents and spraying window cleaner into executives' eyes are among the terrorism tactics that prosecutors said SHAC recommended. "They were the commanders who often got their foot soldiers to go out and do dirty work," U.S. Attorney Charles McKenna said. "And like many wars or engagements, oftentime the commanders don't even know who the foot soldiers are."

McKenna left out a critical detail of this war plan, though. It was not created by SHAC. The Top 20 Terror Tactics list was created by the Research Defence Society, a British animal testing lobby group that supports Huntingdon. In typical SHAC style, the group republished the list online with a note about its origins.

"Their side produced the information," it said. "We're just helping spread the propaganda. Now don't go getting any funny ideas."

Earlier in the trial, defense attorney Andrew Erba warned jurors that they would read some unpleasant web postings. "I'll be honest with you," he said. "It's much more punk rock than Beethoven." His comment was meant as an insult, but he had subtly hit on a deeper truth, critical to any discussion of the radical animal rights and environmental movements: in order to understand them, it helps to know a bit about punk rock.

The mainstream perception of punk is, as Erba suggested, one of insolence. Leather jackets, green mohawks and middle fingers. Lots of middle fingers. It is characterized as either "Fuck the world!" nihilism or "How does my studded belt look?" teenage rebellion. Those things have all had their place in punk subcultures, of course, but there has been much more, just as there was more to hippie culture than peace signs and long hair.

It is undeniable that the punk and hardcore scenes have had a formative, lasting impact on these movements. Rod Coronado became a vegan in 1986 because of the lyrics in a song by Conflict called *This Is the A.L.F.*; he later formed ALF cells himself. Before he became a spokesperson for the ELF, Craig Rosebraugh's first exposure to radical politics was through bands like Crass, Subhumans and Citizen Fish. In the 1980s, at a time when animal rights and environmental issues were far from mainstream, they were being militantly defended by many punk bands.

For the next generation of activists, 1990s hardcore was even more influential. The scene was far from homogenous, but bands like Earth Crisis helped ingrain militant animal rights and environmental politics into the culture: "Destroy the machines that kill the forests, that disfigure the earth / Ecotage when efforts to reason fail and no longer have worth." Peter Young, one of the first activists convicted of animal enterprise terrorism, says this vegan, straightedge culture inspired him to raid fur farms; others clearly felt the same, quoting hardcore lyrics in communiqués. Few people in the outside world knew what the word vegan meant, or how to pronounce it, but within a large segment of the hardcore scene veganism and support for animal rights was expected.

Although there is a shortage of research into punk's impact on animal rights and environmental activism, some connections have been made. An investigation by sociologist Elizabeth Cherry, for instance, showed that "punk vegans" had stronger, better-defined and longer-lasting commitments to animal activism than "non-punk vegans." This is not because of the bands or the fashion, Cherry argues. It is because of the community.

This is not to say there is a direct, causal, Tipper Gore–style link between the music and the movement. Punk records do not turn teens into saboteurs. It might be that the same types of people who are drawn to angry, outcast music are also drawn to angry, outcast activism.

It could also be that the punk scene has a lasting influence on those involved and shapes how they interact with the world. Perhaps the only canon of punk, true across musical styles and subcultures, is that if you want to do something, you should just go out and do it yourself. Don't wait for permission or approval. Start a band, book a show, design a flier, publish a zine, plan a tour. If there is something that needs to be done, do it.

Five of the six SHAC defendants have ties to the punk and hardcore scenes (Kevin Kjonaas is more of a Justin Timberlake fan) and they all embrace this DIY ethic. However, instead of recording a 7″ record, they decided to shut down a multinational corporation.

Self-taught, SHAC activists developed a Wall Street–level knowledge of business that made the anti-apartheid movement appear amateurish. They targeted Marsh Inc., Huntingdon's insurance provider, because without insurance the lab couldn't function. They targeted Bank of New York because it held many American depository receipts, which allow U.S. investors to trade on the London stock exchange. They pressured members of the board of directors to resign, and were so successful that Huntingdon appointed someone thought to be unreachable—the seventy-three-year-old owner of a cement and paper business in Pakistan. SHAC told activists to buy international phone cards. He quit in a week.

As Huntingdon's stock plummeted, it was placed on the OTC Bulletin Board, a trading platform for riskier businesses that cannot meet the financial standards of the world's major stock exchanges. SHAC didn't stop there. They researched arcane financial regulations and learned that trading on the bulletin board requires market makers—go-between companies that match buyers with sellers. Without market makers a company's stock remains dormant. Huntingdon typically used six or eight of them. In one nine-week period, SHAC picked off one market maker a week. Huntingdon's chief financial officer, Richard Michaelson, testified that the company lost fifty market makers because of animal activists. When its final market maker cut ties, Huntingdon fell from the OTC Bulletin Board to be traded with the riskiest investments on the pink sheets, the currency of the moribund.

With each victory and each new tactic, the industry grew increasingly worried. After Huntingdon, would they move on to another lab? Or would they apply the same tactics to another industry? The closure of Huntingdon was no longer a matter of if but of when. In 1999, SHAC UK had set out to close the lab in three years. It could take a bit longer, but the global campaign was on track. Unless these activists were stopped, they would move on to the next lab, and the next, until they destroyed the animal testing industry.

Corporations fought back with court orders to restrict SHAC's protest times and locations. Across the country, they filed restraining orders and injunctions. They even tried to use the Racketeer Influenced and Corrupt Organizations Act, the mob law. Nothing worked. The campaign continued.

Through all these attempts, there was one thing that corporations and the government had not tried. In 1992, Congress passed an obscure law called the Animal Enterprise Protection Act. It received little attention except from the meat, dairy, fur and animal experimentation industries that lobbied for it. The law created a new crime of "animal enterprise terrorism" in response to the growing frequency and severity of crimes by groups like the ALF.

Prosecutors applied it only once, in the case of Justin Samuel and Peter Young, two animal rights activists who released mink from fur farms. Other than that, it remained unused. The law was intended for the prosecution of underground activists, but the government cannot prosecute those it cannot catch. With SHAC, the government decided to try something new. Prosecutors reinterpreted the law's requirement of "physical disruption to the functioning of an animal enterprise" to mean causing the loss of profits; if the anonymous, underground activists could not be caught, they would go after those who vocally supported them.

Meanwhile, there was a bigger strategy unfolding. At the same time multiple government agencies were preparing to use this law against SHAC, top FBI and Justice Department officials were testifying before Congress that the law needed to be expanded precisely because it *could not* be applied to SHAC. The FBI's John Lewis told Congress, "This statute does not cover many of the activities SHAC routinely engages in on its mission to shut down HLS." Either top law enforcement officials did not know about the largest domestic terrorism investigation in the country, or they were intentionally misleading Congress in order to secure new powers.

The corporations targeted by SHAC were some of the biggest and most powerful in the world, and their executives had connections to other powerful people. Two weeks after the SHAC protest in Little Rock against Stephens Inc., Republican Senator Tim Hutchinson of Arkansas introduced a bill to expand penalties in the Animal Enterprise Protection Act. "[Stephens] was not only on the back of my mind, it was on the forefront," Hutchinson said. Arkansas Representative Marion Berry also joined the call for expanded terrorism legislation. Both Hutchison and Berry had received thousands of dollars in contributions from the Stephens political action committee and individual executives. The bill was ultimately passed by Congress as part of another bioterrorism bill.

As the government presented its case in the SHAC trial, it was revealed that Huntingdon's general counsel, Mark Bibi, had built a relationship with FBI Special Agent Jeffrey Farrar and Assistant U.S. Attorney Charles McKenna. In about seventy-five emails spanning three years, he offered website postings, news clips, and commentary on how he thought the government should pursue the case. He advised McKenna that Harper and Kjonaas would be lecturing at Long Island University, because he thought the government should monitor their speeches, and he sent an article by Steve Best, a professor of philosophy, with a warning that defense attorneys may argue that the campaign is protected by the First Amendment.

In another email, he attached a news article about the campaign. "Kevin Kjonaas is quoted in this article as saying, 'the FBI can't arrest us on anything, they can't indict us on anything,'" Bibi wrote to McKenna on October 1, 2003. "Charlie, I'm counting on you to prove him wrong."

After September 11th, President George W. Bush said the terrorists who attacked the Twin Towers did so because they hate our freedom. That, of course, is an incredibly reductionist view of the attacks and of U.S. foreign policy, but a study of First Amendment law adds some authenticity to the president's assertion. I am not sure about Al Qaeda, but if the average American knew what types of activity the First Amendment has protected, there is a good chance they would hate our freedom, too.

The history of the First Amendment is one of protecting the vulgar, the crass, the wayward and unhinged. It has protected Clarence Brandenburg, a Ku Klux Klan leader, when he called for "revengeance" against the courts, Congress and the president, while Klansmen at the rally shouted, "Bury the niggers." At a very different kind of rally, Robert Watts told antiwar protesters that he would refuse service if drafted to Vietnam. "If they ever make me carry a rifle," he said, "the first man I want to get in my sights is L.B.J."

In segregated Mississippi, an NAACP field organizer named Charles Evers helped organize a boycott of white-owned businesses. "Store-watchers" monitored who shopped there. They printed their names in the newspaper and read them aloud at churches. Violating the boycott had serious repercussions: people had been beaten, others had bullets fired through their windows. It was in this climate that Evers warned, "If we catch any of you going in any of them racist stores, we're gonna break your damn neck." *NAACP v. Claiborne Hardware Co.* was strikingly similar to the SHAC case in that it involved political hyperbole, personalized targeting, and a campaign with both legal and illegal elements. The Supreme Court ruled that Evers's speech was protected by the Constitution.

This is how high the bar has been set in First Amendment law. It does not mean the bar is unreachable. In 2002, a federal appeals court ruled that the First Amendment did not protect a website called the Nuremberg Files, which posted pictures of doctors who performed abortions, with their names underneath the photos, and crossed off the names of three of them as they were killed. In another case, an appeals court ruled that Paladin Press was not protected in its publication of *Hit Man: A Technical Manual.* The how-to style book was used in a triple murder, and in a ruling troubling to free speech and journalism organizations, the court decided that the book publisher could be sued for aiding and abetting the crimes. The rulings in these cases remain extremely controversial because they butt against one of the most important tests established by the Supreme Court to separate political hyperbole from unprotected speech. As established in the Brandenburg case, threatening speech is protected up to the point it incites others to "imminent and lawless action."

At Josh Harper's speech at the University of Washington in 2001, the ten attendees—including one FBI agent—were not incited.

They left calmly. There was a much larger audience at the Little Rock speech, and his rhetoric was more fiery. He told the crowd, "What we're here to convince you to do is to take the personal initiative to shut this fucking lab down." People sat and listened, they clapped, and then the next speaker stepped to the podium. There was a riot that weekend, but it was a police riot; when activists refused to enter designated "protest pens," believing that the First Amendment says nothing of speaking from cages, cops in riot gear used batons and pepper spray.

During the SHAC trial, the government called only one witness who actually committed crimes in the name of the campaign. Jeffrey Dillbone learned about Huntingdon when he was fifteen years old. He read about black faxing on a non-SHAC website and decided to fax Stephens using his parents' machine and a phone card.

He visited the SHAC website on a daily basis. The group posted calendars of events. Each day of the week had a different way to pressure businesses, including protests, phone calls and emails. On some days, SHAC advertised electronic civil disobedience. Activists could use computer software to overload corporate websites by sending, at one high point, 800,000 requests for Huntingdon's website in a three-hour period. The SHAC website provided a link to an external website and told activists that if they chose to participate they could click the link at a specified time. The notice came with a warning: "This is not a game. Please read the action justification before starting. Also read the warning of the possible consequences."

Dillbone testified that he learned about electronic civil disobedience approximately one year before participating, and that SHAC posted notices about the actions weeks in advance. He had ample time to think about his actions. In the words of Hal Haveson, Jake Conroy's attorney, "imminence" means that speech sets fire to reason. Dillbone read the disclaimer, thought about it, downloaded the program, blocked his phone number, and participated. SHAC, he said, did not set fire to his reason.

Ultimately, prosecutors argued, it does not matter whether SHAC committed the crimes, nor does it matter whether they incited others to do so. The defendants knew that listing individuals on their website made them a target for underground groups, and when crimes were committed SHAC supported them, because they gave the group bargaining power. SHAC intended for those targeted to perceive the website as a true threat, because through fear came power. It is an ambitious legal argument: past crimes, by other individuals, against other targets, can be a true threat to future targets without meeting the incitement standard. A ruling in the government's favor would be a historic decision on the limits of free speech.

The courts have not made exceptions to the First Amendment lightly or without controversy, believing that the amount of protection afforded to those on the fringes reflects the freedoms of those at the center. In many ways, First Amendment rulings are not really about protecting unsavory speech but about refusing to prohibit it. They are not about the case at hand, but the one that follows: what the government may silence next if the bulwarks at the fringes of free speech are not relentlessly defended.

Because of this, the arc of First Amendment history has bent toward protecting the rights of the Brandenburgs, the Wattses, the Everses and, defense attorneys argue, the SHACs. It is a very long arc, though, for each landmark decision came from higher courts long after the speakers lost at trial.

Lunch breaks gave jurors and defendants about thirty minutes to find some food and rush back to the courtroom. Even if they'd had more time, it probably wouldn't have helped. For all the things Trenton makes, vegan food is not one of them.

During one break in the trial, I visit the Trenton Federal Courthouse "cafeteria" with some of the defendants. They know the routine, and so does the woman behind the counter. The "animal rights terrorists" have a special menu not listed alongside the other items on the rectangular white board with black block-letter stickers.

"Soy hot dog?," she asks, smiling. She snaps on a pair of latex gloves, pulls limp, flesh-colored tofu wieners from their clear plastic wrapper, briefly microwaves them on paper plates, and plops them on bleached white bread. We each pay about $4.

"I already feel like I'm in prison," someone says. There probably won't be tofu hot dogs in prison.

There isn't much talking during lunch. The tactic, I believe, is to finish the Tofu Pup and leave the crinkling linoleum, folding chairs and discolored wall paneling behind as quickly as possible. We head out the door and toward the elevators that lead back to the court-room. As we pass the metal detectors, a group of attorneys stops us. One of them asks: "Are you all law students?"

What else could they be? Andy Stepanian wears spotless suits, often with a bright pink shimmering tie. Jake Conroy looks like who he is: a clean-cut kid from Connecticut more comfortable in cargo pants and a hoodie than court clothes. Darius Fullmer works as a paramedic in New Jersey. Josh Harper wears his thick glasses and carries a stack of skateboard magazines with his court papers. Lauren Gazzola fits the law student image the most, perhaps be-cause she rescheduled the LSAT after cops stormed her house with guns drawn, and she scored in the 97th percentile.

"No," Gazzola says, smiling, and without hesitation. "We're on trial for terrorism."

The security guard scanning briefcases on a six-foot conveyor belt laughs.

Before Harper steps down from the witness stand, he speaks about how he began to rethink some of the flashpoint crimes of the cam-paign, including the stink bombs at the Bank of America tower in Seattle. He applauded the incident in speeches, until he learned that the intense stench induced nausea and fainting. Even more contro-versial were the 2003 bombings of two corporations, Chiron and Shaklee, in California. A new group called the Revolutionary Cells claimed responsibility for the attacks, saying, "This is the endgame for the animal killers, and if you choose to stand with them you will be dealt with accordingly." The Chiron bombings took place while employees were inside, and the pipe bombs used against Shaklee were wrapped in nails. The crimes could have injured someone, Harper says, and actions like that are detrimental to the campaign and contrary to the beliefs of the defendants.

Those were not the only actions published on the website that made him and other activists uncomfortable. One anonymous communiqué targeted Theresa Kushner, a senior veterinarian at Huntingdon. It described Kushner's panties, which the authors had obtained—Fruit of the Loom, size eight, white with purple flowers, and soiled with her blood. They were advertised for auction on a fe-tish website, and the communiqué said: "Even if the item gets taken down from bidding, you can be assured, Terry, tonight some per-vert will be jacking off to your dirty underwear." It ominously ended with, "Oh and did we forget to mention that all interested buyers will also receive your address and telephone number and an invita-tion to come over?"

Outside of the courtroom, Harper and the others will tell me they had backed themselves into a corner with the website. From the beginning, they established a policy of publishing everything sent to them, regardless of whether they felt it was effective or mor-al. Many animal rights activists passionately believed that SHAC or-ganizers had no right to question underground activists who risked their freedom. The publishing policy was designed to insulate SHAC from any accusations of censorship. The Kushner communiqué, in particular, made them question this decision. Supporting animal liberations and sabotage, Harper says, should never necessitate sup-port for veiled rape threats.

After Harper steps down, the jury hears from other animal rights activists about their activism and why they took part in home demonstrations. They are restricted in what they can say. Judge Anne Thompson prohibits them from speaking about Huntingdon's animal welfare violations. She had allowed Brian Cass, managing director of Huntingdon, to say the lab's work saves lives, but she refuses to allow Dr. Ray Greek, one the leading opponents of animal experimentation, to testify. "It would be a confusion," she says.

Jurors are allowed to hear about Lauren Gazzola's involvement in a 2002 protest at the home of Rob Harper, a Marsh executive. She chanted "What goes around comes around," and a group of about ten people responded, "Burn his house to the ground." The chant was used four times during a ten-second period, while protesters laughed and police watched. Gazzola yelled that the police could not protect Rob Harper at all hours, which is exactly what Charles Evers said of boycott violators. The jury is not allowed to hear that a Massachusetts court dismissed Gazzola's charges on Constitutional grounds.

A trial that was expected to last three months winds down in two weeks. The entire defense team, believing that the government had clearly failed to make its case, takes one day to present its witnesses and evidence.

Defense attorneys are about to rest their case when a final witness unexpectedly speaks.

After Kevin Kjonaas relinquished his position as president of SHAC, Pam Ferdin took the helm. As a child, Ferdin appeared in many sixties and seventies television programs and was the voice of Lucy on Charlie Brown cartoons. Later she stepped into a different spotlight. Her husband, Dr. Jerry Vlasak, has made international news for his advocacy of physical violence against animal experimenters. Just a few months before trial, a Senate committee held a hearing titled "Eco-Terrorism Specifically Examining Stop Huntingdon Animal

Cruelty." The committee invited Vlasak to testify. The defendants and SHAC supporters argued that nothing positive could come from it. The hearing was a transparent effort to smear the defendants as terrorists as they awaited trial. Vlasak went forward with the testimony, speaking about SHAC and the campaign to close Huntingdon and then, in the next breath, saying that murder would be "morally justifiable." "The animal rights movement," he said, "has been notoriously nonviolent up to this point."

It is Ferdin's right as SHAC president to take the stand. She feels the trial has been unfair since jury selection, when the judge dismissed a juror for being vegetarian but allowed jurors with ties to companies SHAC targeted. Ferdin says she wants to counter the misleading statements of witnesses and prosecutors.

The other defendants have pleaded against this. With Ferdin comes too much baggage. Throughout the trial the defense has attempted to make clear that, despite all the support of property destruction, SHAC always stopped short of supporting physical violence. Prosecutors tried to align the group with David Blenkinsop, a man who beat Huntingdon's Brian Cass in England, but witnesses made clear that SHAC condemned the crime. Ferdin's comments in support of violence will undoubtedly be brought into the trial, the defendants believe, and they will only help the government's case. They feel it is not a decision that Ferdin, who faces no prison time, has the right to make.

Ferdin testifies anyway, and, as expected, prosecutors question her about media interviews where she said it was only a matter of time before animal rights activists resort to physical violence. She was quoted by *Salon* as saying that she loves legal battles like the SHAC trial because they are a public education opportunity. If the SHAC defendants are convicted, "People, I think, are going to get hurt," she said. "There's going to be a lot of violence."

The defendants face a double-edged sword as attorneys present their closing arguments and the jurors begin deliberations. If they lose, they will go to prison and be labeled "terrorists" for the rest of their lives. If they win, it could become the foundation of an even harsher political crackdown, as corporations continue lobbying for expanded terrorism legislation to stop the campaign.

On March 2, 2006, after three days of deliberation, the jury returns a verdict, for all defendants and on all counts: guilty.

Days later, industry groups signal what is to come. David Martosko of the Center for Consumer Freedom, a mouthpiece for the restaurant industry, says the government should build on the victory against SHAC and take aggressive action against mainstream organizations like PETA and the Humane Society of the United States. He calls these national organizations "farm teams for the eco-terror problem."

"This," he says, "is just the starting gun."

CHAPTER SIX

Are You Now, or Have You Ever Been, a Vegetarian?

May 23, 2006 As I walk through the halls of Congress, I feel like I'm back in the Catholic churches of my youth. Its scent is rich and pungent, pine tar soap and the kind of pomade that only grandfathers use. It smells of dark oak and echoing halls, rituals and rites, faith and fear. It feels old and comfortable, but also foreign, and as I walk I feel the same way now as I did back then: I do not belong here. It's unsettling to be in a historic place and witness its everyday use. Reverence is replaced with routine, and the past becomes intertwined with and indistinguishable from the present.

Outside of room 2141 in the Rayburn House Office Building in Washington, D.C., a long line has formed. Congressional staffers and lobbyists wait to ensure they have seats at a hearing by the Subcommittee on Crime, Terrorism and Homeland Security on the Animal Enterprise Terrorism Act. Many people in the crowd are bike messengers who have been hired as line standers. Moments before the hearing begins, the courier in cut-off shorts with grease stains on his messenger bag will swap places with a corporate executive. In the gospel, "Jesus went into the temple of God, and cast out all them that sold and bought in the temple, and overthrew the tables of the moneychangers, and the seats of them that sold doves."

In this temple the money changers have their seats and their tables, and they don't even need to wait in line for them.

I'm unsure of the protocol at a Congressional hearing, so as soon as I enter the room I walk right up to the other witnesses and introduce myself. Brent McIntosh is a deputy assistant attorney general for the Justice Department. He is the only one to smile. William Trundley, the British vice president of corporate security for GlaxoSmithKline, offers a limp handshake and an up-and-down glance. He wears a pinstriped suit and pinstriped shirt, perfectly pressed. Michele Basso, an animal experimenter from Wisconsin, turns her back to me as I shake hands with the others. I step beside her and introduce myself again, more loudly this time, and she compresses her lips and doesn't say a word. As the three chat and laugh together, I sit and stare at the rows of microphones in front of me. To my left sits a woman who will transcribe the hearing. We talk about vegetable gardening. I pour water from the pitcher on the table. I straighten the pages of my typed testimony and then fold my hands.

It's a strange place, Washington, where people discuss terrorism laws over burritos. Four days before the hearing, I had met a former colleague from the American Civil Liberties Union at the burrito cart on the corner of 15th and K, the heart of the lobby district. She said that Republicans wanted to move the Animal Enterprise Terrorism Act forward, and were holding a hearing. Democrats had invited the Humane Society of the United States to testify about the Constitutional concerns they had raised privately with the Justice Department. The Humane Society declined because, in this political climate, opposing an "eco-terrorism" bill would be spun by adversaries as implicit support for illegal tactics. It would tarnish the group's mainstream reputation and jeopardize a bill to ban horse slaughter—concerns that would prove well founded when the horse industry published full-page ads in *Roll Call* with a photo of a slaughterhouse on fire and the message, "Animal rights groups will stop at nothing to ban businesses they do not want operating in the U.S." The Humane Society deferred to the ACLU, and the ACLU's national security experts responded that they were overloaded. My former colleague knew I had been tracking the bill, so she asked if she could recommend me to the committee. I agreed without hesitation.

I viewed testifying as an honor, both a recognition of my work and an opportunity for it to help shape public discourse. Republicans controlled the committee and selected three of the four witnesses. I would be the lone "opposition" expert witness, selected by Representative Bobby Scott, the senior Democrat on the committee. Scott's website declared he was "known in Congress as a champion of the Bill of Rights to the U.S. Constitution." From my tenure at the ACLU, I knew he had a strong civil liberties record. When I spoke with a Congressional staffer who worked for Scott, my perception quickly changed. I was told that Scott supported the bill.

Although he had the opportunity, and responsibility, to select the only dissenting witness, he wanted someone who would not cause problems. I could be somewhat remonstrative, I was told, but I should remember that Scott supported the legislation and I was his witness. I had wanted to believe that members of Congress respected and valued, however begrudgingly, the fourth estate's autonomous role as a watchdog in democratic processes. I had naïvely thought that lawmakers had invited me to listen to my testimony, ask questions, and then come to their own conclusions. But Republicans and Democrats alike had already been swayed by more influential players. It was becoming clear that I was being invited to appear as a token gesture of dissent in their spectacle of democracy.

I began to second guess my decision. If I challenged the legislation, I would do so as a sacrificial lamb. It was clear that I would not be warmly welcomed, but I began to wonder if the experience could turn out much worse. Would I be smeared as an "animal rights terrorist," as the Humane Society had feared? Would FBI agents fulfill their promises from years ago and tell members of Congress that I was on a domestic terrorist list? Would the representative from Wisconsin turn to me and ask, "Mr. Potter, are you now, or have you ever been, a vegetarian?"

It had been three years since the FBI threatened me in Chicago, and fear had followed me. It didn't paralyze me as it had before, but its mere existence, even fleetingly, was a reminder that I had been dishonest with myself. After Chicago I had moved to Washington to cover Congress and politics for another newspaper, and I had continued living a compartmentalized life. There was Activist Will Potter and Journalist Will Potter. Sometimes the lines blurred, such as when I wrote an essay on the SHAC 7 for a progressive website. But for the most part I maintained the borders of my life as if it were a Victorian garden, my professional voice and personal voice each cultivated in clearly defined and separate plots. I had made some small efforts to reconcile the two, such as leaving the "unbiased" newsroom to use my writing for very biased purposes at the ACLU, ghostwriting op-eds and speeches on issues like the Patriot Act. I enjoyed the challenge of writing in another's voice, but it was no substitute for using my own.

The historian Howard Zinn always advised his students, "You can't be neutral on a moving train." The Republicans and Democrats on the committee all supported this dangerous legislation. Corporations had been awaiting this moment for years and wanted nothing more than for their bill to proceed unchallenged. This train is moving, I thought, whether we like it or not. It's no use feigning neutrality as smoke rises from the engine. The only question is if we'll safely stay in our seats as the cliff approaches, or if we'll take action, no matter how small or seemingly futile, to change course. It was time for me to reconcile my personal and professional lives.

Terrorism legislation targeting animal rights activists had been proposed for more than twenty years prior to this Congressional hearing. The chrysalis had been formed on April 16, 1987, when the ALF set fire to a veterinary diagnostic laboratory under construction at the University of California at Davis. Animal rights activists had used arson in England for at least a decade, but this was believed to be the first time the ALF had burned in the United States. At the time, this was the most destructive underground animal rights crime in U.S. history. Davis demonstrated an increasingly sophisticated, bold and effective underground movement that demanded a comparable response.

This was a watershed moment, and it triggered two responses. First, law enforcement changed how it classified and investigated crimes by animal rights and environmental activists. The FBI, for the first time, labeled an animal rights crime "domestic terrorism." Davis marked the beginning of the ALF's official classification as a domestic terrorist organization.

Second, corporations and industry groups, which had made that semantic shift long ago, used Davis as the impetus for legislation that carved out special protections for animal enterprises. They began their fight at the state level. Beginning in 1988, two states passed laws specifically crafted to target animal rights activists. Then two more states followed in 1989. Then eight more in 1990. Then eleven more in 1991.

Proponents argued that animal rights activists could not be prosecuted without this new legislation. In the history of the radical animal rights movement in the United States, only nine people had been convicted of animal rights–related crimes, according to government statistics. Only one person, Fran Trutt, had been convicted on federal charges—and she had been set up by the corporation she targeted. There had only been one ALF conviction. On October 25, 1986, Roger Troen drove a car full of lab animals from the University of Oregon psychology department to safe homes. He was convicted in 1988, at age fifty-six, on theft and burglary charges. The judge said that Troen's role in the transportation of 125 rabbits, hamsters and rats was nothing less than "an act of terrorism," yet sentenced him to only five years probation.

Through it all, ALF attacks continued. The FBI officially labeled two other incidents in this period as domestic terrorism. On April 3, 1989, the ALF set fire to two University of Arizona buildings in Tucson after removing more than a thousand animals. The arson caused at least $150,000 in damage. On July 4, 1989, the ALF broke into the Texas Tech lab and office of John Orem. Orem had been studying sleep apnea and sudden infant death syndrome by experimenting on cats, bolting electrodes into their skulls and bolting their heads into restraining devices. He had also forced them to balance on a wooden plank over a drum of water to see how they responded to sleep deprivation. ALF activists destroyed about $70,000 worth of Orem's equipment, rescued five cats, and in three-foot-high letters on the walls spray-painted, "Don't Mess With Texas Animals."

There had been talk of federal legislation since the mid-1980s, even before Davis, but it had mostly been only talk. As state-level lobbying gained momentum and ALF crimes continued, federal legislation began to seem feasible. To pave the way for a new national law, proponents used the media and Congressional hearings to label animal rights activists as terrorists; in a study of all *New York Times* coverage of animal rights issues through 2007, and a similar content analysis of Congressional hearings, Jen Girgen of Florida State University found that the most common claim by adversaries was that "animal rights activists are violent, criminals, and/or terrorists."

Politicians seized the national attention generated by high-profile crimes to push their legislation. Four days after the Arizona raid, a Democratic senator, Howell Heflin of Alabama, introduced a bill amending the Animal Welfare Act to target people who rescue animals from labs. Soon after the Texas raid, a Democratic representative from Texas, Charles Stenholm, introduced a similar bill.

In 1990, Congress held a hearing in which law enforcement

and industry groups called for a new federal law to target animal rights attacks. The bill should have slipped through, greased by the spate of arsons and the sympathetic White House of George H.W. Bush. Instead, the proposal was challenged by an unlikely source: Bush's own Justice Department. It may be difficult, post-9/11, to fathom the government declining new terrorism powers. For the U.S. deputy assistant attorney general at the time, though, it was a traditional, conservative defense of limited government. "Despite our sympathy to the aims of some of these bills," Paul L. Maloney said, "the [Justice] Department cannot endorse the creation of new federal criminal legislation, which, in our view, would add nothing to the prosecution of these types of offenses."

In a highly unusual move, the White House issued a letter rebuking the Justice Department. The Bush administration had not made animal rights crimes a priority, but within the White House was someone who cared deeply. James B. Wyngaarden, a coauthor of the letter, was an associate director in the Office of Science and Technology Policy. He had advocated federal legislation targeting animal rights "terrorists" since 1985, when he was head of the National Institutes of Health. His proposal had gone nowhere, but this new position in the Bush administration offered a better opportunity for his voice to be heard. However, even with pressure coming from the White House, there was still not enough congressional support for the bill, and it stagnated in committee.

Supporters needed lobbying leverage, something to refocus national attention on animal rights terrorists. They needed another Davis.

On February 28, 1992, the ALF raided mink research facilities at Michigan State University, pouring sulfuric acid on research equipment, setting fire to a professor's office, and destroying more than thirty years of fur farm research. The crimes caused approximately $125,000 in damage. What set the action apart was that it capped a systematic, multi-state attack on fur farms and research that cost the industry millions. The ALF had also set fire to the Northwestern Food Cooperative in Washington, which supplies feed to fur farmers; an experimental mink farm at Oregon State University; and a mink farm in Yamhill, Oregon. Dubbed "Operation Bite Back," the crimes were led by Rod Coronado, who had been a legend of the environmental movement since 1986 when, as a crew member for the Sea Shepherd Conservation Society, he sank two unmanned Icelandic whaling ships.

Operation Bite Back was national news. Groups like the National Animal Interest Alliance and National Association for Biomedical Research pointed to the crimes as a reminder of the growing threat of animal rights extremists and the need for new laws. That summer of 1992, against the wishes of the Justice Department, Congress passed its first version of animal rights terrorism legislation.

The 1992 Animal Enterprise Protection Act created the crime of animal enterprise terrorism for anyone who "intentionally causes physical disruption to the functioning of an animal enterprise by intentionally stealing, damaging, or causing the loss of, any property," and causes economic damage exceeding $10,000. The focus was ostensibly on illegal, underground actions by groups like the ALF. The law was meant to deter crimes and lead to more convictions. It failed on both fronts.

A year after its passage, the Departments of Justice and Agriculture released the first in-depth look at crimes by animal rights activists. The report surveyed attacks from 1977 to June of 1993 and found that more than half—160 of 313 documented incidents—were petty vandalism. The second most common activity—77 incidents—was stealing or releasing animals. No incidents involved weapons, none resulted in death or injury.

Most important, the report revealed that leading up to the passage of the Animal Enterprise Protection Act, crimes by animal rights activists had been declining. The number of crimes had steadily increased for most of the 1980s, spiking in 1987 and 1988 and then dropping off a cliff. By 1992, incidents had reached their lowest level since 1986. The underground had been slowing down. Contrary to the message of corporations and industry groups, there was no urgent problem, no need for new legislation.

After the law passed, crimes spiked. There were more crimes in the first six months of 1993 than in all of 1992. The new law was meant to deter underground actions, but instead of diminishing they were on track to double. Instead of retreating from the terrorism rhetoric in fear, underground groups didn't seem to be paying any attention.

Those who had called the new law essential immediately began calling it inadequate. Before prosecutors had even attempted to use the law, groups like the National Animal Interest Alliance, American Psychological Society and Americans for Medical Progress demanded more. More penalties, more federal regulations, and more terrorism laws.

A bill introduced in 1993 would have amended chapter 13 of title 18 of the United States Code, which deals with civil rights abuses, to include "blocking access to animal enterprises." That proposal was derailed by the murder of an abortion provider; the very same section of the U.S. code was instead amended by the Freedom of Access to Clinic Entrances Act to include blocking access to abortion clinics.

Efforts to expand the Animal Enterprise Protection Act turned into a long-running campaign. Bills had names like the "Environmental Terrorism Reduction Act," "Researchers and Farmers Freedom From Terrorism Act," and "Stop Terrorism of Property Act." One proposal created a national "eco-terrorist" criminal database. Another, the "Hands Off Our Kids Act," called on the attorney general to identify animal rights and environmental groups who recruit young people. Many added the death penalty for animal rights crimes. Most failed at the subcommittee or committee level; a few died on the House or Senate floor.

Along the way there were some successes. In 1998, Peter Young and Justin Samuel were indicted under the Animal Enterprise Protection Act for releasing thousands of mink from Wisconsin fur farms. Congress also approved some new penalties and restitution provisions. These were only piecemeal victories, though.

By 2000, animal experimenters and businesses had had enough. Edward J. Walsh, a member of the board of directors of the National Animal Interest Alliance, released an analysis of the law that would guide future legislative efforts. He said the law must be expanded beyond the ALF. It should include "not-so-savage acts" that he said were taking a bigger toll on the industry, including a media stunt popular in the late 1990s: "pies in the face." Walsh urged readers to sign a petition requesting that Congress hold hearings about animal rights terrorism, and in an eerie forecast of President George W. Bush's "you're either with us or against us" rhetoric in the War on Terrorism, he warned politicians who might stand in the way: "Congressmen and women who are sympathetic to the cause of animal rights must be reminded that they are aiding and abetting terrorism when they work to dilute the language of criminal statutes written to protect scientists, businessmen and women, entertainers and farmers, as well as law-abiding citizens in general, from hate-inspired violence."

A year later, on September 11, 2001, animal enterprises and politicians seized on the tragedy as an opportunity to advance their political objectives. On the day the Twin Towers fell, Don Young, a U.S. Representative from Alaska, told the *Anchorage Daily News* the attacks might have been the work of the ALF or ELF. "I'm not sure they're that dedicated, but eco-terrorists—which are really based in Seattle—there's a strong possibility that could be one of the groups," he said.

The nation was focused on Al Qaeda, though, not animal rights and environmental activists. Congress increased some animal enterprise terrorism penalties in 2002, but momentum had stagnated. Animal enterprises reorganized, solicited the aid of a little-known right-wing lobby group, and moved the front lines of their legislative battle from the federal government back to the states.

The American Legislative Exchange Council was founded in 1973 by Paul Weyrich—a conservative activist who famously coined the term "moral majority" for Jerry Falwell—in order to take his culture war to statehouses. Over time the mission of the organization changed. The focus shifted from winning cultural hot-button issues like abortion to advancing a legislative agenda palatable to corporate benefactors. ALEC evolved into an efficient, well-funded and little-known conservative powerhouse. According to an exposé by the Natural Resources Defense Council and Defenders of Wildlife, ALEC became a Trojan horse used to roll a corporate agenda through statehouse gates undetected.

More than one-third of all state lawmakers are ALEC members. With membership, they receive perks like free trips for spouses and children, Broadway theater tickets, and dinners at expensive restaurants. A 1994 ALEC conference included a golf tournament sponsored by R.J. Reynolds Tobacco Company, skeet and trap shooting sponsored by the National Rifle Association, and a trip to Busch Gardens sponsored by Anheuser-Busch Companies. If state lawmakers need help traveling to ALEC events, they can obtain "scholarships" from corporate sponsors. State lawmakers are short-handed and cash-strapped, with most only paid to work part-time and many with no paid staff, so the luxuries offered by ALEC are alluring. In addition, state legislatures have sparse lobbying disclosure laws and public reporting requirements, so the true extent of ALEC's junkets and perks goes undetected.

In return, lawmakers pay dues, but not enough to even litter the bottom of ALEC's coffers. Dues from state legislative members are a token amount of the overall operating budget, contributing about 2 percent of total revenue in 2000. About 97.9 percent of ALEC's $5.69 million in total revenue that year came from corporations and charitable foundations. Corporations including Philip Morris, R.J. Reynolds, Amoco, Chevron, Shell and Texaco pay nearly all of ALEC's expenses. The more they pay, the more power they have. Basic membership is $7,000 per year. Joining at increasingly elite levels—the Washington Club, Madison Club, or Jefferson Club— costs up to $50,000.

"Our members join for the purpose of having a seat at the table," said Dennis Bartlett of ALEC in 1997. "That's just what we do, that's the service we offer. The organization is supported by money from the corporate sector, and, by paying to be members, corporations are allowed the opportunity to sit down at the table and discuss the issues that they have an interest in."

This is the heart of the Trojan horse. Power in ALEC does not come from political acumen, it comes from brute financial force. Corporations buy their way onto one of ALEC's specialized task forces. There, "legislators welcome their private-sector counterparts to the table as equals," according to one ALEC publication. Actually, the corporate counterparts are more than equal. They have veto power. No bill is released from a task force without their approval. The results of such an arrangement are predictable. The task force on criminal justice, for example, has been co-chaired by a representative of Corrections Corporation of America, the nation's largest operator of private prisons. In 1996, ALEC issued model legislation to deregulate utility markets: the legislation was pushed by Koch Industries and Enron.

After corporate members use ALEC to draft dream legislation, the "model" bills go home with state legislators. The ALEC bills are introduced, debated and voted on by other lawmakers who think the proposals are democratic creations. The method is ruthlessly efficient and effective. According to ALEC, it resulted in enactment of

450 state laws during the 1999 and 2000 legislative sessions. *Mother Jones* described it as a "chain-restaurant approach to public policy, supplying precooked McBills to state lawmakers."

ALEC is a pay-to-play system, and the pharmaceutical industry has been one of the players willing to pay the most. Johnson & Johnson, Procter & Gamble, Aventis Pharmaceuticals, Bayer, Eli Lilly & Company, GlaxoSmithKline, Pfizer, Wyeth, Merck are all ALEC members. And they, along with other members like Cargill, the National Pork Producers Council, Wendy's and McDonald's, all have a vested financial interest in using ALEC to pass legislation labeling activists as terrorists.

In 2003, ALEC issued a report titled "Animal & Ecological Terrorism in America." The Private Enterprise Board Chairman at the time was Kurt L. Malmgren, a senior vice president of the Pharmaceutical Research and Manufacturers of America. The editor of the report, Sandy Liddy Bourne, would later become vice president for policy and strategy at the Heartland Institute, which calls climate change "scare-mongering." In a section titled "From Books to Bombs," the report outlines the history of animal rights and environmental extremism, beginning with Darwin's publication of *The Descent of Man.* According to ALEC, the voyage of the Beagle charted a course that led to the Animal Welfare Act and then to the ALF. The next step, the report warns, is physical violence. The authors make this warning repeatedly and dishonestly; the section on the ALF lists all of the group's guidelines except for the fourth, which is "to take all necessary precautions against harming any animal, human and non-human." Instead, ALEC says of activists: "If their voice isn't heard by burning buildings, perhaps it may be heard by cutting throats."

Federal legislation is too constrained to effectively target these movements, ALEC argues. The Patriot Act's broad new powers cannot be used, because federal terrorism definitions require death or harm to human beings, "an element not characteristic of eco-terrorists." In other words, ALEC says that the lack of violence by these allegedly violent groups is what necessitates new laws.

ALEC's solution is a model bill, the "Animal and Ecological Terrorism Act," heavily influenced by a similar bill from the U.S. Sportsmen's Alliance, a pro-hunting group. It includes an ambitious, and likely unconstitutional, list of restrictions and punishments. Among them are three main proposals.

The first is to expand the definition of terrorism to include not only property destruction, but any action intended to "deter" animal enterprises. That includes nonviolent civil disobedience, and witnessing and documenting corporate misconduct. The model bill prohibits "entering an animal or research facility to take pictures by photograph, video camera, or other means with the intent to commit criminal activities or defame the facility or its owner." Anyone—including journalists—could be labeled a terrorist for exposing activities that industry would rather keep secret.

The second key element of the model bill is to widen the net. A major weakness of existing federal legislation, ALEC says, is that it does not target the financial and ideological structure of eco-terrorist organizations. The model bill outlaws any action that may "publicize, promote or aid an act of animal or ecological terrorism," language so nebulous that the Sierra Club has said "holding a bake sale to support tree sitters could be a terrorist offense."

The final element of the plan is to create a "terrorist registry." Under ALEC's proposal, anyone who has violated the bill must register with the state attorney general, who shall maintain a public website with name, current address, photograph and signature of each eco-terrorist. The terrorist registry would operate much like a sex offender registry, except that instead of alerting communities to the presence of known pedophiles, it would be a tool for stigmatizing people because of their political beliefs—a blacklist.

Variations of ALEC's model bill have been introduced across the country by lawmakers who know little of the issue outside of

ALEC talking points. Frank Niceley, a member of both the Tennessee House of Representatives and ALEC, introduced the "Tennessee Ecoterrorism Act." The bill would have created a list within the Tennessee bureau of investigation for "wackos," as Niceley described them. It also spelled out prohibitions against eco-terrorist weapons—which do not exist—including "guns attached to trip wires or other triggering mechanisms."

"Eco-terrorists are, I guess, left-wing eco-greenies," Niceley told the General Assembly. "They don't have a leader. They're a leaderless terrorism group. They just kind of spring up sporadically. They do things like turn research animals out on the interstate, turn farm animals loose from semis in the middle of town. They drive spikes in logs going into the saw mill so that it will knock the teeth out of the saw mills. They put sugar in firefighting equipment in the national forest, and just, it's a different type of terrorism. They don't have Osama bin Laden leading them."

It is difficult to precisely determine the impact of ALEC's model eco-terrorism legislation. Whenever similar bills are introduced, ALEC's fingerprints have been wiped clean. Sometimes the bills tweak the model, or leave out entire sections. Sometimes they are handed off to non-ALEC members for introduction. When Niceley was questioned by other lawmakers about his bill, he replied that he received his information about eco-terrorism from Rush Limbaugh. That might be the case, but he received his bill from ALEC.

A conservative assessment—relying on ALEC documents, news articles citing ALEC officials, and an investigation of state criminal codes—shows that bills substantially similar to ALEC's have been introduced in at least sixteen states: Arizona, Arkansas, California, Hawaii, Missouri, Maine, Montana, New York, Ohio, Oklahoma, Oregon, Pennsylvania, South Carolina, South Dakota, Tennessee, and Texas. There has been mixed success. In Arizona the bill was vetoed by the governor. In some states the bills failed at the committee level or on the floor only to be reintroduced again and again.

In Arkansas, California, Missouri, Montana, Ohio, Oklahoma, and Pennsylvania, some variation of the proposal became law.

A focus exclusively on ALEC and its model bill, however, does not reflect the true scope of state eco-terrorism laws. ALEC is a well-funded, corporate-supported organization protecting vested financial interests, but it is one among many. Another key player has been the National Association for Biomedical Research. NABR monitors any and every attempt to restrict the animal experimentation industry. Its "members only" database tracks, for instance, states that have restricted the use of shelter dogs in experiments. The group also tracks all eco-terrorism bills and lobbies for them. The collective effort has had a significant impact on the legal system. By 2010, thirty-nine states had passed laws carving out special protections for animal and environmental enterprises and special penalties for activists.

There have been plenty of failed attempts along the way as well. An Oregon bill, which nearly passed, would have made it a felony for environmentalists to conduct any kind of protest within a quarter mile of a logging site. In Maine, the animal enterprise terrorism law was repealed. In Washington, there was a proposal to revise the state's criminal sabotage laws (first drafted in 1903 to combat a growing anarchist movement) to specifically include eco-terrorism. No laws stretch quite as far as ALEC's model, but that's not the point. Legislative changes are made incrementally, first setting a foundation and then slowly, relentlessly expanding that framework until it changes the nation's legal infrastructure. Each subsequent law has validated a manufactured threat, making increasingly draconian proposals, such as the Animal Enterprise Terrorism Act, appear quite ordinary and palatable.

Members of Congress and their staff begin to file into the room. Howard Coble takes his seat at the center and top of the tiered rows. He is a Republican from North Carolina and chairman of the committee. His cream-colored seersucker suit contrasts so sharply with the dark wood of the chambers that it appears white.

He speaks with a thick Carolina drawl that shakes his thick jowl, and when he pauses his heavy breath reverberates in the microphone. The Animal Enterprise Terrorism Act was introduced in response to a growing threat of eco-terrorism, he says. He quotes a professor from North Carolina Wesleyan College who says, "Environmentalists work within the system for preservation, and eco-terrorists seem to want to destroy civilization as we know it."

To stave off these end days, his bill would make a few changes to the existing law. It expands the Animal Enterprise Protection Act to include any business connected to an animal enterprise, which the government calls secondary and tertiary targeting. It also edits the language from "physically disrupting" the operations of an animal enterprise to "damaging or interfering with," a change that explicitly widens the law's scope beyond sabotage. Finally, it includes a new clause prohibiting actions that instill a "reasonable fear" in people connected to animal industries.

The first witness is Brent McIntosh of the Justice Department. He immediately delves into the issue I expected him to gingerly avoid—the fact that the existing law has already been used successfully. SHAC adopted secondary targeting techniques, and two months ago the SHAC 7 were convicted of animal enterprise terrorism charges. Meanwhile, more than a dozen activists, including Daniel McGowan, have been indicted for ALF and ELF crimes without any specialized legislation. McIntosh acknowledges this, but simultaneously argues that the government needs more power to go after activists. The U.S. Attorney in New Jersey prosecuted SHAC under a combination of the existing statute and interstate stalking laws; with this new legislation, McIntosh says, SHAC could have been hit harder.

William Trundley of GlaxoSmithKline says executives have been terrorized because of the company's ties to Huntingdon. In

Baltimore, an employee received a hoax telephone call from the morgue, asking her to identify a relative's body. Another employee's mail was stolen, and thieves learned that the target's wife had recently completed an alcohol treatment program. Someone later left a bottle of beer at the front door with a note that said, "Have a drink, bitch." Trundley shows an image of a leaflet he says has been distributed at animal rights protests. It lists some of the actions committed by underground groups, and warns corporations to stop doing business with Huntingdon. Trundley refers to the leaflet as a "terror card."

Michele Basso of the University of Wisconsin conducts brain experiments on primates to study Parkinson's disease. She does not recount incidents like those described by McIntosh or Trundley. Her first encounter with animal rights extremists, she says, was when two organizations tried to purchase a building adjacent to two labs on campus. They wanted to create a memorial museum for primates tortured and killed next door.

Basso says she never had a protest at her home, but at other homes activists used a truck with a video monitor to show undercover footage of animal experimentation. While the video played, activists chanted with bullhorns, distributed fliers and talked to neighbors. Basso says they shouted obscenities and "went and rang the doorbell and ran away and various activity like that." Basso also says she received more than fifty magazine subscriptions and various books such as *Oh, What a Slaughter*. At one point, someone wrote "Basso Animal Abuser" outside her home with chalk.

Members of Congress have invited Basso to testify about her firsthand experience with terrorism. These are the incidents she lists. Real estate deals, protests, magazine subscriptions, and sidewalk chalk.

There are a few reporters here today, and I wonder how they will perceive my testimony. As I will acknowledge in my prepared comments, I am not a lawyer, I am not a First Amendment scholar, and

I am not a spokesperson for the animal rights movement or underground groups. I am here because of my freelance reporting, although today I'm not covering this story; I'm part of it. If any of them speak to me afterward, I'm sure their first question will be, why is a journalist taking a position?

The ideal of objectivity has become a trademark of modern journalism, and although I respect many colleagues who espouse it, I've increasingly felt that there are times when clinging to these professional conventions is a disservice to the public. Too often, journalists report "both sides" as if they are equal, even when one side is riddled with lies and motivated by self-interest. Over-reliance on "official" government and corporate sources, and deference to their word, has taken precedence over critical, investigative reporting that speaks truth to power. Journalists must always strive for fairness and accuracy, and I'm not suggesting a return to yellow journalism or tabloid sensationalism, but at some point there are issues that require a firm stance. The First Amendment is one of them. Eric Newton, the director of Journalism Initiatives at the Knight Foundation, describes this well: "If we ever reach the point in this country where a journalist being in favor of the First Amendment is seen as special pleading and advocacy," Newton says, "we're in deep, deep trouble."

As I listen to the Justice Department spokesman mislead Congress about the need for new legislation, and as I hear the others label speech as terrorism in order to push their agenda, these feelings are reaffirmed. When it's my turn to speak, I begin by telling the committee that I have closely followed the animal rights and environmental movements, and the corporate-led backlash against them, since 2000. "I have documented an increasingly disturbing trend of terrorist rhetoric, sweeping legislation, grand jury witch hunts, blacklists and FBI harassment," I say, "reminiscent of tactics used against Americans during the Red Scare. The Animal Enterprise Terrorism Act is a continuation of that trend."

The broad range of attacks on "subversives" during the Red Scare affected all aspects of American life. Parallel to today's crackdown on the animal rights and environmental movements, the Red Scare operated on three levels: legislative, legal and a third I would call extralegal, or scare-mongering.

Congressional hearings elevated the perceived threat of subversives, and Congressional legislation rolled back First Amendment protections while expanding government power. The investigations of the House Committee on Un-American Activities led to the blacklisting of the Hollywood Ten. The Internal Security Act of 1950, also known as the McCarran Act, required the Communist Party and so-called front groups to register with the Attorney General (much the way ALEC's model legislation creates an "eco-terrorist" registry). President Truman called it the greatest threat to civil liberties since the Alien and Sedition Laws of 1798, and said: "We will fail in this, and we will destroy all that we seek to preserve, if we sacrifice the liberties of our citizens in a misguided attempt to achieve national security." Congress overrode his veto.

Legal efforts in this political climate were frequently less about defendants' conduct than about their ideology. The Smith Act targeted anyone who "prints, publishes, edits, issues, circulates, sells, distributes, or publicly displays any written or printed matter advocating, advising, or teaching the duty, necessity, desirability, or propriety" of revolution. Between 1941 and 1957, hundreds of people were prosecuted. In 1948, twelve board members of the Communist Party were indicted not for attempting to overthrow the government, but—much as with the SHAC defendants—for conspiring to advocate those ideas. In other legal cases, such as the trial and execution of Julius and Ethel Rosenberg, there was evidence of criminal activity. However, the true nature of the threat was lost in the media smear campaign. The Rosenbergs' son, Robert Meeropol, says the Operation Backfire defendants have been treated much like his parents, tarnished in the press before they had even stepped into a courtroom. "Terrorist" has replaced "communist" as the most powerful word in our language; the term automatically skews public opinion against the accused and makes it impossible to receive a fair trial.

The final component of the Red Scare was by far the most dangerous. It included a wide range of activity outside of Congress and the courts, with the sole intention of instilling fear. It was Senator Joseph McCarthy waving lists of names on camera, and employers requiring loyalty oaths. It was propaganda about the Red Menace, and campaigns urging people to report their neighbors. The word communist was used so relentlessly, so virulently, that it became a political albatross to hang around anyone's neck. The true meaning of the word melted away; communism became a malleable brand that could fit the enemy of the hour. Court cases and legislation sent people to prison, but these tactics, leveraging the weight of fear, incarcerated many more.

There once was a law that required anyone receiving "communist political propaganda" through the post office to authorize the delivery of each piece of mail. This legislation did not say it was illegal to send or receive communist literature. It just said you had to sign for it. But that has the same effect, does it not? Only the truly fearless or clueless would voluntarily add their name to a list of people who received communist propaganda during the Cold War. So people didn't do it. The Supreme Court struck down the law. Justice William O. Douglas wrote in *Lamont v. Postmaster General*: "The regime of this Act is at war with the 'uninhibited, robust, and wide-open' debate and discussion that are contemplated by the First Amendment.'" Douglas called this a "deterrent effect," and it would later become the legal concept known as a "chilling effect." The law was unconstitutional not because it banned subversive speech but because it chilled it, turning the free flow of ideas into a crystallized mass, silent and cold.

Some of today's extralegal campaigns have been silly, such as the backlash against *Hoot*, a children's movie in which teenage protagonists fight a development project that threatens endangered owls. Opposition groups called the movie "soft core eco-terrorism for kids." Ron Arnold, the self-proclaimed creator of the word eco-terrorism, said *"Hoot*'s so-called harmless 'mischief' is training a generation to look cute while burning homes and cars and stores." When a new film adaptation of *Charlotte's Web* is released, the Center for Consumer Freedom says it promotes animal rights extremism. These comments would be laughable if they weren't part of a much larger campaign, including a constant barrage of press releases and advertisements. In this post-9/11 climate, it's impossible to talk about "reasonable fear" as stipulated in the bill, because the unreasonable has become reasonable.

I tell the committee that through my reporting I have already seen the chilling effect of eco-terrorism smear campaigns, and heard the widespread fears of activists that they may soon be labeled terrorists. When you learn that the FBI has surveilled Greenpeace and local peace groups, you start to look more skeptically at those around you. When you learn that the SHAC defendants have been convicted on terrorism charges for running a website, you start to wonder if it could happen to you. And when you learn that nonviolent activists like Adam Durand have received 180 days in jail, plus $1,500 in fines, plus probation, plus 100 hours of community service, all for producing an undercover documentary about a factory farm, you start to wonder if you will be next.

"This legislation will add to this climate of fear and distrust," I say, "and it will force Americans to ask themselves, is it worth it? Is standing up for my beliefs really worth the risk of being labeled a terrorist? That is not a choice that anyone should have to make."

Others may soon find themselves facing similar decisions. Targeting animal rights activists as terrorists sets a legal precedent that will be used against other social movements. To use a very non–animal rights analogy, these activists are the canaries in the mine. If they run out of air, others will soon find it difficult to breathe. This has been the historical pattern both within the United States and abroad. Author Naomi Wolf has researched some of the most notorious periods of government repression in world history and identified common patterns. They all followed a similar model. "The state will start by abusing people that no one in the mainstream really identifies with much," she says. "In Germany it was anarchists, communists, homosexuals . . . then what always happens is that there's a blurring of the lines, and the noose starts to catch up more and more members of mainstream society, and it's always the same cast of characters: us."

Singling out one group of people based on their beliefs puts far too much power in the hands of the government. This should concern every American, regardless of how you feel about animal rights or the ALF. It is a path we have traveled before, and one we should not tread again.

"Public fears of terrorism since the tragedy of September 11th should not be exploited to push a political agenda," I say in my concluding remarks. "I urge you to reject this bill and ensure that limited antiterrorism resources are used to protect national security and human life, not profits."

The question-and-answer period proceeds as if it has been rehearsed. Lawmakers ask McIntosh if the Justice Department's support of the bill is political, and he responds, "We are apolitical in this." They ask Basso about whether animal experimentation is necessary, and she responds that it is. In 2009, she'll be suspended for what university officials call a "clear pattern" of animal welfare violations, but today she is asked to explain how much experimenters care for their animals. As I listen to these exchanges, I begin to wonder if my analysis has been too simplistic. My testimony focused on corporate profits, but I begin to wonder if the root motivation of this legislation grows much deeper.

The questions directed at me have a much different tenor. The low point is when Representative Tom Feeney, a Republican from Florida, interrupts to say I need a logic course. The questions I am most dreading, though, come from Bobby Scott. He invited me to testify and, according to his staff, expected me to raise only mild objections to the bill. Instead I called for its complete rejection and said it was a witch hunt reminiscent of the Red Scare. I'm not sure how a congressman who considers himself a champion of civil rights will respond to his actions being compared to such dark days.

Scott asks if I've seen the latest discussion draft of the bill. At the last minute, a provision was added that said the bill does not prohibit any activity protected by the First Amendment. I did see the edits, only moments before testifying. I tell him I have read the new version, and he asks if it has addressed my concerns.

"No, it does not, sir."

"Why doesn't it?"

"The main changes I saw in the discussion draft were, at the end, the specific exclusion of activity like picketing or lawful demonstrations," I say. "I'd like to point out that we would hope that would already be included under our conception of protected activities. So to point it out almost implies and acknowledges the overly broad and vague language of this legislation and the true danger it poses to First Amendment activity. And furthermore, that language still does not prohibit the use of this animal enterprise terrorism clause against things like civil disobedience, and perhaps even whistleblowing and undercover investigations."

Scott is calm. He briefly presses the issue with a few questions about the penalty and definition sections, which I have said are too vague, and then the hearing continues. He does not mention my comparisons to previous eras of government repression, and neither he nor any other committee member addresses the constitutional implications of terrorism rhetoric's chilling effect. Their silence is more effective than rebuttal.

As Coble concludes the hearing, Bill Delahunt, a Democrat from Massachusetts, asks to make a final comment. All of the crimes Basso and Trundley have listed in the hearing are already crimes under state law. Redundant statutes burden the federal government and shift power from the states, Delahunt says. Federal resources are limited. He says industry groups should instead lobby state officials, because they could address these crimes more efficiently and quickly than their federal counterparts.

After the hearing ends, supporters of the bill don't take his advice. They already have state legislation. What they want is a new federal law. In support of this, a long list of corporations and associations submit written comments to the Congressional record. The list includes the Biotechnology Industry Organization—the world's largest biotechnology association—and the California Healthcare Institute, which alone represents 270 biotech and pharmaceutical companies.

One letter of support is from Mark Bibi, general counsel for Huntingdon. He says SHAC's campaign has been "enormously successful," and new legislation is needed because the group's model poses a continued threat to other corporate interests. "The risks posed by SHAC and its ilk should not be underestimated," Bibi says.

"Imagine the impact if SHAC tactics were used by those opposed to various other industries from defense, to mining, to oil, to timber, to who knows what else."

CHAPTER SEVEN

Guilty by Association

April 28, 2006 Lauren Gazzola should not be laughing right now but, as she has said so many times throughout this ordeal, she can't help it. I'm walking out the front door on my way to Connecticut to visit her when she calls. "Have you seen it?" she says. I tell her I have. She laughs and tells me that this morning she was eating breakfast and reading the newspaper when she turned the page. There, in the front section, across from the national report, was an anonymous, full-page ad that said "I Control Wall Street" with the photo of a man in a black ski mask and black leather jacket. Her sentencing is about a month away, and the *New York Times* has published a full-page ad labeling her a terrorist.

"Can you believe this?" she says, still laughing. "I mean, what kind of animal rights terrorist would wear a *leather* jacket?"

The campaign against Huntingdon sank the company's share prices so low it had to be removed from the New York Stock Exchange in 2000. Huntingdon pleaded with stock exchange officials and attributed its financial plight to "economic terrorism," but the company was dropped from the Big Board. On September 7, 2005, Brian Cass and the board of directors gathered at the exchange and prepared to celebrate Huntingdon's relisting with champagne. Minutes before the scheduled announcement, they were told it had been delayed.

The stock exchange blamed Huntingdon's finances; this full-page ad blames animal rights terrorists. "In March, six of the campaign's leaders were convicted on federal terrorism charges," the ad says. "But the NYSE is still running scared."

Ads appeared in the *New York Times*, the *Wall Street Journal* and the *Washington Post*, three of the most expensive media markets for print advertising in the country. When groups spend that amount of cash for an ad, they typically want credit, but those responsible for these ads, whoever they are, have kept their identities hidden. There is no mention of sponsors, and the website listed, NYSEHostage.com, was registered anonymously. The website only says it is "a project of individuals and businesses who were disturbed by the New York Stock Exchange's decision to abandon Life Sciences Research International," which is the new name for Huntingdon.

Industry leaders deny responsibility. NYSEHostage.com links to Americans for Medical Progress, a group that has also labeled activists as terrorists. Jacquie Calnan, president of the group, will tell the *Washington Times*, "I can only say every instinct, after ten years of being in this field, is that it's not any pharmaceutical company behind this." Richard Michaelson of LSRI will speculate that the ad is an activist ploy: "The first we learned of the ad was when we opened the newspaper. . . . Animal rights activists are the only ones I can fathom that might be behind this."

Animal experimentation groups have purchased ads like these many times before to coincide with key events. In advance of national protests by SHAC in Little Rock, the Foundation for Biomedical Research published newspaper ads with three men in black masks wielding axes that said, "Some people think that the best way to protect animal life is to make scientists fear for theirs." A judge will soon decide how long Gazzola and the others will spend in prison, and animal industries are trying to push the Animal Enterprise Terrorism Act through Congress. Fear of the defendants, and animal rights activists more broadly, will aid those efforts.

Gazzola asks me to download the website, since by court order she is not allowed to access the Internet. Bring the files to Connecticut, she says, and hurry. On Monday, May 1st, she turns twenty-seven, and I can't miss her last birthday party before prison.

Before the trial, there was no Lauren Gazzola independent of SHAC's Lauren Gazzola. The campaign was her life. She did not spend time pursuing personal interests, because that would mean time away from SHAC. She didn't spend money on clothes and entertainment, because it would be better spent on the campaign. Anything not directly tied to closing Huntingdon was an indulgence, and that often included food. I remember talking to her on the phone as she rummaged through cupboards at the SHAC house. Once, when she found a lone jar of pasta sauce hidden away someplace, she shrieked so loudly she dropped the phone. When she remembered they had no pasta to go with it, she laughed.

Now Gazzola carefully monitors pots and pans on all four burners of the stove in her father's kitchen, stirring and seasoning while she preps vegetables for the grill. She offers warm pita with hummus along with tomato salsa heavy on the cilantro, and motions for me to sit. The hummus and salsa both have such a sharp, clear taste I ask where she bought them. She smiles at me and rolls her eyes. "Oh, Will Potter," she says, "I don't buy pre-made." House arrest has forced her to slow down and reclaim some parts of her life independent of the campaign. She now allows herself the luxury of food.

Gazzola prepares meals like she prepares court documents: methodically, precisely, but not without flair. She has had a hand in all of SHAC's legal battles, either closely working with attorneys or, in their absence, preparing cases herself. She would often find motions from other cases, identify the necessary ingredients, and then create her own. In early 2004, when she lived at the Pinole house, Gazzola asked me to mail her some of my writing. "The sharing of one's art deserves the same in return," she wrote in reply, and included a motion to dismiss she filed in a Huntingdon lawsuit. In one section of the document, she rebuts claims that SHAC is "affiliated" with underground groups because of shared beliefs. "Unfortunately, there are places in the world where such a theory might prevail," she wrote. "However . . . this country is not one of them."

The dining room table in her father's home is piled with boxes of legal materials. On house arrest, she has been rereading court transcripts, studying First Amendment case law, and aiding the early stages of the appeal. She has been intimately involved in every step of the trial, and I have relied on her, more than any attorney, to guide me through SHAC's legal history. No matter how much she wants to continue this level of involvement from prison, she knows that she must soon step back from the stove.

I feel uncomfortable because I'm not sure what role I play in the kitchen. I offer to help chop or cook, and Gazzola steers me out the back door to the grill. She says I need to figure out why it won't light. It has grown increasingly difficult to characterize my involvement in the SHAC trial and the lives of the defendants. When protesters gather outside at court dates, I feel like I should put down my notebook and carry a sign. This weekend, I'm staying at Gazzola's home. I'm here as a friend, not a journalist. Sitting in the backyard, attaching a new propane tank to the grill, I wonder whether my work has stopped me from being a better friend to her and the others during such difficult times. The grill ignites and begins to warm.

After the picnic everyone lounges in the backyard, birthday cake comatose. Gray dusk has settled on the lawn. We had planned on being on the road to visit Jake Conroy by now, but no one shows interest in moving. His mother's home is about an hour away. Gazzola funnels her friends out the front door. "Get going," she says, "Jake needs to see you too."

She follows us down the front walkway toward the car and

abruptly stops. I look back and she points down to a black box the size of a pack of cigarettes strapped to her left ankle. The electronic device notifies police if she leaves her home. For court dates, she sometimes conceals it with a floral scarf.

"This is how far I can go," she says, as she points ahead at a spot in the yard. That's how the SHAC campaign operated. Gazzola and the others knew the law, they knew their rights, and they marched up to that legal line—with bullhorns and tough talk and puffed chests—and then stopped. They say they never crossed it. As we climb into the car, I notice that Gazzola has sat down and is waving goodbye a few paces short of her imaginary line.

When we arrive, Jake Conroy's mom greets us with hugs and offers to make us up plates of dinner. As we pass through the dining room of their country-style home, his aunt and uncle stop me to chat about working for newspapers, and what I think of life in Washington, D.C. Upstairs, Conroy and a handful of friends listen to punk records, talk about video games and brainstorm movie and book recommendations for someone who, after months of house arrest, seems to have seen and read everything twice. Until this moment at the end of the evening, we could have been carless high schoolers on a suburban Saturday night.

His time on house arrest has been a war against boredom. His girlfriend, Andrea Lindsay, has traveled from California, and they've spent afternoons competing at Scrabble and trying not to think about prison. One evening they used children's modeling clay to make miniature ALF figurines. Lindsay uploaded photos to Conroy's support website, one with the caption, "House arrest makes you creative. Support the CLAY.L.F." In one of their creations, a figure in a white lab coat and black mask carries a sledgehammer, and another figure in camouflage pants carries a small monkey with a device on its head and bandages on its eyes.

It was a miniature version of one of the most famous ALF

raids in history. On April 20, 1985, the ALF deactivated the security system of a research laboratory at the University of California, Riverside. "Diane," a member of the cell, said an inside contact had alerted them of animals being abused in sight-deprivation experiments. Underground activists in white lab coats and black masks entered the laboratory predawn, prying open doors as they went. Video footage released after the raid shows that they worked swiftly and walked confidently, crowbars in hand and the white tails of their lab coats flapping behind them.

They removed about 260 animals, many with their eyes sewn shut or damaged, including one infant primate named Britches. Experimenters had taken Britches from his mother on the night of his birth and sewn his eyes shut with thick black sutures. They attached a sonar device to his head that let off a screeching sound and placed him in a steel cage, alone; the isolation and sensory deprivation caused neurological disorders. Britches would lurch and shake, shrieking. After spray-painting "FREE! ALF," activists wheeled racks of animals and carried cages up from the basement and into the darkness, with Britches, small enough to sit in the palm of a hand, clinging to one activist's fingers.

Footage of Britches's recovery, released by PETA, showed his eyes healing, his hair growing back, his neurotic episodes diminishing. One scene showed people in black masks holding Britches in a soft, white blanket and nursing him with a bottle. In the lab, Britches clung to and nursed from a faux mother, a contraption of metal and wire wrapped in cloth. After the raid, video showed Britches clinging to an adoptive primate mother who wrapped both arms around the infant and pulled his head to her chest.

The break-in cost about $683,500 in theft and damage, and animal experimenters hit back. State and national groups called for new legislation. The rescue of Britches was a critical step in the long march toward convincing the government, twenty years later, to apply the terrorist label to the SHAC 7.

Conroy looks tired. Lindsay says something about how it has been a long day and that we have a drive ahead of us. Time is running out before sentencing, and she rations these days and nights. Privately, she mentions to me that, in addition to spending time with those he loves, Conroy needs time to read. He has been studying books and pamphlets about how to survive in prison.

After sentencing, Conroy and the others will probably await their prison designation on house arrest and then self-surrender. If not, they will be remanded into the custody of U.S. Marshals straight from the courtroom. The latter option is dreaded. It means that they would await their Bureau of Prisons designation while in holding facilities—city and county jails—which are more crowded and more violent. Inmates who have arrived at the prison where they will spend years of their lives want to accrue time served with good behavior. With the transitional nature of city and county jails, inmates lack that motivation.

When he arrives, Conroy will be placed in a holding cell, booked, strip-searched, issued linens and khakis, and told to place any pieces of his previous self away in a box. Then he will be thrown in the deep end and expected to swim. Former prisoners often say they only served two days in prison: the day they went in and the day they came home. If you survive the first day, they say, you can make it to the last. Knowing that prison officials will not provide any guidance, nor will they care if he drowns, Conroy has turned to books to learn about head counts, call-outs, cell blocks, phone calls, shot callers, commissary, shoes, gangs, black markets, the hole, prison health care, prison tattoos and prison etiquette.

Rule number one: Don't snitch. Ever. Snitches are the lowest of the low in the prison hierarchy, somewhere at the bottom with the pedophiles. For some of the Operation Backfire defendants who have chosen to cooperate with the government and turn in their friends, this means they will have a difficult and dangerous time. Other rules of inmate etiquette sound like those of elementary school, but they are potentially dangerous, even lethal, if broken. Don't cut in line. Don't reach across someone's food. Don't touch personal property. Don't hog the phone. Don't whine. Don't owe debts.

Older inmates may help in this re-education. Prisoners who are from the same hometown, have mutual acquaintances or just remember what it was like being thrown in on the first day will step up and offer guidance. They will teach Conroy and the others where to sit in the cafeteria, how to buy stamps, and how to negotiate what is one of the most dangerous areas in any prison—the TV room.

Ultimately, though, there will be situations where no amount of book learning or inmate advice will help, and the activists will have to rely on gut instincts. There are two rules every prisoner must internalize, writes David Novak in *Downtime*. The first: Do your own time. When a fight breaks out, walk away. If someone is stabbed or beaten with a rock from the prison yard, turn your head. Your only responsibility is to yourself. The second rule: when in doubt, blend. If you aren't sure how to stand or what to do, look around. "The one thing you want to do in prison," writes Novak, "is not stand out."

Downtime is one of the most popular books about preparing for prison. The copy I obtained is a computer scan of a photocopy of the original. It looks like it has been passed through many nervous hands. David Novak wrote it after spending about ten months incarcerated at Eglin Federal Prison Camp, the facility that inspired the term "Club Fed." Public outrage over prison amenities led to its closure. Novak was a white-collar criminal doing ten of the easiest months possible. Incarcerated life for these activists will certainly be much different, but there are no books to prepare for what it's like to serve time in prison as a terrorist.

September 12, 2006 Hijackers flew planes into buildings five years and one day ago, and the morning talk radio hosts are still discussing it. Lauren Ornelas's fingers fidget with buttons on the car stereo only to return to NPR's fifth anniversary coverage of September 11th. She turns down the volume so post-9/11 white noise hums in the background and then squeezes the wheel with both hands. Nobody in the car says a word about September 11th as we drive north on Interstate 295. We are heading to Trenton, N.J., to watch a judge sentence the SHAC 7, and no one wants to hear that word.

When my bus pulled up to the Takoma Park metro station near Washington, D.C., at 5:02 a.m., I had immediately pulled my *Washington Post* out of my bag and prepared to wait. Activist time is usually about thirty minutes behind what the clock says. Instead a small car, idling in the parking lot with foggy windows and no headlights, awoke and pulled in front of me. Ornelas and Patrick Sullivan, considered veteran animal rights activists even though they are only in their thirties, had agreed to let me tag along for the sentencing if I chipped in for gas. And tolls. New Jersey loves tolls.

Now, three and a half hours later, we're late and lost. Taking a wrong exit had spat us into crawling traffic and more tolls. We can't tell if this concrete horizon is New Jersey Gray or Delaware Gray or some other monochromatic state entirely. Finally, we see "TRENTON MAKES, THE WORLD TAKES." "I don't know what Trenton makes," Sullivan says, "but they better make me some goddamn coffee."

The six defendants in their thrift-store court clothes work the room like hosts at a dinner party. Activists have traveled from Los Angeles, Seattle, San Francisco, Portland and Chicago for the court date. Around the room, old friends hug and laugh and then, as if remembering where they are, straighten their shirts and lower their voices. I approach Conroy as he leans against the dark wood wainscoting and watches supporters sift through the metal detector into the courtroom. Court pews begin to fill, and the guards turn people away. Kevin Kjonaas brings water to his mother. He places his left palm on her back and then opens her hands so they can receive his paper cup. They sit together on a pew and she shakes.

At a previous court date Conroy had pleaded that, on my next reporting trip, I bring him vegan cinnamon buns from Sticky Fingers Bakery in D.C. Vegans have a way of circling every conversation back to food, much like born-again Christians have a way of returning every conversation to the scripture. I start asking him questions about today's sentencing and realize I forgot, once again, to make the holy sticky bun run.

"I covertly tried to sneak in a cinnamon roll with a file baked inside," I say, "but the cops confiscated it at the metal detector."

"You're really sick, that's not funny," an eavesdropper says.

"Yes it is," Conroy's mother says, tears in her eyes. "You have to laugh. This is insanity."

The cops break up the crowd and say everyone has to find a seat, and those who cannot find a seat must leave. Some New Jersey activists in the back row recognize me from previous court dates and squeeze together so I can sit with them.

I spot Michael Drewniak, spokesperson for the United States Attorney's Office, with his trademark bald head, tanning-salon orange. He stands near Huntingdon executives, men who look like they sleep in suits. Drewniak takes mental snapshots of the activists in the courtroom. He stares at one for three seconds, shifts to the next for three seconds, one by one, row by row.

While we sit in silence waiting for the judge to make her appearance, a local reporter quietly opens his notebook and asks activists near him, "So, what did you think about the trial?" as if he is chatting up someone at the grocery checkout line. They turn him down one by one, verbally or through their body language. On his fourth or fifth attempt he turns to an activist with uneven facial hair and canvas sneakers.

"Are you a reporter?" the activist asks, leering at his notebook. "I can't answer any of your questions. Why? Why do you think? These guys are on trial for guilt by association. Nobody in their right mind is going to talk to a corporate reporter."

The reporter harrumphs and puts down his pen. Occasionally, laughter or bits of non-terrorism small talk break the silence, reminders that this is a courtroom of young people awkwardly struggling with the gravity of the scene unfolding before them. Across the room, I see Harper catch Gazzola with her nose to the armpit of her black sweater. She wrinkles her nose, and Harper covers his face. He tries not to smile. Gazzola tosses her head back and laughs.

Here is how a sentencing hearing for a federal case usually works. The judge makes a statement about the federal sentencing guidelines, whether they apply, and their parameters. The prosecutors then generally ask for sentences somewhere in the middle or on the high end of those guidelines. Defense attorneys respond with a series of nitpicky points about the sentencing recommendations, using legal jargon the defendants and family members do not understand, and argue that their client should receive a reduced sentence. Sometimes they submit letters from friends or family members saying that Johnny is a "fine young man" or that Jane is an "upstanding person who made a poor decision." Sometimes defendants say they have seen the light, and realized the error of their ways. Sometimes they cry.

Here is how a sentencing hearing for animal rights "terrorists" works. The judge makes a statement outlining the sentencing guidelines. Some defendants face up to thirteen years in prison—in comparison, the average sentence is about twenty-one years for murder, eight and a half years for sex offenses and six and a half years for arson. Attorneys boil years of the defendants' lives down to point systems outlined in a pre-sentence investigation report, or PSI.

Prosecutors ask the judge to throw the book at these "extremists," defense attorneys fight for scraps of time, and then the judge sides in favor of the government or knocks off a few months.

Charles McKenna, the assistant U.S. attorney for New Jersey, rises from his seat to make the government's sentencing recommendation for each defendant. Behind him sit corporate representatives from Huntingdon and Stephens.

Kevin Kjonaas was "drunk with power," McKenna says. "He could go in and push around multinational corporations." He was the leader, a "cunning manipulator" who used the website to encourage illegal actions because he was "too cowardly to go out and do them himself." The corporate executives targeted by protests or underground actions "can never feel safe again."

Lauren Gazzola "had the bullhorn and was clearly the person in charge," McKenna says. The government wiretapped a phone conversation she had with activists in Texas. She told them where to protest, he says, which shows her leadership role. On a job application, she listed herself as SHAC's "campaign coordinator."

McKenna argues with defense attorneys about details in Conroy's paperwork, including the address on his driver's license, before moving on to sentencing recommendations. Conroy's attorney says that if these activists committed a crime, it is a "crime of compassion." McKenna bursts from his seat to rebut: "I don't think he's a man of compassion."

Pressed up against activists in the back row, I can feel and see their muscles tense. Across the aisle, I spot Greg Bennick, a close friend of Conroy's and the lead singer of Trial, a vegan straight-edge hardcore band. In this crowd, he is something of a celebrity, a punk rock luminary. He sits at the end of the row, near more of Conroy's friends, with a freshly shorn head and pinstriped suit. He bites his clenched fist and flexes the muscles in his left hand. He leans over in the pew, with one foot in the aisle, as if he is poised to jump and disrupt the scene.

Watching Bennick makes me think of one of SHAC's campaign videos. Conroy and Harper produced the film, *This Means War*. They used a Trial song to narrate footage of activists storming offices and screaming through bullhorns. There's an explosive release of drums and then Bennick screams, "The wreckage of humanity has been strewn across the land and now the hour of desperation is at hand."

Bennick doesn't leap from his seat now, nor does he relax. He remains on the edge, fists clenched. McKenna continues. "The Internet was key to these crimes, and Jacob Conroy was key to the Internet." He turns to the judge and says, "Your Honor has often been called upon to sentence people, perhaps people from the inner city that grew up in lives of deprivation." But Conroy and the others had "good homes, good schools," and they "chose to throw it all away."

"What the fuck," a woman next to me says to herself. "They're not drug dealers. They're activists."

The defense attorneys had not just submitted letters of support for the defendants, they submitted tomes. The judge raises a bound book from Conroy's attorney, with letters from professors, friends and activists as far away as Cambodia who say they have been inspired by his compassion. The judge says she has rarely seen anything like this in any case.

Conroy declines to make a statement in his defense; he is sentenced to four years in prison. Gazzola's sentence, after she tells the court she still will pursue law school, is four years and four months. Kjonaas, depicted by prosecutors as the leader, receives six. Darius Fullmer and Andy Stepanian, who each were charged only with conspiracy, will later be sentenced to a year and a day and three years, respectively. At the next court date, Harper will tell the court that he will fight for animal rights and defend direct action until the day he dies. He will be sentenced to three years in prison. The defendants are collectively ordered to pay $1 million in restitution to the lab they devoted their lives to closing.

The only other sentences that have been meted out under the Animal Enterprise Protection Act were for Justin Samuel and Peter Young, who released mink from fur farms. Samuel and Young each served about two years in prison. The SHAC defendants—who only wrote and spoke in defense of those who used illegal tactics—are sentenced to double and triple the amount of time given to those who have carried them out.

Activists who had been turned away from the overflowing chambers rush in to ask what happened. None of the defendants seems to know what to say. They put their game faces back on, standing tall with shoulders back, and when friends with tears in their eyes say they are sorry, they reply, "It could have been worse."

The local press swarms the defendants with skinny notebooks in hand. I stand on the periphery and hold my questions. What do you say to someone who has just been sentenced to years in prison? It reminds me of my time at the *Chicago Tribune*, writing about murders and dead bodies found in storage lockers and having to ask people how it made them feel.

Outside the courthouse, a woman weaves through the camera crews and up the courthouse steps with her teenage son, for their own court date. He does not look much younger than the SHAC defendants, and wears a dress shirt, belt and pleated trousers all made for a much larger man. His oxford drapes off his shoulders like a rain poncho. The woman asks a reporter along the way, "What's all this? They some superstars?"

Conroy and Gazzola invite Ornelas, Sullivan and me to a grocery store fifteen minutes away with the best vegan options New Jersey has to offer. For their post-sentencing farewell feast, they eat tempeh salad, hummus and nondairy ice cream with chocolate swirls in little plastic cups, the type elementary school students receive on special occasions in the cafeteria.

Gazzola moves from table to table, cracking jokes and trying to lighten the mood. She flexes her upper arm muscles and tells us, "On the upside, I'm going to come out of prison like Sarah Connor in *Terminator 2*. I'm going to be totally ripped."

An activist from New York takes photos with her cell phone, and the defendants pose with their supporters while an attorney from California takes a more formal group photograph in the middle of the bakery. Nearby, a customer squeezes and sniffs loaves of French bread while her toddler begs for a chocolate chip cookie. "Is this some kind of going-away party?"

Silence. "Yes," the attorney says, "I guess it is." She smiles politely at the woman, turns and walks away without explanation.

Later, in a motel room, seven California activists sit on a bedspread covered in cigarette burns, flipping through television channels. They're looking for any mention of their friends. "Tonight's game will be" CLICK "a new train service" CLICK "with sunny weather on the way" CLICK "a dog was rescued from a dumpster" CLICK "this was a brutal act, a savage act."

"Oh, this must be us," someone jokes and grabs the remote control to turn up the volume. After about twenty-five minutes, they find a mention of the trial on the local evening news. It lasts about ten seconds, accompanied by a graphic that says "ANIMAL RIGHTS" in white block letters imposed over images of puppies and kittens.

Andrea Lindsay, who heads up the SHAC support committee in addition to working full time and attending law school, doesn't pay much attention to the news coverage. She sits with her legs crossed and back against the headboard, typing on her laptop. While others watch the news looking for some recognition of what has happened, she is looking forward, typing notes from the sentencing, editing a previously drafted press release, uploading photos to the website, and emailing animal welfare and civil liberties groups to help her partner and her friends prepare for their appeal.

———

One warm, foggy night in early September, as the SHAC 7 awaited sentencing, underground activists drove through the rolling hills of rural Massachusetts. They pulled up to a strip of land that looked as though it had been shaved out of the surrounding forest of white pine, sugar maple and eastern hemlock. The activists hopped the fence and headed straight to the rabbit sheds. They did not dodge security guards, pick locks or break windows. They walked right in through the mist and began opening cages.

New Zealand white rabbits are one of the most popular house rabbits. People love them for pets because they're chubby and cuddly. They're also affectionate to a fault, making them one of the most popular rabbits for experimentation, because they're easy to stick, prod and cut. Selective breeding for albinism has given them bright white coats, a clean canvas to experiment with dyes and cosmetics. As a consequence of being bred for a genetic defect, a lack of melanin, their eyes burn red.

Capralogics is a company that uses these rabbits to create antibodies that are sold to animal experimenters and other testing labs. The process: inject proteins into the rabbits, allow them to build antibodies in their blood, drain the blood, extract the antibodies, then sell 100 microliters, about half a cup, for between $250 and $295. Capralogics prides itself on taking the time for multiple test bleeds. "Be patient," the company advises prospective clients on its website. "This is where antibody production has much in common with wine making."

The anonymous activists moved row by row, shed by shed, until every cage door had been opened. In their black hoods and black masks, with both arms wrapped around fat, white bunny bellies, they stepped back into the mist. The few rabbits they could not steal were let loose in the nearby field.

Some had warned that this could happen. The private intelligence firm STRATFOR advised that the SHAC 7 conviction "could serve to inspire more illegal activity, rather than less, and the trend could spread to involve larger numbers of groups and industries." Andrea Lindsay made a similar comment to the press after sentencing. The government scoffed. "That's the kind of twisted logic we've been dealing with from these militant animal rights followers who can rationalize their behavior, inspire others to do likewise, and refuse to take responsibility for their actions," said Michael Drewniak, the government spokesman. "It's just unbelievable that they can view harsh prison sentences this way."

One week after the SHAC 7 sentencing, an anonymous communiqué is released. It includes photographs, which activists say were taken by Capralogics employees, of a rabbit with its head in a restraining device, a rabbit with chunks of fur shaved off and raw skin exposed, and lab technicians bleeding a rabbit's ears. Twenty-three rabbits were removed from Capralogics and placed in new homes that night, the communiqué says. Six have been named Jake, Lauren, Kevin, Andy, Josh and Darius, after the defendants.

"The government and the industries it represents hate us so much because no matter who they surveil, raid, defame or imprison, they cannot kill the idea and so they cannot stop us," the communiqué says. "And while the SHAC 7 will soon go to jail for simply speaking out on behalf of animals, those of us who have done all the nasty stuff talked about in the courts and in the media will still be free.

"So to those who still work with HLS and to all who abuse animals: we're coming for you, motherfuckers."

CHAPTER EIGHT

Un-American Activities

November 13, 2006 On a cold, wet morning, politicians and celebrities slog through the muck of the National Mall to pay tribute to the Reverend Dr. Martin Luther King Jr. and break ground for his memorial. Democrats and Republicans, Clinton and Bush, Oprah and Jesse, they are all here in soggy wingtips and muddied pumps, praising the legacy of the slain civil rights leader. The new memorial will, for the first time, honor an African American alongside the dead white men of the mall. Lincoln, Jefferson and Roosevelt flank Dr. King's plot, just a half mile from where he gave his "I Have a Dream" speech on August 28, 1963.

"By its presence in this place, it will unite the men who declared the promise of America and defended the promise of America with the man who redeemed the promise of America," President George W. Bush says at the ceremony. "Dr. King showed us that a life of conscience and purpose can lift up many souls."

Forty years ago, not even a liberal Democrat, let alone a Republican president, would have dared to compare Dr. King to the founding fathers. At best there might have been angry letters and phone calls. At worst, riots. Now a president who has allowed "civil rights enforcement to wither and die," according to some civil rights groups, lets his praise roll like a river and his thanks like a never-ending stream. The five thousand people in the crowd cheer or cry while the cameras roll.

"Martin Luther King, Jr. inspired me and thousands of other Americans to get in the way," Representative John Lewis, a Democrat from Georgia, says to the crowd. "He inspired us to get in trouble. But it was good trouble; it was necessary trouble."

Today is the first day back at work for lawmakers after the midterm Congressional elections, when Democrats took control of both chambers of Congress. Election night was not kind to supporters of the Animal Enterprise Terrorism Act. Of the many Republicans who lost their seats, six were co-sponsors of the House legislation. (Another co-sponsor, Randall "Duke" Cunningham, resigned from the House a year earlier after pleading guilty to accepting at least $2.4 million in corporate bribes.) The change of Congressional leadership might not mean defeat, considering that ten of the forty-four co-sponsors of the House bill are Democrats, but the political landscape will certainly shift.

The next few weeks will be calculated chaos as Republicans scramble to enact their priority legislation. Democrats will try to stall until January when newly elected officials take office and they have the majority. Unless the Animal Enterprise Terrorism Act is on the Republicans' agenda, it will be lost in the melee.

For months, supporters have been telling members of Congress that unless they act now, animal rights terrorists will strike again. The National Association for Biomedical Research purchased a full-page ad in *Roll Call*. The paper covers Capitol Hill and is read daily by Congressional staff. The ad featured a black-and-white photograph of a vandalized office. On the wall, in bright red spray-paint-style lettering, it said "Your home is next." At the bottom of the page, it said "SUPPORT THE ANIMAL ENTERPRISE TERRORISM ACT."

Behind the scenes, NABR has also been coordinating the lobbying efforts of corporations and trade associations, forming an umbrella organization called the Animal Enterprise Protection Coalition. Members include corporate powerhouses like Pfizer, Wyeth, GlaxoSmithKline and industry groups like the Fur Commission and National Cattlemen's Beef Association. The coalition is a front group representing tiers of businesses, industries, and other groups that have the ears of members of Congress, formed solely to lobby for the Animal Enterprise Terrorism Act.

Despite all of their resources it seems the coalition has skimped on security, and an anonymous source has leaked many of the group's internal documents, which reveal a carefully orchestrated campaign to label activists as terrorists by spreading disinformation. Its sample letter to Congress states that animal rights activists have found loopholes in the existing legislation, yet does not mention that the conviction of the SHAC 7—a major victory for animal enterprises—was secured under the existing law. Its template news release says animal rights activists are the "largest domestic terror threat," yet does not mention that no one has ever been harmed.

Its Capitol Hill Toolkit includes an Illegal Incidents Report by the Foundation for Biomedical Research, released as part of the group's lobbying efforts. The report claims that from 1995 to 2006, illegal actions by animal rights and environmental activists increased by more than *one thousand percent*. That's an astronomical increase and begs the question what, exactly, the group is tracking. The foundation's database reveals that the organization has included a broad range of conduct—including pranks, civil disobedience and crimes in other countries—in order to inflate the numbers. They have been cooking the eco-terrorism books.

Incidents include releasing birds from cages in Russia, hanging banners in an arena to protest the circus and wearing bunny suits for PETA. Many of the incidents in the database are actually protected by the First Amendment. For instance, one of the categories for incident tracking, "harassment," is subdivided to include "demonstrations." The database includes a college event where activists "handed out propaganda." It also includes the June 11, 2005, protest outside the courthouse where SHAC activists were arraigned. I covered this court date as a reporter. Nothing illegal took place and no arrests were made. Activists held signs that said things like "free speech on trial." This lawful, nonviolent protest—a protest against the prosecution of First Amendment activity as terrorism—is itself labeled terrorism.

The coalition's internal talking points are written with startling candor. They reveal these groups' description of what they see as the true threat of the animal rights movement. Activists are dangerous not because of violence, or the potential for violence. "These tactics have been very successful," the talking points say, in "damaging the financial footing of corporations involved in animal enterprise."

Even with this coordinated campaign by multinational corporations and industry leaders, the Animal Enterprise Protection Coalition knows it still does not have the votes it needs. Two of the coalition's internal lobbying documents are political scorecards. They have rows for every member of Congress, and columns for support of the Animal Enterprise Terrorism Act: "Yes," "Leaning Yes," "Leaning No" and "No." According to the scorecards, only four of one hundred senators support the legislation. That explains why the Animal Enterprise Terrorism Act was rushed through the Senate, on the last business day before Congressional recess for the elections, with no discussion or debate. As a result, it passed by "unanimous consent."

On the House side, support is equally scarce. According to the scorecard, only 27 of the 435 members of the House—6 percent—support the legislation. One should treat that tally conservatively. Most of the rows and columns on the scorecard are blank, and only solid "yes" votes are marked. Lobbyists were clearly erring on the side of caution, which is normal, and only tabulating the most solid votes. That being said, even if the number of supporters is eight times higher than the coalition has recorded, the legislation will fail on the House floor.

There is not much time. Congress is in session this week, then out two weeks for Thanksgiving, then lawmakers have a few weeks to resolve remaining business. In the final days of the 109th Congress, Republican leadership will have competing priorities—Iraq, the Mark Foley sex scandal, domestic spying and a host of other issues have put the party on the defensive. This is the best opportunity supporters of the Animal Enterprise Terrorism Act will have to pass their bill while Republicans still control the House, the Senate and the White House. To overcome the lack of votes and capitalize on this fleeting opportunity, supporters of the Animal Enterprise Terrorism Act need a new, post-election strategy. And they need it fast.

As politicians and celebrities gather on the mall to celebrate Dr. King, Alex Hershaft heads to Capitol Hill with about a dozen volunteer lobbyists to oppose legislation that would have labeled the civil rights leader himself a terrorist. They begin working down their list of members of Congress. They have been told by Congressional staffers that the bill could come up for a vote at about 6:30 this evening. It will be a crunch, Hershaft thinks, but if they move swiftly they can each visit about twenty or thirty offices.

Hershaft leads FARM, a national animal protection group that focuses on factory farming and vegetarian outreach. Born in Warsaw, Poland, he survived the Warsaw Ghetto and immigrated to the United States from Italy in 1951. He speaks meticulously with a soft, dense accent in a voice that shakes his thick salt-and-pepper beard.

Hershaft has lived in the D.C. area for thirty years, but only ventures to Capitol Hill for events like the Great American Meatout, where volunteers give lawmakers free tofu hotdogs. He feels out of place in the halls of Congress. The inside-the-beltway baseball of roll call votes and committee markups is an arcane, intimidating world for him, he says, but one he is willing to tackle if it means stopping this law.

By early afternoon, his group has visited the offices of every Democrat in the House, and about one-third of the Republicans. Hershaft has personally spoken to staffers in twenty-eight offices, a breakneck speed for even a veteran lobbyist. Lawmakers and their staff say calls, emails and faxes have been rolling in about the legislation, and the public has been overwhelmingly against it.

As Hershaft waits to speak with another Congressional staffer, an office assistant points to a screen. "Hey your bill is on TV. Do you want to watch it?" Hershaft is stunned. There it is, on C-SPAN. Supporters of the Animal Enterprise Terrorism Act had bumped the legislation ahead of schedule by about four hours. Few, if any, of the lawmakers Hershaft had visited this morning would know of the change.

A Congressional staffer offers him a pass for the House floor, and he begins to run.

It is 2:46 p.m., and lawmakers who spent the morning grandstanding about causing trouble are back in their offices, or at events related to Dr. King's memorial. Only five lawmakers have gathered here on the House floor. They are barreling through a string of bills, assembly-line style, as part of an obscure procedure called "suspension of the rules." Members of Congress have busy schedules, and this procedure lets them, as the Congressional Research Service says, "act expeditiously on relatively noncontroversial legislation." Each bill gets forty minutes of debate, then an up-or-down vote, then a push out the door.

It's usually so uneventful that many members of Congress don't bother attending. Representative Sheila Jackson Lee made an appearance to praise the Houston Dynamo, "who are now the 2006 Major League Soccer Cup champions, as they won it just yesterday in front of thousands of soccer fans at Pizza Hut Park." A few minutes earlier Representative Mike Castle urged his colleagues to rename a bridge in Delaware after the man who created the Roth IRA.

The next bill does not cheer sports teams or rename bridges.

Representative James Sensenbrenner hopes to use this quick-and-dirty procedure for the Animal Enterprise Terrorism Act.

Jaws rarely drop in this town. Washington, despite the occasional scandal or legislative upset, and contrary to the BREAKING NEWS! nature of political coverage, is methodical and predictable. When a bill comes to the floor, lawmakers have already counted their votes and know if it will pass or fail. Before a report is released or a bill drops, the wonks are talking about it. Press conferences and political speeches are always the same verbal caricatures, language exaggerated by party lines. There is excitement, of course, but it is the excitement of watching a long-running soap opera; there are twists and turns, but as soon as a familiar character appears on the screen, viewers know how they will behave.

It should surprise no one that Representatives James Sensenbrenner and Thomas Petri sponsored the Animal Enterprise Terrorism Act and are leading today's efforts to rush it through the House. They are political hawks—tough on terrorism, weak on civil liberties, cozy with industry. They both hail from Wisconsin, home of fur farms and the dairy industry. A jaded political observer might attribute their stance on this issue to money. The American Veterinary Medical Association political action committee—Sensenbrenner's second-largest source of campaign contributions—is a member of the Animal Enterprise Protection Coalition. Sensenbrenner also cashed checks from GlaxoSmithKline and Wyeth, two corporate supporters of the law. PACs from the industries this law protects have helped keep him in office: in 2005–2006, the pharmaceutical and health industry gave him $41,000 and agribusiness gave him $20,000.

Petri has similar coffers. Then again, so do most members of Congress. The industries protected by this law are some of the most powerful, and generous, political operations in Washington. In 2006, PACs representing the agribusiness industry gave $20 million to members of Congress, and the pharmaceutical industry gave

$11.5 million. By comparison, the Humane Society's Humane USA PAC gave $123,000, and all environmental PACs combined gave about $514,000.

Lobbyists from these industries have lengthy legislative agendas on which the Animal Enterprise Terrorism Act is but one small part, but their political influence is clear. In 2006, the Humane Society spent about $90,000 on lobbying, and FARM, Alex Hershaft's group, spent about $40,000; Pfizer alone spent $11.8 million.

This is how the game is played. These industries have the money to help elect politicians, and they have the money to ensure that those politicians vote favorably. It's not surprising to see bipartisan support for legislation these industries deem a top priority. What is surprising, though, is what Representative Bobby Scott, a leading Democrat and ideological rival of Sensenbrenner and Petri, says next.

In a move he would never have considered making at the Dr. King memorial ceremony just hours ago, Scott—a prominent figure in the Congressional Black Caucus, a go-to guy in the House on civil rights and civil liberties issues—acknowledges that this "terrorism" law could target nonviolent civil disobedience. "There are some who conscientiously believe that it is their duty to peacefully protest the operation of animal enterprises to the extent of engaging in civil disobedience," he says. "If a group's intention were to stage a sit-in or lie-down or to block traffic to a targeted facility, they certainly run the risk of arrest for whatever traffic, trespass or other laws they may be breaking. But they should not be held more accountable for business losses due to causes such as delivery trucks being delayed any more than a boycott or protest against any other business.

"To violate the provision of the bill, one must travel or otherwise engage in interstate activity with the intent to cause damage or loss to an animal enterprise. While the losses of profits, lab experiments or other intangible losses are included, it must be proved that such losses were specifically intended for the law to be applied."

In other words, those who conscientiously believe that it is their duty to peacefully protest through civil disobedience could be labeled terrorists, but only if they *intend* to hurt corporate profits.

When the words civil disobedience are spoken now, it is with a soft reverence, a genuflection to the noble history of the act as embodied by Dr. King. Those who utter the phrase know it necessitates lawbreaking and arrest, but it has become a socially accepted, even honored, form of resistance. At the time, Dr. King's actions were not so lauded.

In his 1963 letter from a Birmingham jail, Dr. King responded to those who had condemned his tactics in Alabama. Breaking the law had become a moral duty, he said. It was part of a long history of civil disobedience that extended from Jesus of Nazareth, through the tea party of Boston, to the lunch counters of the South. Dr. King reserved his harshest words for clergy who refused to stand by him, and for the "white moderate," who is "more devoted to 'order' than to justice; who prefers a negative peace which is the absence of tension to a positive peace which is the presence of justice; who constantly says: 'I agree with you in the goal you seek, but I cannot agree with your methods of direct action.'" Moderation is a luxury of the privileged, Dr. King said. Patience is not possible at the end of a rope.

Forty years later, at the groundbreaking ceremony for his national memorial, the buffer of history has made it easy, even expected, for politicians to support Dr. King's direct action. Everyone is willing to become a radical in hindsight. Detaching his memory from his life makes it easier for politicians—moderate, right and even far right—to invoke Dr. King's name without acknowledging the uncomfortable truth that he was, undeniably, an extremist.

In his "I Have a Dream" speech, Dr. King defended his extremism in the face of what he called the "tranquilizing drug of gradualism." By 1967, every drop of that drug had been purged from his body. He had begun pushing the civil rights movement to not just target buses or lunch counters, but the entire economic system. In his speech at Riverside Church in New York City, he railed against the "individual capitalists of the West" and called the United States "the greatest purveyor of violence in the world today." Whereas the white moderates had ostensibly supported his goals but condemned his tactics, this speech prompted black allies like the NAACP to distance themselves from his holistic vision of a movement that addressed race alongside class and empire.

"I am convinced that if we are to get on the right side of the world revolution, we as a nation must undergo a radical revolution of values," Dr. King said. "We must rapidly begin the shift from a 'thing-oriented' society to a 'person-oriented' society. When machines and computers, profit motives and property rights are considered more important than people, the giant triplets of racism, materialism and militarism are incapable of being conquered."

Placed in a different historical and political context, Dr. King's tactics and beliefs would undoubtedly have been targeted by terrorism legislation, had Strom Thurmond only thought of it first. Perhaps the law would have been called the Lunch Counter Terrorism Act or the Bus Enterprise Terrorism Act. Supporters would have said that civil rights was a noble cause, but a new law was needed to crack down on the radicals.

When I testified before the House Judiciary Committee, lawmakers bristled at such a comparison. Animal rights activists are *extremists*, they said. They clearly are not "good trouble." They are not "necessary trouble." I imagine that is what white moderates and civil rights opponents said when Dr. King compared his own actions to the Boston Tea Party. In a different time, civil rights activists were not "good trouble," either. J. Edgar Hoover, former director of the FBI, obsessed over Dr. King. The government placed him under a national security microscope until his death. They wiretapped, they harassed, they compiled 3,165 pages of surveillance.

The MLK memorial foundation does not talk about that Dr.

King. To do so would certainly hurt fundraising drives. Checks have rolled in from the "capitalists of the West" that he decried, and their vaults of opportunity have funded the $100 million memorial project. Procter & Gamble ($2.95 million), DuPont ($1 million) and McDonald's ($1 million) are just some of the corporations using Dr. King's memory for bulletproof PR. And they are just some of the corporations that would be protected by a new law under which Dr. King's style of activism would be labeled terrorism.

Hershaft arrives at the House floor in time to see Representative Dennis Kucinich of Ohio speak against the legislation. Kucinich could not be more different from James Sensenbrenner. He is the only vegan member of Congress and one of the most consistently liberal, even if it means sometimes bucking the Democratic Party. He voted against the Patriot Act and called for its repeal, and he voted against the invasion of Iraq. Next year, he will introduce impeachment articles against Vice President Dick Cheney.

All of the crimes listed in the bill are already crimes, Kucinich says. Trespassing is trespassing, theft is theft, harassment is harassment, regardless of the industry targeted. He asks Sensenbrenner why some corporations need designer legislation.

They go back and forth briefly about the purpose of the bill, and Sensenbrenner says it is needed to combat tertiary targeting. Kucinich says lawmakers could more effectively fight extremists by addressing the extreme cruelty that motivates activists. "I just think that you have got to be very careful about painting everyone with the broad brush of terrorism who might have a legitimate objection to a type of research or treatment of animals that is not humane," Kucinich says. "This bill is written in such a way as to have a chilling effect on the exercise of peoples' First Amendment rights."

"Mr. Speaker, I am afraid that my distinguished colleague from Ohio hasn't read the bill, so I will read it for him," Sensenbrenner replies. He is annoyed. Sensenbrenner's views on animal rights and environmental issues are well known. He thinks climate change is a hoax and that the growing international consensus on the issue is due to what he calls "scientific fascism." He also believes there is an "international conspiracy" to bury the truth that global warming does not exist. He is not happy that this pacifist vegan is holding up his bill.

Sensenbrenner reads sections of the bill that he says exempt lawful protests, boycotts and speech. Kucinich's claims are simply unfounded, he says. This bill has nothing to do with free speech. "Now, let's look at what the people this bill has been designed to go after have been saying," he says, and begins to read quotations attributed to animal rights activists defending illegal tactics. The list of sound bites, all out of context and many disputed, have long been used in talking points by industry groups and corporations. They appear on the website of the National Animal Interest Alliance, on a page titled "Quotes from animal rights extremist leaders." Sensenbrenner reads them in the same order they appear on the website. He or his staff seem to have copied and pasted talking points from one of the industry front groups.

"To calm the gentleman's concerns," Kucinich replies, "I have read the bill, and I underlined the sections that I expressed concern about. I am concerned about, as you are, anyone who wants to commit violence against anyone. Remember, I am the author of the bill to create a Department of Peace and Nonviolence. I share your concern about violence. I am suggesting that carving out a special section of law here has a chilling effect."

Sensenbrenner becomes exasperated. He reads, again, the sections of the bill that he says protect the First Amendment.

Kucinich says those provisions are no safeguards, evidenced in Sensenbrenner's claim that the law does not target First Amendment activity—followed by his list of activists' First Amendment activity as proof of their threat.

Sensenbrenner plays his trump card. He says he has a letter

from the ACLU. The group advocates minor changes, but says it does not oppose the bill.

"Now, if there ever was an organization that really goes all the way on one side in interpreting the First Amendment as liberally as it can, it is the American Civil Liberties Union," Sensenbrenner says, as if he has been a card-carrying member all along. "My friend from Ohio, whom I have a great respect for, is even outside the definition of the First Amendment that the ACLU has eloquently advanced in the halls of this Capitol for decades and will do so for decades to come. This is a good bill. I think that all of the fears that the gentleman from Ohio has placed on the record are ill-founded by practically everybody who has looked through this bill, including the ACLU."

Support from the ACLU can be golden; for some legislation, particularly national security bills, a lack of ACLU opposition can be just as valuable. When the civil liberties watchdog says, "The ACLU does not oppose this bill," as it did in an October 30, 2006, letter to Sensenbrenner, it's like a bank security guard turning his back with the vault's doors swung wide.

The ACLU and the Humane Society had both discussed the legislation with the Justice Department in its early stages. They both raised nearly identical sets of concerns in letters to members of Congress opposing the legislation. No amendments to the bill addressed the substantive concerns raised in these letters. Yet the ACLU did not oppose. Later, when I speak to my former colleagues, I will hear various explanations. Some will say that there were too many other civil liberties issues demanding critical attention; others will say that lobbyists didn't think the bill had a chance of passage this session. They will say it was a combination of bad timing and aggressive lobbying.

Or perhaps history repeats itself. The ACLU has had a long, venerable life defending the civil liberties of even the most unsavory characters, including the Ku Klux Klan. To some, though, the organization has always been dogged by its darker days. The ACLU was formed in 1920, just weeks after the Palmer Raids of the first Red Scare. During the hysteria of McCarthyism, many looked to the organization for leadership. Instead, the ACLU was paralyzed by internal divisions. Members and local leaders found themselves fighting their own organization. The ACLU leadership passed a resolution in 1940 barring communists from top positions and voted to remove Elizabeth Gurley Flynn from the board because she was a member of the Communist Party. In the 1970s, the full extent of the organization's complicity became clear when it was revealed that some ACLU leaders even supplied documents on the group's activities to J. Edgar Hoover.

Meanwhile, the National Lawyers Guild took a beating for refusing to name names and purge its membership of suspected communists. Most of the attorneys in key Red Scare court cases were guild members. Because of its vigilance, the organization became a top target of surveillance, harassment and disinformation campaigns by Hoover. FBI agents broke into guild offices at least fourteen times. The House Un-American Activities Committee released a report in 1950 that labeled the guild "The Legal Bulwark of the Communist Party." These government attacks took a heavy toll, and by the 1950s the organization had lost about four-fifths of its membership. Through it all, the National Lawyers Guild stood its ground.

It continues to do so today. National Lawyers Guild members have been representing "eco-terrorists" in court, and the guild's executive director, Heidi Boghosian, has firmly positioned the organization on-record against the Animal Enterprise Terrorism Act, the FBI's "Operation Backfire," and the broader campaign to persecute animal rights and environmental activists. "The government is engaging in Orwellian newspeak by labeling activists as terrorists," Boghosian has said. "It's wrong to enact legislation that punishes the same action more severely if it is committed for political reasons. The AETA is a misguided and dangerous piece of legislation."

This time around, the National Lawyers Guild has been out front opposing the labeling of activists as eco-terrorists.

This time around, the silence of the ACLU gave the green light to the Green Scare.

"I was in the elevator with Sensenbrenner and Petri afterwards, and I turned and said, 'Are you Sensenbrenner? I'm here to oppose this bill,'" Hershaft says. "He says, 'Don't blame me, I was just managing the bill.' He was smiling a little bit. He said, 'It's this guy's fault,' and turns to Petri."

"I walked out with them, followed them, and said 'What's the status of the bill now?' Petri said it's on its way to the White House. I was speechless. He wasn't in the mood for chatting. He was walking briskly like he was trying to get away. Petri said, 'It's done. Kucinich could have asked for a roll call vote, but he didn't.'"

Passing a bill through a suspension motion requires that a quorum is present. Asking for a roll call vote would have required a tally of the names and votes of every member in the room, and revealed the presence of only a handful of lawmakers—not the majority needed. It would have stalled passage of the Animal Enterprise Terrorism Act and forced it either to the House floor or to the next suspension calendar.

Hershaft continues, his voice rising. "We were playing by the rules and doing all the things you're supposed to do in a democracy and they, these people basically shit on us." He takes a long pause. "I understand some win and some lose, but it has to be a fair fight."

Two days later, legislation honoring the St. Louis Cardinals for winning the World Series comes to the House floor under the suspension of the rules. More members of Congress attend and make comments about baseball than were in the room for the terrorism legislation at the start of the week. To record where members of Congress stand on this issue, Representative Virginia Foxx wants a tally of the vote, a move not made for the Animal Enterprise Terrorism Act.

"Mr. Speaker," she says, "on that I demand the yeas and nays." There were 395 yeas, no nays, and only 37 members not voting.

Representative Charlie Norwood, a Republican from Georgia—Dr. King's home state—could not make it to the terrorism vote or the baseball vote. To let the American people know he was not shirking his democratic responsibilities, he submits a "personal explanation" to the congressional record on December 5th. "Mr. Speaker, on roll call No. 523, H. Res. 1078, congratulating the St. Louis Cardinals on winning the 2006 World Series, had I been present, I would have voted 'yes.'"

A week after passage of the Animal Enterprise Terrorism Act, the Fur Commission distributes an announcement proclaiming "Mission Accomplished!" It says the new legislation will give law enforcement the tools needed to catch eco-terrorists. "And more eco-terrorists in jail will help others too, from miners and loggers to recreationists."

Corporations have been eager to appropriate War on Terrorism rhetoric for their own war against political activists, but this is an interesting public relations choice. President George W. Bush stood on the USS *Abraham Lincoln* in front of a banner proclaiming "Mission Accomplished" in 2003, only to be dogged by that hubris months and years later as insurgent attacks continued to rise.

As months pass, it becomes clear that the mission is far from accomplished. On November 27, 2006, fourteen years after his father endorsed the first animal enterprise terrorism bill, President George W. Bush signs the Animal Enterprise Terrorism Act into law. That same day, underground activists vandalize thirty windows at a pharmaceutical corporation with glass etching solution, and dedicate the action to the SHAC 7. This is just the beginning.

December 14, 2006: the Animal Rights Militia claims that it tampered with 487 bottles of Pom Wonderful juice and consumers will suffer from diarrhea unless Pom pulls the juice from the shelves. The company has been under attack for funding animal experiments to tout the health benefits of its juice. The communiqué says, verbatim: "thanks to feinstein and inhoff and the stupid animal enterprise terrorist law that violates the principles that this country is supposed to be founded on, more and more activists like us will choose to retreat into the shadows and fight for the animals underground."

December 19, 2006: underground activists claim responsibility for clipping through the fence at a quail farm in New Jersey. "The farm is located by a waterway and open fields, and we wish our friends the best of luck in establishing new lives," the communiqué says. "To the animal abuse industry, welcome to post-Animal Enterprise Terrorism Act America: not one damn bit different."

January 5, 2007: the ALF distributes an anonymous communiqué after vandalizing six windows and a door at the home of a University of Utah animal researcher. It concludes: "PS. To all the vivisectors we have yet to visit: don't bask in your recent legislative victory for too long. This new animal enterprise law means NOTHING."

In some ways the era of the Animal Enterprise Terrorism Act coincided with a more radical period in the animal rights movement, especially in California. Aboveground and underground groups had both been escalating their tactics against animal experimentation. A few months before the law passed, UCLA professor Dario Ringach had announced he would no longer test on animals, after being harassed by calls and home protests that he said made him fear for his family. In late 2007 and 2008, UCLA professor Edythe London would be targeted for feeding liquid nicotine to monkeys, killing them and examining their brains as part of experiments funded by Philip Morris; underground activists will flood her home with her garden hose and later leave an incendiary device on her porch, setting fire to her front door. No one will be home, and no one will be hurt, but such potentially lethal crimes will occur more frequently.

The North American Animal Liberation Press Office will claim that illegal actions doubled in the year after the passage of the ter-rorism law. Industry groups will also claim increases. The Animal Agriculture Alliance will report that attacks on food retailers by animal and environmental activists increased by 377 percent from 2007 to 2008. Jacquie Calnan, president of Americans for Medical Progress, will invite the leader of a UK animal testing group to the United States to help teach Americans how to deal with animal rights activists.

But are the attacks actually increasing? Or are both sides spin-ning numbers for different purposes, one to inspire radical activists, the other to show the continued threat? As some business groups claim increases, Ron Arnold of the Center for the Defense of Free Enterprise says the radical environmental movement has been de-clining. He attributes the decrease not to legislation but to better sharing of information between federal and local authorities. As the ALF press office touts a spike in ALF crimes, Nick Atwood, the edi-tor of the pro-ALF magazine *Bite Back*, tells me that his data shows the new law has had very little, if any, impact.

Corporations and politicians using this war to target animal rights activists carefully walk a line between success and failure. They want to claim a decline in animal rights crimes, because do-ing so would prove the efficacy of their work. They also want to claim an increase in activity, in order to demonstrate the need for additional government resources and legislation. In the UK, for in-stance, both messages have been used: a report by the Association of the British Pharmaceutical Industry claimed a sharp drop in animal rights activity due to a government crackdown, yet concluded that the decrease shows the need for sustained efforts against the animal rights movement.

This is the political brilliance of the War on Terrorism: it's a war that can never be won. The government can foil plots and make ar-rests, but terrorism as a practice can never be "defeated," any more than all violence or all crime can ever be eliminated. If animal rights opponents can continue walking this line, claiming victories while maintaining the threat, they will have access to a well of money and power that can never run dry.

The day the bill passed the House, I published an article about it on my website. More than one hundred people left comments in response. Many were consumed by fear, cold and bleak, anticipating police roundups and mass arrests. Some warned that I had drawn too much attention to myself, and I should stop writing. For many the beast of government had broken its chains, and this was another footprint as it lumbered toward fascism. The sound of those steps alone was reason to retreat into hopelessness and despair.

To my surprise, though, the overwhelming majority of website comments and emails demonstrated resilience. True, they were afraid, but it was a fear tempered with rage. They called for increased organizing, community building, outreach, lobbying and protesting. They shared the tenor of "Jersey," who wrote: "do they really think everyone is going to crawl into the woodwork and stand for this?" One after another, as the comments streamed in they were buttressed by those prior. People seemed to derive strength not just from the outrage of others, but from their courage to admit their own fears.

Just one week after passage of a law specifically crafted in response to the SHAC campaign, some activists began a "SHAC 7 Week of Action" with protests in Denver, Salt Lake City, New York, Long Island, Philadelphia, D.C., Portland, Los Angeles and Tampa at the homes and offices of those who were doing business with Huntingdon. A slide show of protest photographs posted online showed activists scuffling with security guards while Johnny Cash sang in the background, "You can stand me up at the gates of hell. But I won't back down."

On the anniversary of the Operation Backfire arrests, activists around the world organized dozens of protests and community forums, from Austin to Athens. In Durban, South Africa, protesters gathered at the U.S. Consulate office with a banner reading "Durban Against the Green Scare."

Student activists in Massachusetts protested the Animal Enterprise Terrorism Act outside the office of their U.S. Representative, James McGovern. They demanded answers, and they got some; the headline in the local paper summed it up: "Animal protesters get results." After meeting with McGovern's staff in his office that afternoon, protesters were given a statement from the congressman stating that he does not support the law, he would have voted against it if he had known about a vote, and he would advocate for repeal. Outside McGovern's office, a young woman held a cardboard sign that read, "You can't scare the green out of me."

When? Prosecutors used the previous version of the legislation only twice, and they attribute their inactivity to what they called loopholes in the law. The Animal Enterprise Terrorism Act, the tool prosecutors said they needed and the expansion industry hoped would usher in a political crackdown, has finally arrived. When will prosecutors test their new power? When will the government make the first arrest? When will it all begin?

Industry groups maintain pressure. They use the passage of the law to continue marketing fear to their constituents, as if the new legislation validates the eco-terrorist threat. At the 2007 BIO International Convention, chemical warfare specialists patrol the exhibit hall with equipment to detect poison gas and biological weapons. Outside, armored police vehicles sit ready. The National Association for Biomedical Research distributes fliers with a blood-red background and a black-masked face. They warn attendees to be prepared for attacks by animal rights terrorists.

Frankie Trull is the president of the organization that made those fliers. She tells *Wired* that Constitutional concerns about the law are misguided. New terrorism laws are not intended to make people afraid to use their rights, she says: "All this legislation is not to quell cherished First Amendment activities; people can write, demo, picket, boycott all they want."

This is the public message from supporters about how the legislation will, and will not, be used. Privately, some animal enterprises perceive the law much differently. Among the first indications of what is to come surfaces in Portland, Oregon. For about a year, Portland animal rights activists had been protesting Schumacher Furs and Outerwear. The protests usually involved a dozen people on Saturday afternoons, and there had been about a dozen arrests, none for violence. Sometimes the protests got ugly, with screaming, name calling and threats on both sides. Activists said the owners and employees spat on them, threatened them, and even followed them home. Greg Schumacher put signs in his window threatening violence. One read: "ALL PROTESTERS SHOULD BE! * BEATEN * STRANGLED * SKINNED ALIVE * ANALLY ELECTROCUTED," the fate suffered by the animals that became his coats.

The mayor and police intervened and offered to mediate. Schumacher refused. "I don't think it is reasonable to ask me to mediate with a terroristic organization," he said. When City Commissioner Randy Leonard tried to help the owners, he couldn't. "The Schumachers carry at minimum—at minimum—equal responsibility for what happened outside their store," Leonard said. "I think the case could be made they did what they could to fan the flames at every opportunity."

In February 2007, after 112 years of business, one of the oldest family furriers announced its closure. Greg Schumacher says he has been terrorized by protesters and urges federal prosecutors to use the Animal Enterprise Terrorism Act. The National Animal Interest Alliance supports him and questions whether the protests should have been protected as free speech.

Despite Schumacher's pleas and despite the fur industry warning that animal rights terrorists will make the economy scream, prosecutors wait. Are they waiting for a better case? Do they want public attention to dissipate before using it? Some local activists worry that they might be arrested for terrorism at any moment, but they have no choice but to continue. They put a notch on their bullhorns and turn their attention to Nicholas Ungar Furs, the only remaining fur salon in town.

Meanwhile, Ricardo Solano, one of the lead prosecutors in the SHAC case, gives the keynote address at the Animal Agriculture Alliance's Stakeholders Summit. Conference sponsors include the National Pork Board, United Egg Producers, Monsanto, and the American Veal Association. The attendees, the same groups who supported the Animal Enterprise Terrorism Act, warmly welcome Solano and thank him for helping to convict the SHAC 7. Solano promises that the government will continue its efforts and use the new law. No news outlets report on this wooing of corporations by a federal prosecutor, except for trade publications like *Dairy Herd Management*.

"The fact of the matter is that there are extremist individuals and groups that will go through great lengths to put you out of business," Solano tells the executives of animal industries. "The recent passage of the Animal Enterprise Terrorism Act sends a clear signal to animal rights extremists that if their activities cross the line, the federal government will not stand idly by."

By May 2007—six months after President Bush signed the new terrorism law—it still has not been used. It will be another year and a half before the government decides to prosecute activists. It will be the type of case that supporters of the law had promised would never occur, a case based on what are normally classed as legal activities, such as allegedly protesting, creating leaflets and chalking slogans on the sidewalk. Until then, the law sits unused, a grenade without a pin.

CHAPTER NINE

Loyalty Oaths

May 15, 2007 The Northwest is a story of extremes. The Cascade mountain range extends down from British Columbia through Washington, and on its way to California it creates two Oregons. The Cascades trap cool, moist air from the Pacific Ocean, creating a maritime rain forest in the western third of the state that is wet and green, dripping with life. It can be gray and it always rains, but the land is lush and alive. The western slopes of these mountains can shed two hundred inches of a snow a year, but cross the summit and the clouds drop only a fraction of that moisture. Travel down the slopes of the Three Sisters or Mount Hood, head down into Redmond and deeper down into the playa, and life withers. The land is rough and bitten. Rocky mountain ash, black cottonwood, sagebrush, chokecherry: the trees are short and the bushes gruff, their needles sharp like devil tongues.

Oregon is Portland, the bicycling capital of the country, and Eugene, the "anarchist capital of the United States," according to former Mayor Jim Torrey. It is organic produce, vegan restaurants, compost and biodiesel. Interstate 5 is a lefty-liberal corridor established by "Californicators" and hippies, and a road frequently traveled by the most active cells of the Earth Liberation Front as they sabotaged property across the state.

There is another Oregon. Veer off the road and the attitude is less commune and more frontier. The Ku Klux Klan is strong here and so are militias. In 2001, after an extreme drought, the federal government cut off the irrigation water flowing to farmers in the Klamath Basin Irrigation Project. Scarce resources were redirected to Upper Klamath Lake to protect the endangered suckerfish. Militia leaders declared, "We are at war," and used the Internet to organize convoys of antigovernment protesters from Montana, Nevada, Idaho and beyond. Militia members siphoned water and sabotaged the headgates. When the government repaired them, they were sabotaged again with chain saws and blowtorches. Some militia members threatened bombings and assassinations of federal officials.

This Oregon is not the subject of today's hearing, though. Militia members who have used ELF-style tactics, and gone even further with threats of physical violence, are not a government priority. Today is about a group of environmentalists who have been labeled "terrorists" from day one. Since their arrest for a string of property crimes in the name of defending the environment, the Operation Backfire defendants have been relentlessly branded eco-terrorists and domestic terrorists in government press conferences, Congressional hearings and the media. Up to this point, use of the word has been for political posturing and public relations purposes. Today in Eugene, though, a federal court will hear arguments about whether the label will follow the defendants into their sentencing hearings and throughout the prison system.

The court's decisions will have grave implications for the defendants. If the government successfully argues for the application of the "terrorism enhancement" to their crimes, it could add up to twenty years to their sentences, in some cases quadrupling prison time. It could place them in prisons next to more traditional terrorists and allow harsh restrictions on contact with family and friends. It would legally redefine them.

There is no "terrorism" crime on the books. No one is brought before a U.S. court and charged with it. Instead there are more than fifty offenses—such as kidnapping, dispersing biological weapons and attempting to assassinate the president—that, in some circumstances, qualify for additional penalties because of the motivations of the defendant. Over the years, this corner of the law has evolved to reflect cultural perceptions of terrorism. Beginning in 1989, the U.S. sentencing guidelines allowed for an upward departure in sentencing for a crime "in furtherance of a terroristic action," but terrorist actions were left undefined. That changed in 1994 when Congress created an enhancement for international terrorism, the predecessor of the policy at issue today—but the bombing of the Oklahoma City federal building the following year made clear that the law needed to account for domestic threats as well. As part of the Antiterrorism and Effective Death Penalty Act of 1996, Congress replaced "international terrorism" with the more flexible "federal crime of terrorism."

Now, a crime qualifies for the terrorism enhancement if the government proves two things. First, prosecutors must show the crime "involved or was intended to promote a federal crime of terrorism." That phrase, "federal crime of terrorism," has a specific definition. It has to be one of a laundry list of offenses, such as assassination, kidnapping, torture, bombings and nuclear threats. Second, prosecutors must show that the crime was "calculated to influence or affect the conduct of government by intimidation or coercion, or to retaliate against government conduct." The two-part test for the terrorism enhancement seems straightforward. In practice, the criteria are open to the interpretations of those in the courtroom.

Early in today's hearing, it becomes clear that one of the key questions is whether the terrorism enhancement should apply to crimes that did not involve violence. In their written arguments, defense attorneys said that the precautions taken to avoid harming people separate these crimes from the heartland of the terrorism enhancement. "A terrorist acts from hate and aims to create fear," wrote Marc Friedman, the attorney for Kevin Tubbs. "A terrorist's goal is to cause death, because death is the ultimate tool. Death is the ultimate source of fear." In the government's sentencing memorandum, prosecutors acknowledge that the defendants took precautions to avoid harming anyone.

Arson is an inherently dangerous crime, though. The government argues that the defendants were not capable of knowing, without a doubt, that no employee or firefighter would be harmed. Assistant U.S. Attorney Stephen Peifer tells the court that it was "pure luck" that no one was killed.

Defense attorneys call on the only witness in today's hearing, Dr. Zelda Ziegler. She was one of Stan Meyerhoff's instructors at Central Oregon Community College. The government says that the ALF and ELF committed 1,200 crimes between 1990 and 2004, with no injuries or deaths. Ziegler performed a statistical analysis, using a random sampling of data. Her conclusion: the probability that this many crimes resulted in no injuries is 1 in 90 septillion, or ten thousand trillion times better than picking all six winning numbers in the lottery. This is an exaggeration, because the government does not specify how many of the 1,200 crimes committed by the ALF and ELF were arsons. However, even if one out of every four of those crimes involved arson, the probability is one in three million. If it is pure luck no one has ever been injured, the ALF and ELF may be the luckiest people on the planet.

As part of her research, Ziegler replicated incendiary devices used in the arsons to determine the risk they posed. Attorneys play a video of her experiment to the court. It shows Ziegler using two small yogurt cups with dimensions proportionate to the five-gallon buckets the defendants used. She fills one with pure gasoline, and the other with a mixture of diesel fuel and gasoline—a mixture chosen by the defendants because it burns slowly. She places unlit matches next to the cups; if the fire spreads, even slightly, the matches will ignite. The flame burns, but the cup does not melt away, the nearby cup of fuel does not ignite, and the unlit matches do not ignite. There is no explosion, no fireball, no mushroom cloud. The government has argued that a propane tank at a crime scene, about twice the size of the large table in the courtroom, could have exploded and harmed someone. Ziegler proves that would not have been possible. "It's notoriously boring, unfortunately," she says, referring to the incendiary device she replicated. "We called it the yule log for a while."

Peifer says that even though the ELF exclusively destroys property, their conduct ultimately targets people such as loggers, researchers and forest service employees. He does not question Ziegler's statistical analysis but says that these crimes threatened people's livelihood and, by extension, them.

"The defendants' argument is there was no injury to human beings, no danger to humans, and therefore, there was no terrorism," Peifer says. "If that's the standard, the Ku Klux Klan did not commit terrorism when they traveled in the dark of night, three, four o'clock in the morning, burning black churches in Mississippi. No one was inside the churches, no one was there to be injured. They may not have wanted to injure anybody. They just burned buildings."

Defense attorneys are not sure what to say. The hearing continues, but later Amanda Lee, one of Daniel McGowan's attorneys, says she cannot sit quietly. The Klan did not just burn buildings. They burned churches and burned people and held neither of greater value than the other.

On September 15, 1963, the Klan bombed the Sixteenth Street Baptist Church in Birmingham, Alabama. Klansmen had planted nineteen sticks of dynamite outside the basement of the church with a timing device so that it would explode after Sunday school. The explosion shattered stained glass and flicked concrete like hymnal pages. Four teenage girls were murdered as the congregation prepared for a sermon on "The Love That Forgives."

"There's a word for this, your honor," Lee says, "and it's over-reaching. It's stretching. It's attempting to force the concept of terrorism to fit a set of facts and a group of people that it does not fit."

"This is not a political prosecution," Peifer says. He claims he has never spoken with anyone in the Justice Department about whether to seek the enhancement. Peifer and other prosecutors are tight-lipped, though, about why they seek the terrorism enhancement in some cases but not others.

Stephen John Jordi received it for the attempted arson of an abortion clinic. And Jack Dowell received it for acting as a lookout as some drinking buddies set fire to an IRS building in Colorado Springs, Colorado, and spray-painted "AAR," for Army of the American Republic.

Yet the government did not seek the terrorism enhancement in the case of Zacarias Moussaoui, convicted of conspiracy in connection to the September 11th attacks.

And in the same district where these ELF cases took place, a self-avowed white supremacist named Jacob Albert Laskey threw swastika-etched rocks through the windows of a Eugene synagogue while members were inside. Among the many charges against him, Laskey also solicited help in murdering a potential witness and called in a bomb threat to a federal courthouse in order to disrupt a grand jury. While he awaited sentencing, Laskey sent a letter to *Resistance Magazine* advocating for execution cells to break into homes and kill their targets in front of wives and children. He advocated using "shoot and scoot" tactics to kill political officials as they returned home from work, because the televised funerals would amplify the message. Soliciting a bomb threat against the federal courthouse is listed as a federal crime of terrorism, and Laskey admittedly intended to influence the government, but prosecutors never sought the terrorism enhancement.

The government has aggressively pursued the enhancement in

Operation Backfire. During plea discussions, prosecutors refused to negotiate on this point. Defense attorneys say they do not know of any pre-9/11 cases in which the government sought the enhancement for property destruction alone. This would mark the first application of the terrorism enhancement to environmentalists.

The impetus for the government's commitment to the terrorism enhancement is unclear, but some motivations can be ruled out. The first: increasing prison sentences. The enhancement would automatically increase a defendant's criminal history to the highest level, but prosecutors say they will immediately request an identical decrease due to the plea agreements. Seeking the enhancement is also not a matter of public safety. Jacob Ferguson set more fires than any other defendant. Because he wore a wire and entrapped his friends, he will receive a sentence of no time in prison and five years probation. He will return to Eugene, continue playing in his band Eat Shit Fuckface, and resume his previous life. "I believe that people deserve punishment for their crimes," Amanda Lee says during the hearing, "and I pray that my government is not making the kind of deals with real terrorists that it made with Jacob Ferguson."

Regardless of motivation, a few things are clear. In the last several years the rate at which prosecutors seek the terrorism enhancement has been increasing, and when the government asks, it usually receives. An investigation by the *National Journal* revealed that judges have upheld the terrorism enhancement far more often than they have denied it. Prosecutors successfully obtained the enhancement in twenty-seven of the thirty-five cases reviewed by the *National Journal*, a success rate of about 75 percent.

Accompanying this increased use of the terrorism enhancement has been the creation of a new, secretive prison facility in Terre Haute, Indiana. Not much is known about the facility except that it is for so-called lower-risk terrorists. The government will not reveal which prisoners are housed there or why. Daniel McGowan fears that if the court labels him a terrorist, he could be locked up in such a facility. He would be hidden from public view and isolated from family and friends, without recourse. The government dismisses these concerns as political scaremongering, but his attorneys argue that it is a real possibility.

"I've got to tell you, this concept alone would have boggled our minds a few years ago, and it still boggles my mind," Amanda Lee tells the court. "It is one thing to say we need a special facility in Florence, Colorado, a supermax facility for the most dangerous terrorists we know of, but now we need a facility for low-risk terrorists. I believe the term is an oxymoron. I don't know what a low-risk terrorist is, and yet now we have whole new facilities for them. You know, next we are going to have camps for terrorists."

One week after the terrorism enhancement hearing, U.S. District Court judge Ann Aiken issues her ruling. She's in a difficult position. She must untangle the meaning of a knotted legal history, and in doing so straighten out a legal definition of the word. If she rules in favor of the defense, she will undoubtedly be labeled "soft on terrorism" and soft on those who have targeted the economic backbone of this region. If she rules in favor of the government, Aiken, a Clinton appointee known as one of the more liberal judges on the federal bench, will tacitly be supporting the expansion of the Bush administration's War on Terrorism.

In an acknowledgment of her predicament and an attempt to slip out of it, Aiken begins her decision by redefining her role. She says she is not here to determine if the government is using the law to push a political agenda. Her job is not to determine how the word should be applied, nor what most people feel it means. This is not a political case, she says, and it is not a political decision. Aiken treats the most politicized, nuanced word in the language as if it's straightforward and universal, saying she is "bound by the canons of statutory construction." This is much like a priest saying he is bound by a literal interpretation of the book of Revelations, albeit less straightforward; these legal canons remain largely unwritten.

Congress has not revisited the law since its creation in 1996. The Supreme Court has never heard a single case involving its application. In situations like this, judges often evaluate lawmakers' intent when they passed the law.

The Congressional debate that preceded the enhancement focused on the bombing of Pan Am Flight 103, the 1993 attack on the World Trade Center, and a cult's gassing of the Japanese subway system. Defense attorney William Sharp has catalogued every incident that witnesses and lawmakers said the law should cover, and says no one proposed then that people who solely damage property should be labeled terrorists. "Terrorism is about killing people," Sharp said during the terrorism enhancement hearing. "That is what our members of Congress thought, and that is what the witnesses before the judiciary committee said. It is not a close call. It is simply not possible for anyone to read this history and come up with any other conclusion."

In her forty-six-page decision, Aiken answers the question of whether the enhancement applies to environmental saboteurs with a resounding—maybe. It is possible, she says, but the burden will heavily fall on prosecutors to prove during sentencing that the defendants targeted the government. She will weigh the enhancement for each defendant and their crimes individually.

It's a positive sign to hear Aiken say she might be persuadable. Yet attorneys had expected more from a judge who, in a few months, will strike down part of the Patriot Act dealing with secret searches and surveillance; Aiken will be praised for providing checks and balances on the terrorism powers of the executive branch. Defendants had hoped that, of all possible judges, she would be one of the few willing to rebuke the government for overreaching with terrorism laws. Now all they can do is wait.

June 1, 2007 "Exile" and "Sadie"—Nathan Block and Joyanna Zacher—sit in a Eugene federal courtroom, waiting to find out how many years they will spend behind bars for admittedly torching SUVs and a research facility as part of the ELF. This is the part of the story where the defendants are supposed to see the light, atone for their sins and complete the legal dénouement. Block and Zacher look like they have been typecast for the "eco-terrorist" role: Block with his long, jet-black mane and four-inch black beard, Zacher with red-and-brown streaked hair, pulled back into a bun to look more presentable than the dreadlocks in her mug shot. A cast of cops and prosecutors sits stage left. The case fits the mold of a prime-time courtroom drama, yet something's missing. Block and Zacher are refusing to behave. The terrorists are not following the script.

Judge Aiken has been through plenty of sentencing hearings, has seen the most defiant defendants cower and beg for leniency. The I-swear-to-God-it-wasn't-me defendants apologize and talk about the hard life that took them down the wrong path. The maybe-I-did-it-but-it's-not-my-fault defendants grovel and talk about the lessons they have learned. When the question of prison is no longer *if* but *how long*, most people swallow hard and grovel. They cry. They beg. They vow to get their lives on the right track, set things straight.

This is the seventh sentencing of Operation Backfire defendants, and so far the others have followed this model, with a twist. Because of the political nature of these cases, Aiken has been asking for something more than she would of typical defendants. It's not enough for them to admit their guilt, provide evidence against their friends, and apologize for their actions. She wants them to condemn the radical environmental movement and militant tactics.

When she sentenced Stan Meyerhoff, a lead arsonist in the case, she told him that his actions had given legitimate environmentalists a bad name. For Darren Thurston, she read an excerpt from a book about Thurgood Marshall and spoke about how the Supreme Court justice fought within the legal system, not outside of it. She told him to take classes on U.S. democracy and the proper ways of social change. At the next and final hearing, for Jonathan Paul, she will tell him that as part of his sentence he must read *Three Cups of Tea*. He must then turn in a book report to the court detailing what he has learned about nonviolent activism.

Aiken's message is one that corporations and politicians have been sending for years. In October 2001, U.S. Representative Scott McInnis and other Republicans sent a letter to the Sierra Club, Greenpeace, National Wildlife Federation, Earthjustice, World Wildlife Fund, League of Conservation Voters and Natural Resources Defense Council. "As our Nation begins the recovery and healing process following the tragedy of Sept. 11, we believe it is critical for Americans of every background and political stripe to disavow terrorism in all its forms and manifestations," the letter said. The organizations were told that they must publicly denounce the ALF, ELF and similar groups, which have committed sabotage "no less deplorable" than the World Trade Center attacks. They were given a deadline, and it was implied in press statements that if they declined they would be investigated. The leaders of the national environmental movement all pledged their loyalty oaths.

Some bristled in their responses. Others jumped at the opportunity to show they follow the proper channels. The National Wildlife Federation not only responded to McInnis's letter, but sent their own to the *New York Times* urging others to issue condemnations. The Sierra Club had previously offered monetary rewards for information that led to the capture of environmental saboteurs, and Greenpeace has long gone out of its way to condemn underground activists. Representative George Nethercutt, a Republican from Washington and sponsor of eco-terrorism legislation, has perhaps captured this guilt-by-association mentality best. "National environmental groups need to know, you are either with us or against us," Nethercutt said during a Congressional hearing in 2002. "You need to choose which side you are on, and know we will be watching. Financing and harboring terrorists is no different from directly committing the acts. These dangerous and misguided zealots must be left without aid or comfort. This is the moral framework."

The moral framework has developed as everyone, it seems, is "going green." Judge Aiken herself noted in one of the previous sentencing hearings that there are perhaps ten years before an environmental "tipping point," and Al Gore, one of the most respected and mainstream faces of the environmental movement, has called for lawbreaking, saying, "I can't understand why there aren't rings of young people blocking bulldozers." A report prepared for the Pentagon advised that climate change "should be elevated beyond a scientific debate to a US national security concern," and these concerns will lead to the establishment of a new Center for the Study of Climate Change at the Central Intelligence Agency. If the state of the planet is indeed so dire, it would logically pose some unsettling questions. If total environmental collapse approaches, is another petition the appropriate response? Is switching to compact fluorescent light bulbs really enough? How far is too far when life on the planet is at stake?

In this political context, being "with us," as Nethercutt said, means not asking such questions. There is a right way of social change, and a wrong way. The wrong ways—and the radical beliefs that inspire them—are simply not open for discussion. The right ways, the "with us" ways, are conventional, slow, lawful and, above all, nonthreatening. Activists should address the inconvenient truth without overly inconveniencing anybody. Anyone who believes otherwise, or who refuses to condemn those who believe otherwise, is "against us" and will be punished accordingly.

For Block and Zacher, even the most contrived statement and renunciation of radical tactics might knock off months of prison time. Aiken has already ruled in previous sentencings that both of

Block's and Zacher's crimes qualify for the terrorism enhancement, so a public statement will not help on that front. But Meyerhoff's political about-face certainly helped him during sentencing. He began a statement to the court by saying, "I apologize to you, victims and fellow citizens, for three years of extremist barbarity." He condemned the ELF as "thuggish" and concluded by pleading for mercy. Aiken commended his renunciation of direct action. She sentenced him to thirteen years, about two and a half years less than the government offered in his plea deal.

They sit silently. Block, twenty-six, and Zacher, twenty-nine, had planned on not reading a statement, but to Aiken that is not acceptable. She tells the defendants that she wants to hear something, anything, from both of them. Their attorneys look at each other and shuffle papers. Awkward pause. The court will take a long lunch, Aiken says, so the defendants can think about what they have to say.

As they waited for the sentencing hearing to begin this morning, friends of Block and Zacher gathered outside the courtroom, holding hands in some kind of a pagan prayer circle. Their appearance turned heads, even the heads of the other young supporters familiar with activist subcultures—punks, vegan straight-edge hardcore kids, Earth Firsters. They could not quite figure out the prayer circle crowd. Long black ZZ Top beards. Harry Potter spectacles. Facial piercings. Celtic-inspired tattoos. Silver bracelets. Natural fiber vests and tunics in purples, greens and of course black. Grateful Dead meets death metal. All of the defendants have been marginalized and labeled terrorists, and among them the noncooperating defendants are even more isolated because even their friends turned against them. Block and Zacher are the blackest of the black sheep.

Multiple defendants have been labeled "anarchists" in the press and in court documents—their sentencing memorandum declared, "Block and Zacher were dedicated anarchists who, by definition, were anti-government"—and this morning Assistant U.S. Attorney Kirk Engdall made sure these defendants wore their scarlet circle "A." They met in November 1999 at the World Trade Organization protests. During his sentencing presentation, Engdall showed a video segment from KIRO-TV in Seattle titled "Anarchist Rampage." People in black clothes, calling themselves the Black Bloc, vandalized corporate chain stores. A very excited female reporter shouted into her microphone, "Oh my gosh! They just broke the Starbucks window!" Block did protest at the WTO, but police never arrested him, and he has said he did not break windows or even witness this scene. Zacher said it's true she was there, but before the riots and four blocks away. Engdall went on to tell the court that a CD was found at their home with liner notes that said "to hell with property, to hell with the State." Police also found "anarchist literature."

Zacher's attorney, Bill Sharp, has ignored the government's allegations of reading-while-anarchist and, in an attempt to deflect attention from his client's silence, poked fun at the excuses made by cooperating defendants. He listed "whiner factors," justifications made by the others, including "my frontal lobes are undeveloped," "my love for a conspirator" and "I was sexually abused." "Buildings don't burn less when nice people burn them," Sharp said, so excuses do not matter. Nothing should matter, he said, except the extent of damage, the number of crimes and how long each defendant participated. Stick to the numbers.

This may look good on paper, but the system doesn't work this way. Aiken wants an apology, an admission of ideological guilt, and she is determined to get it.

After lunch, Block's and Zacher's shackled legs hobble back into the courtroom. Here it comes. This is what Aiken has been waiting for. The fear just needed to steep for two more hours.

They take their seats, look at each other and look back at their friends. Block tugs at his forest-green inmate scrubs and fidgets with his beard. Zacher adjusts her knot of hair. They sip water, then force out statements that only last about a minute each. Block says he respects the "sacredness of human life alongside all other life." Zacher says she "only wants this harrowing chapter of my life to be closed" so she may live sustainably among the air, trees, water and animals, a sly reference to Charles Manson's "ATWA" and a subtle commentary on the government's demonization of the pair.

If the defiance surprises prosecutors, they don't show it. By all accounts, it should. The two should have been the weakest links in the group of co-conspirators the government calls "The Family." The other defendants sometimes called Block and Zacher, the youngest of the bunch, the "punk kids." Daniel McGowan wanted to track them down years after the crimes to make sure they kept their mouths shut. Youth and naïveté could have screwed everything up.

Now the punk kids, the young ones, stare down the judge and the prosecutors. They view the entire legal process as a sham, friends and family say, and refuse to cooperate with a corrupt system in any way. One year from now, they'll release a joint statement from prison about their cooperating codefendants: "Perhaps these vile turncoats deserve compassion, in the same way that all creatures deserve compassion, and indeed they once deserved acclaim for their physical deeds, but now they deserve neither praise nor forgiveness, for in the hour when the struggle returned for them, when the predator had once again become the prey, they failed in spirit and resolve, cowardly breaking long held oaths and begging for mercy from their captors, hoping to gain leniency by offering as a sacrifice to the alter of a perverted 'justice' their former friends, trusted colleagues and any dignity they once held."

Block and Zacher will not budge. Aiken is not happy. She breaks for another recess.

"This has been totally anticlimactic," says one animal rights activist who has traveled from the Midwest for court, as he walks past the prayer circle crowd holding hands again. "I totally thought a Norse god was going to swoop in and whisk them both away to freedom."

Block's dad, Lee, sits in the front row, in a gray houndstooth jacket, gray hair, graying handlebar mustache, arms folded across his chest. He waits quietly for Aiken to return and sentence his son. He turns to one of Block and Zacher's friends, a pregnant woman in a green shirt with tribal tattoos on her arms and fingers, and shows her the red button on his key chain. "It's for the rental car. What do you think?"

"I don't think the panic button is going to help you now."

Lee Block stands and walks to the press benches on the left side of the courtroom. He begins talking to Bill Bishop, a reporter from Eugene's *Register-Guard*, without introducing himself. He wants Bishop to write about the government paying Jacob Ferguson to wear a wire and then letting him walk free even though he was involved with fourteen of the twenty arsons.

His wife Maureen, Block's mother, grabs the sleeve of his sport coat and snaps at him to sit down. They are not supposed to talk to reporters, or to anyone. Nathan's orders. Mom and Dad have fierce opinions about the government labeling the ELF—and, by extension, their son—a domestic terrorist threat. But Nathan made it clear that nothing good can come from trying to persuade reporters or from pandering to the court. That has been the strategy all along. Keep your mouth shut and don't give anyone any rope unless you want to get strung up. All his mom will say on the record is that she's "proud as punch" of her son.

Aiken returns a few minutes later, dumps a stack of manila folders on her bench, leans back in her chair, puts her bright red eyeglasses on top of her head, rests two fingers from her left hand on her cheek, and glares at the defendants.

She still cannot figure them out. "Your view of the world has stunned me," she says. They have not used any of the "whiner factors" to explain their actions, so she tries to do the explaining. She says they are not mature. They do not have heroes. They do not understand social change. They are young. She reads some Tennyson: "Ah, what shall I be at fifty / Should Nature keep me alive, / If I find the world so bitter / When I am but twenty-five?"

What upsets friends and family more than anything is when Aiken says Block and Zacher are not well read. "For many of us old people, we read books," she says. "I wonder if people read. . . ." the last word or two in her thought gets lost in the grumbling, whispering and shifting on the wooden benches. Friends who were unfazed when prosecutors described the arsons nearly become incensed when the judge questions their erudition.

"Really at this moment I don't understand who you are, what you are, your belief system," she says. "I don't think you even really understand what life is about."

Block and Zacher stare ahead.

"I didn't hear anyone say they're sorry," she says. "I didn't hear anyone apologize. I didn't hear anyone say they would work to pay restitution." Aiken pauses and glares at the defendants. One last chance. One last chance to condemn sabotage and embrace compact fluorescent light bulbs. "Pregnant pause. You could have stood up right now and addressed these things, but I noticed no one is moving."

More silence, as tense as the seconds of quiet delay between a lightning flash and the thunderclap.

They do not move when Aiken sides with prosecutors on the terrorism enhancement. They do not move when she sentences them to ninety-two months in prison—about seven and a half years, or one quarter of the life they have lived. They barely move through the attorneys' back-and-forth legalese and fine print.

As Nathan Block is led out of the courtroom, though, he stops and turns toward the rows of benches. In the end, he and Zacher did not fare much worse than the cooperating defendants. Block pauses and stares at his friends, then begins to smile. He crosses an "X" with his forearms, makes two rock-on devil's horns with pinkies and pointers on each hand, and sticks out his tongue.

June 3, 2007 Down in the Whiteaker neighborhood a teenager with facial tattoos and top hat sprawls out under a tree and a girl in a dirty prom dress and a hoodie dances around him. Over at Sam Bond's Garage some guys nursing pints talk about early eighties anarchist punk rock. The greasy bar food is organic and the regulars talk about beer like New Yorkers talk about wine. Eugene is still, and always will be, Eugene. But somewhere deep the tectonic plates of this town have shifted, and nothing feels stable anymore.

I had never been to Eugene until these court cases; yet even to an outsider this place feels like it has changed. The activist community is wary of strangers, especially journalists, but after mutual friends vouch for me, no one can stop talking. Everyone remembers where they were when the indictments came down. They are still trying to piece things together, not just what happened then but what happens now.

I've been staying with Lauren Regan, the executive director of the Civil Liberties Defense Center and perhaps the most visible spokesperson for the defendants. She has seen strength, the community response to the arrest of their friends. She has also seen fear. The other night there was a house party with bands and a bonfire and tables of food, welcoming all the Earth Firsters who have traveled to town for court. We tried not to stay long—heavy drinking and pot smoking have long been part of Eugene activist culture, but they play a different role now, a perpetual wake. When drunk or high the partygoers turn to Regan, either to vent or to pull her off to a corner and ask quietly: Did my name come up in any court documents?

Many old faces have slunk into the shadows, either because

they need to keep a low profile now or because they're just plain scared. It's hard to tell which. A young activist with a Food Not Bombs patch on his ball cap says he has had a hard time joining political groups at his college. "People are so distrustful," he says. "They look at you and wonder where you came from, what you're doing." Locals oppose the government's labeling of environmentalists as terrorists, but don't want to publicly be associated with Regan or the defendants. Sometimes, after speaking events, people will approach her, slip a wad of bills into her pocket in support of her work, then turn and disappear.

Yesterday a group of Earth Firsters and I went rafting down the Willamette hoping to float away from all of this, for even a few hours. There was cool water and colder beer and a sun that burned without feeling hot. Regan would remind us that nobody is allowed to talk about the case, the crew would paddle a few strokes, and then the conversation would return to the arrests. Today, hiking in Fall Creek with Daniel McGowan was also supposed to be a break, a final chance for McGowan to experience the natural world before prison. Nobody could talk about anything except the case.

We drive down the long winding road to Lauren Regan's home in unincorporated Franklin, past a trailer that seems to have been abandoned. We've passed that trailer at least a dozen times now, and each time Regan says to herself, "I need to talk to the neighbors about that." We drive under a bridge and on the concrete wall are the words "NO TRESPASSING." McGowan had spray-painted the warning for her years ago, and she jokes that this is where he practiced his spraycan penmanship.

"The Ranch," the home of Regan and her partner Jim Flynn, was once the office of the *Earth First Journal*, when the publication moved to Eugene. It was a crash pad for tree sitters and travelers. Most of the defendants were public activists whom nobody suspected of being involved in clandestine activity. They all had slept at the Ranch at some point. Hadn't they? Regan and Flynn run down the list and then give up. It's hard to remember the details from so long ago; it feels like it was a different world then.

One of the most vivid memories of that period that Regan recounts is McGowan meeting her dog, Nakaia. Nakaia is named after a matriarchal tribe of the Pacific Northwest. She has a long snout and thick white fur and regards most humans with indifference. McGowan was determined to win her affection. He spent hours preparing vegan, heart-shaped dog treats from scratch—a peace offering in hopes of wooing a wolf.

Daniel McGowan mingles around the front porch at his farewell party. He smiles and shakes hands with the older Earth Firsters and younger punk rockers. Inside the house, Jenny Synan stands in a corner; the sun has set and she says she can't stop thinking about tomorrow. She and McGowan argued in the woods because she wanted to spend time alone working on her statement to the court, and McGowan wanted her to stay with him. She says she wants to edit the statement because she's afraid it's too long. "It's the only thing I have control over. Just a little bit," she says. "It's the only thing that can make a small difference." Once the sentencing is over, she thinks she'll be able to focus more on their time together. She'll have two weeks off work to spend with her husband before he reports to prison. Maybe they'll stay in the city and find a hotel with a good pool, she says in between sneezes. A chlorinated, allergy-free pool, not a hippie Oregon swimming hole. They might take in a Mets game, or walk Rockaway Beach and then visit the Cloisters.

In the kitchen the host, Shelley Cater, quietly prepares tea. She won't reveal all of her ingredients. There might be rosemary, an herb for remembering better days while in prison; there might be violets, a flower for remaining faithful, even when tested. She pours from a glass jug with a handmade paper label that says, in fine, black script, "Courage in the face of Adversi-Tea: for strong hearts and steady nerves." A homeopathic remedy, she jokes, an extra dose of what McGowan will need when sitting before the judge.

Lauren Regan and I leave the party and drive to her law office so she can print press releases. In the back seat is Mike Roselle. Roselle is a cofounder of Earth First, the Ruckus Society, and the Rainforest Action Network, and has had a role in nearly every major campaign of the modern environmental movement. He's had a few drinks, as most everyone has, and is telling war stories about sit-ins and civil disobedience. This one is about receiving a call from Greenpeace because they had a dangerous media stunt and Roselle was the go-to guy for things like that. He had to smuggle himself into Canada. Or was it out of Canada? Maybe both, he says, grinning. Roselle has been read Oregon's 1875 Riot Act and has been arrested for "Interfering with an Agricultural Operation" and everything in between. He's no stranger to jail cells or to government surveillance. When he worked with the Yippies, they found out one of their housemates was a federal agent—but they kept him around because he had a car.

Roselle knew all of the defendants at the time they were committing their crimes, and some even attended his nonviolent direct action trainings. But they were living double lives—he had no idea about their underground personas until his friend William Rodgers committed suicide after his arrest. Years from now, Roselle will condemn the defendants and the ELF in his autobiography, writing, "It takes more courage to sit in front of a bulldozer than it does to burn one." Tonight, he will not say much about the defendants except that they are all good people, with good hearts, and that it's a shame they have ended up behind bars.

When we get to the law office, Roselle says he'll watch the car.

"I don't go into law offices unless I'm in trouble," he says, "and I haven't gotten in trouble tonight."

———

June 4, 2007 The sun has refused to rise compliantly today, dragging its feet into a gray, threatening sky. McGowan and Synan, perhaps believing that their only protection is in each other, walk without umbrellas in the rain. The rain quietly rails against the new Wayne L. Morse United States Courthouse, five stories of ultra-modern glass and steel. Some environmentalists praised the designers of the courthouse for using the latest green technology when it was built. The U.S. Green Building Council awarded it a gold certification, and the American Institute of Architects would later name it a Top Ten Green Project for 2007. When juxtaposed with its massive façade of steel and glass, though, the building's recycled and locally produced materials, natural lighting, and native plants seem like more of an acquiescence to the local culture than any real bond with it. It is as if the building itself is saying, "You might have a point with some of this environmental stuff, but you can't take these things too far."

McGowan, who always has a story or a joke and dominates most conversations, is silent now. He and his wife walk up the gray concrete steps, push open two sets of glass doors, pass through metal detectors, climb the stairs and enter the courtroom. Outside, the raindrops cling to the building's façade in streaks that shimmer faintly, like the water in Fall Creek.

Jenny Synan's eyes redden as she moves through the courtroom. She sits on a wooden pew, the front row of four rows, behind McGowan and his two attorneys. Next to her sits one of McGowan's sisters and his father. His father's gray hair is slicked back, with a few hairs starting to pull out of place in the front. He wears thick bifocals, the kind with an extra metal bridge across the top, and on the lapel of his blue sport coat is an American flag.

In the back row, against the wall, sit the parents of Jeff "Free" Luers. Luers's mother fans herself, although the room is quite chilly. They sit near the door, as far away as possible, perhaps because they've been too close to a scene like this already. On the pews between Luers's parents and Synan sit McGowan's friends and local activists, shoulder to shoulder, some holding hands. Some sit on padded shipping envelopes taped together, an improvised court cushion. They've been through so many court dates that they know a long afternoon is ahead, and the courtroom is stiff and unforgiving.

To the far left, in four miniature rows, sit reporters and two courtroom sketch artists. In front of them is a waist-high wooden wall, and beyond the wall sits an L-shaped formation of prosecutors, FBI agents and local cops.

Judge Aiken enters the room and everyone rises, then sits again. Prosecutors begin a one-and-a-half-hour presentation of Daniel the Terrorist, including a Power Point slide show, twenty minutes of wiretap conversations and eighteen exhibits. Assistant U.S. Attorney Stephen Peifer says McGowan may be funny and witty, but another side comes out at night. He says McGowan has a "Jekyll and Hyde personality."

Peifer talks about McGowan's activist history and reads a list of mile markers from his journey underground. The claims are not part of the case, and will not be proven, but prosecutors argue that they show the career of a criminal and the profile of someone worthy of being sentenced as a terrorist.

'97: Broke windows at a Macy's store protesting the sale of fur.
'98: Threw a crème pie at the president of the Sierra Club for being too soft in the defense of the environment.
'98: Tossed etching fluid on the windows of a Fidelity building because of ties to Occidental Petroleum.
'99: Drew a diagram of an experimental corn crop at UC Berkeley, used by others to destroy the experimental corn.
'99: "Planned" the riots in Seattle against the World Trade Organization meeting.
'00: Became a "full-fledged anarchist."

And on, and on. There are bits of truth in Peifer's story,

McGowan will later say, and some portions are flat-out wrong. But now is not his time to speak.

The government plays some of the conversations recorded by Jacob Ferguson, the lead arsonist. Ferguson asks McGowan if he's worried about the connections between all the defendants, whether that makes them vulnerable. No, don't worry, McGowan says. That's long in the past. He says the only way they'll ever get caught is if someone opens their mouth and snitches. "It's not worth it, man," McGowan says. "That's just Judas shit man."

In sentencings for other defendants, Aiken has already ruled that one of McGowan's crimes, committed at Jefferson Poplar tree farm, qualifies for the terrorism enhancement because the communiqué mentioned legislation. The other, at Superior Lumber, does not, because it did not have a clear link to government conduct. In all, Aiken applies the terrorism enhancement to five of twenty crimes, and seven of ten defendants. There is little chance she will deviate from her previous analysis, and McGowan expects that he will receive the terrorism enhancement.

Nevertheless, Synan has said that she hopes the statements of her husband's friends, family and professors will help sway the judge. She has been sitting with her typed statement resting on the floral pattern of her dress, her hands crossed and resting on the statement. She occasionally smooths and straightens the papers. When she has her opportunity, she tells the court about meeting McGowan, going on a date, falling in love.

"I come from an upper-middle-class family and have a respectable education. I have always considered myself a fairly intelligent and compassionate person, but I have learned a lot about compassion from Daniel," Synan says. "Before I met Daniel, I thought one's intentions were adequate enough to make one a good person, an exemplary citizen in our society. If you donate to charities and give a homeless person money once in a while, you were doing good.

One thing I had never even considered was stepping outside of that comfort zone."

She says the day of his arrest is a blur. She did not know what was happening. She did not know about his past, and after his arrest she never asked. She waited for him to come to her and explain it all, and he eventually did. "Daniel has talked to me about how he felt about these actions. He has talked to me about how much he regrets everything he did and how it terribly affected all of the people involved. If he could go back and change those years he spent in the Northwest, he would. I would like to say to the victims that despite what you know about Daniel from his crimes against you, despite how much he hurt you, I hope my words can convey to you that he is not that person now and that can mean something to you."

As the crowd and attorneys disperse for a recess, Synan kisses her husband on the lips and reaches for his hand.

After the recess McGowan takes his seat, whispers back and forth with his attorneys, clears his throat, and leans into the microphone.

"It is hard to hear tapes of conversations I had with Jacob Ferguson, where I speak with false bravado about our past together," McGowan says. "There are no tapes of some of my most private thoughts, about how I got sick to my stomach before these acts, about the fear and discomfort I hid from my friends and family. None of it is an excuse, but I want you to know, Judge Aiken, that when I became involved in the arsons, it was after being involved in environmental activism for a few years, and at a time when I felt utterly desperate as my attempts to change anything failed almost always.

"Moving to Oregon changed my life, as it is so beautiful and the forests are amazing. There is nothing like it on the planet, and it caused me great pain to see the old-growth forests being logged. I wish I had the answers for how to fix this problem, but I didn't and

I took the easy way out. I allowed myself to choose extreme tactics because I felt the environmental situation in the world was getting more and more dire by the day. Things I spoke about and thought about how to fix seven years ago are being discussed on television and online now, and it gives me some hope. At the time, though, I was feeling quite hopeless. This seems now to be a hollow excuse for my actions. But it is the truth."

Judge Aiken says she does not believe it. People "are both clay and angel," she says, and McGowan has shown himself to be more of the former. She says plans to pursue a master's degree while in prison reflect his "self-absorption." Professors wrote letters to the court supporting McGowan; Aiken says he should have made those relationships earlier, and asked scholars to teach him the proper way of social change. During the lunch break, she Googled McGowan's name and saw his media interviews and his website. It makes you look like a celebrity, she says to him, but you are no poster child for the environment, nor are you a martyr or a political prisoner.

She tells him he has the face of Janus, a reference to the Roman god who guarded exits and entrances, beginnings and endings, with two faces looking in opposite directions. Aiken tells him to change his website and tell his supporters that he was a coward for choosing direct action. He must cut off one of his faces, but, as he is sentenced to seven years in prison, as a terrorist, it's not clear if it's the one looking to the past or to the future.

Outside the courthouse, McGowan walks down the stairs and pauses for interviews with reporters, then hugs his friends. Synan stands alone. They walk away with cameras flashing behind them. The rain has stopped, and some sunlight flickers through fast-moving clouds. The façade of the courthouse no longer shimmers like running creek water; instead the steel reflects a dozen shades of gray.

CHAPTER TEN

Enemies from Within

July 26, 2010 Prisons are always hidden away from us—out of sight, and I suppose that means the hope is that they'll be out of mind, too. They're generally relegated to outlying towns whose populations are in desperate need of the jobs their constant stream of occupants brings. Within these incarcerated economies, the prisons are often further concealed by a screen of forests, fields and winding nameless roads. On maps they are the blanks spaces. If you ask for directions at any nearby gas station or fast-food restaurant, though, all of the locals will know how to get there. They'll pause for a moment, since if you have to ask you must be an out-of-towner, which means you must be visiting a prisoner. You'll receive a quick once-over as they wonder what it is that the prisoner did, and why it is that you care. Then the directions are given politely, but tersely—no one likes to remember the razor wire and guard towers, rifles and cages, hidden just out of sight from the rows of chain restaurants, chain stores, chain everything.

If you were to visit the federal penitentiary in Marion, Illinois, of your own free will, you'd head down Grassy Road, past the general store selling bait and tackle, and the pickup trucks full of coolers. You'll turn onto Prison Road and cross Justice Drive and then you will see it, and it's nothing like you expected it to be.

The strangest thing about a prison is that it's so shockingly, horribly normal. The sun still shines here. Trees still grow. The grass is perfectly trim and green. Pull up to the parking lot and prison guards who just ended their shift are talking about their cars and their families. They say today would be a good day for a ball game and a beer. They laugh and wave goodbye to each other. Behind them a moat of razor wire glistens in the sun like an electric current, light reflecting so brightly off of each razor's edge that you can't help but turn away.

Here in Marion, within the walls of the United States penitentiary, there is a special prison unit that the government won't say much about. It is not a normal prison. It is not listed in the Bureau of Prisons directory. In Freedom of Information Act documents, the government redacts the names of those imprisoned here. All U.S. prisons must be legally authorized by the Bureau of Prisons national program statement, but it makes no mention of this place. This is one of two special prisons on U.S. soil, called Communication Management Units, or CMUs, that house prisoners the government has decided are terrorists. The second CMU is in Terre Haute, Indiana. Because the prisoners in the Marion CMU live on an island of concrete, hidden from the rest of the world and isolated from other inmates in a prison-within-a-prison ringed by razor wire, the prisoners and guards call this place "Little Guantánamo."

Here, halfway between his past in Oregon and his future in New York City, is Daniel McGowan.

Since 9/11, it's generally known that people the U.S. government has deemed terrorists are imprisoned at either Guantánamo Bay, Cuba, or ADX-Florence, the "Supermax." For example, the Supermax holds Al Qaeda operative Zacarias Moussaoui and Olympic Park bomber Eric Rudolph. The government will say little about the identity of the twenty-five prisoners at the CMU in Marion or the thirty-six prisoners at Terre Haute, but through information gleaned from government documents and interviews with former and current prisoners, it's clear that they are not the Moussaouis and Rudolphs of the world.

Until recently, the Marion CMU housed Andy Stepanian, one of the SHAC 7. Stepanian was convicted of conspiring to commit animal enterprise terrorism by campaigning to close Huntingdon Life Sciences. By the admission of prosecutors, he had a minor role in the campaign. He destroyed no property and committed no violence, and in prison he had no disciplinary history. Stepanian is the only animal rights or environmental activist other than McGowan to be housed in one of these prisons, and the first CMU prisoner ever released.

Among the prisoners at the Terre Haute CMU is Sabri Benkhala. Benkhala is an American citizen, born and raised in Virginia and a graduate of George Mason University. He was studying law in Saudi Arabia when he was arrested and charged with providing support to the Taliban. In 2004, he was found not guilty, but less than a month later he was forced to testify before a grand jury and then convicted of perjury. He was sentenced to ten years in prison. At his sentencing, U.S. District Court Judge James C. Cacheris praised his "model citizenry" and said "Sabri Benkahla is not a terrorist."

The Terre Haute CMU is also home to Rafil A. Dhafir, an Iraqi-born physician who created a charity called Help the Needy. He was sentenced to twenty-two years in prison for conspiring to violate the economic sanctions on Iraq by sending food and medical supplies to children. "No one seems to know about this top-secret operation until now," he wrote in a letter to his family when he was transferred to the CMU. "It is still not fully understood. . . . The staff here is struggling to make sense of the whole situation."

"We are told this is an experiment," Dhafir said. "So the whole concept is evolving on a daily basis."

This "experiment" involves a radical restriction of prisoners' communications to levels that meet or exceed the most extreme in the country, including the Supermax and the Special Housing

Units ("the hole" in other prisons). McGowan, Dhafir and the others in the CMUs are allowed one fifteen-minute telephone call per week. By comparison, in their previous prisons they were entitled to about three hundred minutes per month, or five times that amount. Additional CMU restrictions make this handful of minutes even more inaccessible. Phone calls must be scheduled one and a half weeks in advance and must take place between 8 a.m. and 2:30 p.m., Monday through Friday, a time when most family members are working. Prisoners have been told that this makes sure their calls can be live-monitored by staff and counterterrorism officials in Washington, D.C.

Visits are limited to four hours per month; before McGowan was transferred here, he had fifty-six potential visiting hours per month. Even at the Supermax, prisoners receive up to thirty-five visitation hours per month, more than eight times what prisoners receive at the CMUs. Visits are non-contact, behind glass and live-monitored. They must also be conducted in English, which places an additional burden on prisoners who speak English as a second language.

Such extreme restrictions on inmate communications, including not allowing them to hug family members, go against a body of research and official government policy on prisoner treatment. Generally, the government encourages contact visits by family because they improve prisoner behavior, increase morale and further rehabilitation. Embracing their family and holding their children is a reminder that there is warmth and good outside these walls. Prisoners, psychologists and prison staff unequivocally say that phone calls, mail and visits are important flecks of light in the darkness.

The government has reason to be secretive about this program, because similar experiments have not been well received by civil rights and human rights organizations. The Bureau of Prisons has a history of operating pilot programs outside the confines of the

Constitution. For example, the High Security Unit in the federal women's prison in Lexington, Kentucky, was created in the 1980s to house political prisoners belonging to an organization that, according to the Bureau of Prisons, "attempts to disrupt or overthrow the government of the U.S." The Lexington HSU existed belowground, in total isolation from the outside world and with radically restricted prisoner communications and visitations. The women were subjected to constant fluorescent lighting, almost daily strip searches, and sensory deprivation. The purpose of these conditions, according to a report by Dr. Richard Korn for the ACLU, was to "reduce prisoners to a state of submission essential for ideological conversion." The Lexington HSU was closed in 1988 after an outcry by Amnesty International, the ACLU and religious groups.

The Marion federal penitentiary—the larger facility that houses the CMU—has its own dark history. It was created in 1963 as a high-tech replacement for the end-of-the-line prison on Alcatraz Island. Over the years, Marion became infamous for its Control Unit, which kept prisoners on indefinite twenty-two-hour lockdown in solitary confinement. There were accounts of widespread brutality. National organizations called the Marion Model tantamount to psychological torture, but the government claimed that it was necessary to maintain safety. However, the Control Unit did not house prisoners solely based on their propensity for violence. As former warden Ralph Aaron stated, "The purpose of the Marion Control Unit is to control revolutionary attitudes in the prison system and the society at large." After a prison-wide strike and then the murder of two guards in the early eighties, government officials called for an even more extreme facility, and eventually the Supermax ADX-Florence was built.

The Communication Management Units in Marion and Terre Haute were created with comparably questionable legality, and in comparable secrecy. In 2005, when press reports revealed that three convicted World Trade Center bombers had been communicating with extremists abroad from within the Supermax, the Bureau of Prisons came under attack. The most restrictive prison facility in the country was not doing its job. An audit by the inspector general's office later revealed that the problem arose not from the inadequacy of the tools available to monitor terrorist communications, but from inconsistent implementation by untrained staff. Nevertheless, a national scandal required a response, and in April 2006 the Justice Department proposed new rules titled "Limited Communication for Terrorist Inmates." Proposals included limiting prisoner communication to one fifteen-minute telephone call per month, one six-page letter per week and one one-hour visit per month. During the required public comment period, the ACLU and other civil rights groups protested that the program was inhumane and contained no checks and balances on government power. The backlash prompted the government to drop the proposal. Or so it seemed. A few months later, the Justice Department quietly transferred seventeen men to Terre Haute. The government called the new operation in the prison's former death row a Communication Management Unit.

The CMU was opened in apparent violation of the Administrative Procedures Act, and outside of the Code of Federal Regulations. Since the previous restrictive proposal had created too much controversy, the government simply circumvented the rules. The Bureau of Prisons issued a document in which they described the CMU as a "self-contained general population unit" in accordance with "national policy." It is still unclear what this national policy is, and who authorized the experimental prison.

Whatever the origins, Bureau of Prisons Director Harley Lappin has been questioned by members of Congress about the status of the experiment. In a budget hearing in March 2008, Lappin briefly discussed programs for terrorist prisoners. Congress had provided $17 million to establish a counterterrorism prison unit, and an additional $9 million was pending for 2009. "Now that we know we are going to have these folks long term, a lot of the more serious offenders, terrorists, were housed at ADX Florence," Lappin said, but not all posed the same level of security threats. "So we are ramping up two communications management units that are less restrictive," he said, "but will ensure that all the mail and phone calls of those offenders are monitored on a daily basis."

Two months later, a handful of prisoners were moved without warning to the second CMU in Marion. Daniel McGowan was one of them. Previously at Sandstone, a low-security prison, he had no disciplinary history. He had spent his time there working as a clerk in the psychology ward and studying for his master's degree. One day he was told to pack his belongings. He was sent to solitary confinement, and the next day he was placed on a bus to Marion.

McGowan had feared this could happen. When his attorneys fought the terrorism enhancement in court, they warned of a new, secretive prison unit. Judge Aiken had replied, "Now, defendants raise the specter that anyone with a terrorism enhancement is automatically doomed to a dungeon, so to speak, at the U.S. Penitentiary in Terre Haute, Indiana. It's a very emotional argument, but nothing more, because it's not supported by the facts." In a way, Aiken's comments are true. The argument was not supported by facts, because there were no facts. There are still few now.

The U.S. Bureau of Prisons reports that it houses 211 international terrorists and about one thousand "domestic terrorists." However, the government will not disclose who is housed in the CMU's, why there were transferred there or how they might appeal their designation.

Twelve days after his move to Marion, McGowan received a notice of transfer that provides some indication of the government's motivation. It states that he had been identified "as a member and leader in the Earth Liberation Front (ELF) and Animal Liberation Front (ALF), groups considered domestic terrorist organizations." Andy Stepanian received a notice with similar language. But

McGowan has a dozen other convicted codefendants, and Stepanian has five. Why were these two singled out, and not their codefendants or the other one thousand "domestic terrorists" in federal prisons? More important, why were they singled out when more dangerous prisoners with histories of communications violations were not?

From his cell in the Supermax, Eric Rudolph continues to write essays that are posted on the Army of God website. He mocks his victims, including a former abortion clinic nurse who described the pain of her injuries in court. When Rudolph's victims questioned why he is still allowed to taunt them, government officials responded that there was little they could do. U.S. Attorney Alice Martin said of the prisoner she helped prosecute, "An inmate does not lose his freedom of speech." At about the time McGowan arrived at the CMU, the Army of God published a 9,000-word essay by Rudolph.

"No one got a hearing to determine whether we should or should not be transferred here," said McGowan in a letter from the CMU. And there are still no hearings in sight. In February 2010, after eighteen months at the CMU with no disciplinary problems or communications violations, McGowan requested a transfer. His request was denied, without explanation. He applied again, and was denied again without explanation. Like the prisoners at Lexington's High Security Unit and Marion's Control Unit, CMU prisoners are there indefinitely.

The ACLU and the Center for Constitutional Rights have filed lawsuits challenging the legality of the CMUs. Transferring prisoners to secretive prisons without explanation or opportunity for appeal is a violation of their due process rights, the groups say, and prohibiting contact with family is psychologically destructive, cruel and unusual punishment. The facilities also appear to be in violation of Bureau of Prisons policy that explicitly prohibits discriminating on the basis of "race, religion, national origin, sex, disability, or political belief." About 6 percent of all prisoners are Muslim, according to government data; at the Marion and Terre Haute CMUs, it is about 70 percent. Guards have referred to McGowan and Stepanian as "balancers," non-Muslim prisoners whose presence helps skew the numbers, but the fact is that the CMUs are essentially racially segregated.

In the face of these legal challenges, the Bureau of Prisons has quietly submitted a proposal to make these experimental units permanent—a process that, by law, should have occurred before they were opened. It's a positive development for McGowan and the others imprisoned along with him that the government is recognizing, and being forced to defend, the existence of prison facilities that have until now been kept hidden from the public. This opens the possibility of placing true checks and balances on the government's power to create experimental units.

Unfortunately, this step in the right direction is being negated by a Bureau of Prisons proposal to actually make the CMUs even more inhumane. The proposal includes:

- Limiting telephone communication to a single completed call per calendar month for up to fifteen minutes;
- Limiting written correspondence to three pieces of paper, double-sided, once per week to and from a single recipient;
- Limiting visitation to one hour each calendar month.

As part of this proposal, the Bureau of Prisons publicly explains CMUs for the first time. Prospective prisoners include those with ties to domestic and international terrorism, the government says. The proposal allows for prison officials to act on "evidence which does not rise to the same degree of potential risk to national security or risk of acts of violence or terrorism" which would warrant Special Administrative Measures. In short, the government is arguing two competing claims simultaneously: (1) that CMUs are needed because the inmates are heightened security risks, and (2) that traditional oversight is too cumbersome because these inmates are not dangerous enough.

President Barack Obama has promised to close Guantánamo Bay, a facility that has become infamous for indefinite detentions and human rights abuses. However, as professor Jeanne Theoharis wrote in *The Nation*, Guantánamo is no aberration. "Guantánamo is a particular way of seeing the Constitution," she wrote, "of constructing the landscape as a murky terrain of lurking enemies where the courts become part of the bulwark against such dangers, where rights have limits and where international standards must be weighed against national security."

CMUs are an expansion of this worldview. When the Terre Haute CMU was created, Dan Eggen of the *Washington Post* described it as a facility for "second-tier terrorism inmates." By this Eggen meant that the CMU overwhelmingly held Muslim inmates labeled terrorists, even though they had not done anything most people would consider terrorism. But as the government's proposal makes clear, CMUs are not "second-tier terrorism" prisons. They are political prisons. They are intended to isolate prisoners with "inspirational significance," to use the government's language, from the communities and social movements of which they are a part. These secretive prisons are for political cases the government would rather remove from the public spotlight.

All of the defendants—Muslims, environmentalists, animal rights activists—are housed there because of their ethnicity, their religion, their ideology or all of the above. The mere existence of CMUs should be a warning not just to other prisoners but to all Americans, for the power to create and maintain secretive prisons for political prisoners is antithetical to a healthy democracy. If there is one thing that should be learned from history, from governments that have gone down this path, it is this: secretive prisons for "second-tier" terrorists are often followed by secretive prisons for "third-tier terrorists" and "fourth-tier terrorists," until one by one, brick by brick, the legal wall separating "terrorist" from "dissident" or "undesirable" has crumbled.

I should not be here, sitting in this rental car in the parking lot outside the United States Penitentiary in Marion. I should never have been approved to visit Daniel McGowan. As part of my paperwork, I submitted my social security number, passport number, a list of prisoners with whom I correspond, and an explanation of my arrest years ago, after which FBI agents told me I was being placed on a domestic terrorist list. One would think that if there is anyone who should not be allowed to visit a convicted domestic terrorist, it is someone on a domestic terrorist list.

My status on "the list" has been unclear for years, and I stopped caring long ago. I have submitted Freedom of Information Act requests to various law enforcement agencies and have been told that they have no records pertaining to me. I travel frequently in the United States without incident, so it's possible, if not probable, that those FBI agents' threats were empty. However, I expected a government background check for approval to visit an experimental prison for terrorists would at least turn up *something*.

The odds were simply not in my favor. The government's terrorist watch lists contain more than one million entries, according to the FBI's Terrorist Screening Center and the Office of the Director of National Intelligence. Mainstream media reports have focused on those who have mistakenly appeared on the lists, such as Senator Ted Kennedy and singer Yusuf Islam (formerly known as Cat Stevens), but countless more have been listed intentionally.

My codefendants from Lake Forest are among them. When Kamber Sherrod returned to Texas and attempted to renew her driver's license, the woman at the DMV asked her to have a seat; moments later, three squad cars arrived and police detained her for questioning. She received her license, and they said, "There must have been a mistake, ma'am."

Kim Berardi learned from an airline attendant that a computer program identified her as a security risk in need of additional screening. During another trip, armed police officers from multiple federal agencies detained her as she attempted to board a plane to visit her parents.

Jay Johnson confirmed his status on a trip to Little Rock for a court date. He had been arrested at a protest against Stephens Inc. His car broke down, and a police officer offered to drive him to a repair station. As they sat in the car waiting for a tow truck, the trooper joked around with Johnson and let him use the radar gun. The officer suggested running Johnson's license plate through the computer, "just for fun." On the screen, in bold, flashing letters, it said "member of terrorist organization."

In another case, Utah animal rights activist Jeremy Beckham was detained reentering the United States from Canada. The border agent typed his name into a computer and became alarmed. About half a dozen border agents surrounded the car, ordered Beckham to exit, and then searched the vehicle. Border agents questioned him for hours about which animal rights groups he supports at the University of Utah and whether he knew anyone in the ALF. Beckham was told that the government monitors animal rights "extremists" such as himself because some activists have resorted to terrorism.

Animal rights activists, environmental activists, former activists, attorneys—there are countless stories like these, all from people who have never faced terrorism charges or been convicted of underground crimes.

Even if I have managed to avoid any government list—and if so, I am certainly not complaining—I should have been denied visitation because the CMUs do not allow reporters. Documentary filmmakers have been denied, and so have reporters from national newspapers. Even if I was not flagged in a background check, a quick Google search would reveal who I am and what I write. Why was I being allowed a visit?

Two weeks before my trip, I learned why I had been approved. I received a message from McGowan's wife, Jenny. She said that

Daniel had asked her to relay a message. He had been called into the office by the unit manager and told that CMU officials were aware that I am a journalist. They were willing to approve the visit as long as it was social, they said, and not an interview. I could visit as a friend, not a reporter. McGowan was told that if I were to write an article about the visit they would give him an incident report—a disciplinary violation. He would be punished for my words.

I spoke with McGowan's prison support committee and his wife, expecting to hear that he had sent the message as a formality, a safeguard against punishment, and he actually wanted me to write. The answer returned: unequivocally, no. Absolutely not. This would not be an interview. That could lead to his losing his already meager communications rights, and he could spend the remaining three years of his sentence completely cut off from his family.

It was a strategic move. If the Bureau of Prisons denied my visit, it might have drawn further unfavorable attention to the CMU and its lack of transparency. This way, prison officials allow this visit, but the burden is not on them. It is on me. As I sit in the parking lot I wonder if the ramifications could extend beyond McGowan. The government could use this as evidence of the need for increased communications restrictions for all CMU prisoners. It would buttress the new, harsher proposal. *See, this is what happens when we let these prisoners communicate. This is what happens when we allow them to speak.*

The waiting area of Marion prison is barren except for a miniature model of the prison displayed in a clear plastic case. Occasionally prisoners walk through the area as they pick up trash or vacuum the rug. The guard at the desk is disconcertingly nice. We talk about motorcycles. He apologizes for the long wait and says that preparing for a CMU visit takes longer than usual. The guards should be ready shortly. The conversation gradually shifts to McGowan, and the guard asks which prison previously housed him.

"Sandstone, right?"

"Yes," I say.

"Yeah, I think that's right. Hey, I saw him on a television show a while back. Democracy something, *Democracy Now*?"

"Oh, you saw that, huh?" I say.

He laughs. "Yeah, we all saw that."

"That did not go over well with the judge," I say, thinking that he is talking about McGowan's appearance on the national television and radio program as he awaited sentencing.

"No, no, not that one. This was just about the special prison unit. The guests were a lawyer. And a journalist."

I'm not sure if he is trying to play games with me, or if he does not know that I was the person on the show. "So, you all know about McGowan, huh? Know all about his case?"

"Oh yeah," he laughs.

The CMU unit supervisor arrives and says little except that this is a social visit, not a media visit, and I cannot bring anything into the visiting room except my license and a few dollar bills for the vending machines. He says that if I say anything to McGowan that sounds like an interview question, he will immediately terminate the interview. I ask him to be more specific, because normal conversations involve people asking each other questions and I do not want to say something inappropriate. He repeats himself verbatim.

I am told to place my shoes and belt on the X-ray conveyor belt. It's like the airport, the guard says. But we both know this is not like a normal trip. As author Laurence Gonzales wrote of his visit to Marion when it was a Control Unit: "As I learned, a visitor does not visit USP-Marion; he is led through a warp that winds its way among three dimensions the way a cavern winds through the earth."

After the steel door grunts closed I am asked to show my hand underneath a fluorescent light, to make sure the ultraviolet ink stamp appears. I will need to show this stamp again after the visit in order to leave. With that, I am led down a corridor that connects the main entrance to the rest of the prison. There is a smell of bleach mixed with some other cleaning product, and I immediately think of Andy Stepanian. He has told me that since being released from the CMU, there will be moments where he's standing in a post office or on a subway platform and smells this scent; he fades out of the moment and returns to prison, to moments in prison he would like to forget—someone stabbed, someone beaten, screams he had to ignore—and he will stay in that place until a noise or a stranger's hand brings him back home.

I am directed through a doorway into a visiting room with rows of chairs, children's toys, and a television. The room is empty. Visits with CMU prisoners are scheduled outside the normal visitation hours, to keep them separated from all other prisoners. Through another doorway, and to my left is a small empty booth. On the other side of a wall of plexiglass is Daniel McGowan, standing, arms outstretched, smiling, filling up the space he is given.

The air is hot and thick in here. Above us are two black plastic orbs the size of grapefruits—post-9/11 panopticons. Within them are cameras, and somewhere through the wires and cables on the other end people are monitoring us in real time hundreds of miles away. McGowan motions for me to pick up one of the phones on the wall.

Weeks pass, and I'm still not sure what to say about my visit with McGowan. I cannot, in good conscience, recount any comments he made about the facility or his case, because it wouldn't be worth the potential repercussions for him. At the same time, I cannot redact this experience from my memory; to write nothing would mean nothing happened. No matter how many times I might think I've escaped these compartmentalized roles of being either a friend or a journalist, of either being part of this story or telling it, I find that I'm still trying to walk the line between them.

———

In many ways the government's response to my visitation request created an issue where there was none. My visit with McGowan was never going to be an interview, primarily because I had no questions to ask him. I have known McGowan for years now, and have spoken with him, his family, his friends and his attorneys at length, following them through the woods and through the subways. His case is a high-profile one that received significant media coverage, and he has been followed by multiple documentary crews. McGowan has even written a detailed essay about the CMU from within its confines; it was published on the Huffington Post. I am not sure what the government thought I'd learn about his case that has not been previously reported by me, others or McGowan himself. I have plenty of unanswered questions, but they're questions shared by McGowan, ones that neither of us can answer.

The real interviewer in that visit was McGowan. He spoke more slowly than he once did, his voice calmer and his limbs less animated, but after a few minutes he resumed his old form. He guided the conversation and asked question after question. First among them:

"How are the others adjusting to life post-prison?"

I tried to remain upbeat in my reply, though I have seen the scars prison leaves. Behind the mask of macho posturing and ra-ra rally cries for the movement, former prisoners are not the same people who went in. As Jeff Luers wrote from prison: "It has become part of who we are. I can watch a man get stabbed in the neck and keep eating. I can pretend to not see a man lying helpless in his own blood (along with everyone else on the yard). And I can watch a man die and be completely unmoved. Would someone please tell me how this is supposed to make me a better person?"

"Where are folks working? Oh, he's getting married? How about their family? Where are they living right now?"

He plans to work as a paralegal after he's released, and says he is already prepared for the moment a prospective employer will ask about his past. He is worried about finding work, and also about learning to trust people again. He wonders what role he will have in a movement that fetishes martyrdom, provided that the martyrs do not change their views. I don't say this to McGowan, but I know he'll have a difficult time ahead. Adjusting to life after prison is emotionally arduous for any inmate, and even more difficult as a convicted terrorist. Members of the Weather Underground now teach at prestigious universities and lead community groups, but their war ended long ago. Maybe thirty years from now McGowan will be a Bill Ayers, but right now "eco-terrorism" is too raw.

Some eco-terrorism prisoners have embraced lawful political activism while standing behind radical tactics. Peter Young, one of the first people convicted of "animal enterprise terrorism" for releasing mink from fur farms, has adjusted to life after prison by lecturing at colleges and universities. He runs a website, speaks in defense of direct action, and has published The Blueprint, a state-by-state list of fur farms and their suppliers. Young says that for the fur industry, The Blueprint is a "roadmap to its collapse." He has had his home raided by the FBI on multiple occasions, but continues his work.

Escaping the terrorist label is impossible, no matter how "mainstream" the former prisoners become. John Wade served three years in prison for vandalizing homes and construction equipment near Richmond, Virginia as part of the ELF. He committed the crimes as a high school student and pleaded guilty. He later attended Virginia Commonwealth University and coordinated Richmond's first environmental film series. Then the Style Weekly published an article titled "Former Eco-Terrorist Organized Environmental Film Festival," and in the uproar the Sierra Student Coalition withdrew thousands of dollars of funding.

Rod Coronado has had perhaps the most difficult time leaving his past behind. The former ALF saboteur has been pursued relentlessly by the government. In 2003, he gave a lecture in San Diego for about one hundred people. He had given dozens of similar lectures since his release in 1999 and called this his "standard" speech recounting his personal journey. During the question-and-answer period, someone asked him how he committed his crimes. He picked up a plastic juice container from a table and said he had used a bottle like that one, filled with gasoline and attached to a timer. Then he went on to the next question.

The government charged him with "distribution of information relating to explosives, destructive devices and weapons of mass destruction" and threatened him with twenty years in prison. The jury deadlocked, and the judge declared a mistrial. Prosecutors vowed to dog Coronado, a father of two, until they returned him to prison. He decided to plead guilty. "Such unconstitutional assaults on my free speech beg for a continued legal battle and defense," Coronado said in a statement to supporters, "but I am instead choosing to reach a settlement that will allow me to move on with my life."

"And how are, um, how are their relationships doing?"

A few weeks ago, McGowan had a telephone conversation with his wife that ended in a minor argument. It tortured him for days. He only has fifteen minutes with her, and if those minutes do not flow smoothly and end flawlessly he has to wait a week to remedy them. McGowan knows the burden this has placed on loved ones. He often asks friends to purchase small presents for Synan, sneak into their apartment, and then hide them between couch cushions or on the bookshelf, so that when he talks to her on the telephone, he can tell her where to find them and listen to her surprise.

Until the day he returns home, he tries to remember that the clock only ticks forward. He has tried running to occupy his time, but the perimeter of the CMU yard is one-eighth of a mile. He runs it twisting thirty-two times, every mile straining his knees. He has exhausted every opportunity to take prison classes. His successful completion of a card-making class means prison officials allow him to use glue sticks and colored paper. A long stretch of our visit was

McGowan telling me his method for drawing, coloring, pasting and laminating greeting cards for his six nieces.

"So what have you been reading? When is your book coming out? City Lights, right? Did I tell you about that Ferlinghetti book?"

McGowan has always been well read, but now he is insatiable. I have offered to send him books, and he politely requests that I only *suggest* something. He is ruthless. He maintains a list of "maybes" that he culls and replenishes systematically. When he finds a new author, he reads their oeuvre. Fiction was never his preference, but he needs an escape. He lives nonfiction, he says. He is allowed to have ten books in his cell at once, and he methodically rotates them home. The one that never leaves is *The Legend of Sleepy Hollow* by Washington Irving. He reads it several times a year, because it reminds him of fall. He can feel the wind and smell the leaves, the trees preparing for the freeze.

CHAPTER ELEVEN

The Way Home

The Present On the night of the 2008 presidential election, hundreds if not thousands of people flowed down 16th Street toward the White House. Along the way strangers hugged and couples danced on cars. The crowd at the White House was more diverse than the usual D.C. protests. Fraternity boys from Georgetown joined students from Howard in chanting "Pack yo shit up!" and "Whose house? Obama's house!" The crowd stayed until dawn celebrating change.

Obama was clearly different from Senator John McCain on the war in Iraq, health care and tax cuts for the wealthiest Americans. As for labeling activists eco-terrorists, there seemed to be hope as well. As a senator, Obama responded to a 2005 Congressional hearing on eco-terrorism by saying that the threat from militant environmentalists was dwarfed by that of other groups. There were only sixty eco-terrorism crimes in 2004, he said, but there were, according to the FBI, more than 7,400 hate crimes in 2003. "In our quest to apprehend these criminals, I hope we are not headed down the path of infringing on the ability of legitimate advocacy organizations to express their opinions and to raise funds in order to do so," Obama said in a letter to the committee. "I do not want Americans to equate groups that advocate violence with mainstream environmental organizations."

Obama later had personal experience with guilt-by-association terrorism rhetoric. During the presidential campaign, Republican vice presidential candidate Sarah Palin attempted to link him to Bill Ayers, a former member of the Weather Underground. She said Obama "pals around with terrorists." Politically and personally, there was ample reason to think the new president would take a firm stance against the reckless use of the word and begin a fundamental restructuring of national security policy.

It was hoped that, if nothing else, there would be a reasoned response to policies that have failed to deter underground groups and their supporters. *The Final Nail*, for example, was a zine that listed fur farm addresses across the country, created by Darren Thurston, one of the Operation Backfire defendants. The document had fallen out of circulation, but has since been republished online at FinalNail .com, expanded to include slaughterhouses, lab animal suppliers and trappers, all divided by state. Meanwhile, the Earth Liberation Front Press Office has reopened. One of its first press releases states: "We have one message for the incoming Obama Administration: act to protect the environment or the ELF will."

"Every time a fire breaks out and somebody takes a spray can and writes 'ELF' or 'ALF' on there, then everybody gets all excited that 'Oh this movement has started back up,'" Bob Holland, a retired arson investigator, told Fox News. "The movement," he says, "never really left."

After only a few months of the Obama presidency, it became evident that change would not be coming from Washington. Obama has backtracked on key civil liberties issues. He has maintained the practice of extraordinary rendition—sending people to other countries to be tortured—and he has defended giving telecom giants immunity for their role in warrantless wiretapping. He has preserved the military commissions set up by the Bush administration, blocked the release of photos revealing torture and signed an extension of the Patriot Act. Under Obama's watch, an animal rights activist named Daniel Andreas San Diego, who is a suspect in the

2003 bombing of the Chiron building in northern California, was the first "domestic terrorist" placed on the FBI's most wanted list.

A telling example of how little this political climate has changed under the Obama administration is the case of Marie Mason. Mason was indicted for a 1999 ELF arson at the Michigan State University campus, targeting genetic-engineering research. The arson caused about $1 million in damage and did not harm anyone. Soon after her arrest, news broke that her former husband, Frank Ambrose, had worn a wire to entrap his friends and spy on lawful environmental gatherings. In the lead-up to her sentencing, the FBI warned the press that "terrorists" might gather and protest. Mason was sentenced in February 2009 to twenty-one years in prison with the terrorism enhancement. It was one of the longest sentences ever for an environmental activist.

By comparison, that same week the FBI distributed a press release announcing the guilty pleas of four men who assaulted three African Americans on the night of President Barack Obama's election victory. They received ten to twelve years in prison, or half the sentence given to Marie Mason. And while Mason's arrest was accompanied by a press conference in which government officials said her crimes were a top domestic terrorism priority, the government's news release in this case—for racist, violent attacks meant to retaliate against black voters—did not once mention the word.

When Daniel McGowan is released from prison he will begin the long, slow process of reclaiming his life. Some of the SHAC defendants have already begun that journey. Andy Stepanian works at a publishing company and is a newlywed. Jake Conroy has been released to a halfway house; Darius Fullmer works at an outdoor retailer; Josh Harper works at a vegan cafe in Seattle's University District and has just moved into his own apartment. At the time of this writing, Lauren Gazzola is awaiting decisions from law schools and Kevin Kjonaas remains imprisoned.

The SHAC defendants appealed their conviction knowing that they would likely be released before a ruling. The purpose of the appeal was not to expedite their release, although that certainly would have been welcomed. Politically, the motivation was to ensure that their case did not set a legal precedent. Personally, it was to ensure that the label would not follow them outside the prison walls.

On January 6, 2009, the Third Circuit Court of Appeals in Philadelphia heard arguments in the case. U.S. attorney Glenn J. Moramarco spoke candidly about the government's motivations, acknowledging that "this case was never fought on the basis of what actually happened, by and large. . . . This case was fought on the battleground of 'should we be held responsible for what other people are doing.'" As an example, he discussed a radio interview in which Lauren Gazzola said SHAC supports home demonstrations and property destruction. Moramarco said that such a statement of her political beliefs and her personal views was "tantamount to a confession." Nine months later, in a landmark ruling on what types of political speech are Constitutionally protected, the appellate court upheld the convictions on all charges.

The ruling departed from a long history of First Amendment law in a few ways. The Brandenburg standard holds that even the most controversial and inflammatory speech is protected as long as it not likely to incite "imminent and lawless action." According to attorneys, this is the first time a court has ruled that the written word—disseminated to a wide audience and focused on past conduct—has been construed as promoting, or resulting in, imminent and lawless action.

A second First Amendment standard is whether the speech is a true threat. True threats, as Justice O'Connor defines them in *Virginia v. Black*, are "statements where the speaker means to communicate a serious expression of an intent to commit an act of unlawful violence to a particular individual or group of individuals." In this case, the appellate court ruled that fiery political rhetoric is a "true threat" when illegal conduct has taken place in the same campaign. The court said SHAC pressured corporations to divest and sever ties with Huntingdon, and the defendants' speeches, protests and web posting about past incidents instilled fear in future targets.

The court ruled that it did not matter that the defendants did not break the law; they were part of a conspiracy through their speech. In the case of Josh Harper, the court said his two public speeches were constitutionally protected: "Harper's personal conduct does not cross the line of illegality; to punish him simply on the basis of his political speeches would run afoul of the constitution." However, the court ruled that he was guilty of conspiring to violate the Animal Enterprise Protection Act because of his public support of direct action, combined with his involvement in researching Huntingdon and organizing protests.

Defense attorneys are currently petitioning for the case to be heard before the Supreme Court.

Meanwhile, the key players behind prosecuting the SHAC 7 have gone on to become even more politically powerful. When Chris Christie became the U.S. attorney for New Jersey, he had no trial, criminal law or investigative experience; he had been a top-tier fundraiser during George W. Bush's presidential campaign, and the position was a political reward. He has since returned to politics, becoming governor of New Jersey in 2010. As pundits speculate about a presidential bid, Christie has made headlines with his social conservatism and skepticism about global warming.

Prosecutor Charles McKenna is now the head of the New Jersey Office of Homeland Security and Preparedness, where he has a much larger canvas and a broader brush for targeting terrorists. In his new job, one of his priorities has been the use of computer technology to profile terrorism threats. The targets of this profiling? McKenna told local press: "Jihad, Crips, extreme animal-rights activists, it's all the same: people trying to damage the system."

———

On February 19 and 20, 2009, the FBI's Joint Terrorism Task Force arrested four California animal rights activists, the first arrests under the Animal Enterprise Terrorism Act. There had been a wide range of both legal and illegal tactics against animal experimentation at University of California campuses, including the destruction of university vans. In August, an incendiary device was left at the home of a university researcher; no animal rights group ever claimed responsibility for this crime, but the university, the FBI and others attributed it to activists.

Nathan Pope, Adriana Stumpo, Joseph Buddenberg and Maryam Khajavi were not arrested in relation to these crimes, however. Much like the SHAC defendants, they were not accused of any property destruction or violence. According to the indictment, the defendants allegedly chanted loudly at home demonstrations (including "murderer leave town, terrorist leave town"), and used the Internet to research public information about animal experimenters. They also allegedly wore bandannas at protests, which is an increasingly common response to FBI harassment and photography, and wrote slogans on the public sidewalk using children's sidewalk chalk.

Individually, these acts all clearly fall outside the scope of criminal behavior. Combined, however, prosecutors argued, chanting, researching, wearing masks and chalking slogans amounted to a campaign that instilled fear in those protested. In the lead-up to trial, the government revealed some information about the extent of government surveillance, including the use of DNA testing. At a time when states say they do not have money for the expensive testing in death penalty cases—testing that has exonerated innocent people on death row—the government has acknowledged using DNA testing on protesters' bandannas.

In July 2010, a U.S. District Court threw out the indictment because the government did not clearly explain what, exactly, the protesters had done. The Center for Constitutional Rights and attorney Matthew Strugar had argued that the charges should be dropped because they seemed to involve First Amendment–protected activity, and that in order to make that argument the defendants' speech must be clearly identified. Judge Ronald M. Whyte agreed, saying that the government had not answered basic questions about the defendants' alleged conduct and the activists had the right to know specifically what they did that could be considered a crime. "This is particularly important," he said, "where the species of behavior in question spans a wide spectrum from criminal conduct to constitutionally protected political protest."

The judge made clear that prosecutors have the opportunity to re-indict if they can be more specific about the charges and explain how speech is terrorism. At the time of this writing, the defendants are attempting to move on with their lives. Newlyweds Adriana and Nathan Stumpo—who exchanged vows while awaiting trial—are adjusting to married life, and life without felony charges.

There have been other animal enterprise terrorism arrests. In Utah, William Viehl, twenty-two, and Alex Hall, twenty, were convicted in connection with the August 2008 release of three hundred mink from a South Jordan fur farm. It caused about $10,000 in damage. In another case, a University of Minnesota graduate student named Scott DeMuth is awaiting trial on conspiracy charges. As in the California case, the government has fought disclosure of what, exactly, DeMuth allegedly did.

Meanwhile, just as they did after passage of the Animal Enterprise Protection Act, supporters of the Animal Enterprise Terrorism Act are already lobbying for new legislation. In California, lawmakers passed a bill similar to the federal law. In Utah, a state lawmaker promised to introduce new eco-terrorism legislation targeting not the ALF or ELF, but a University of Utah student named Tim DeChristopher. DeChristopher became an instant environmental celebrity when he disrupted an oil and gas auction by bidding on parcels of land. Republican state representative Mike Noel said interfering with the auction is no different from "burning down a man's cattle operation." The college student "took millions of dollars away from us, and he's laughing at us," Noel said. "It's not right. It's not fair."

In Washington, state senator Val Stevens introduced the American Legislative Exchange Council's model eco-terrorism legislation. It included the most dangerous provisions of that model bill, sections prohibiting any communications that "encourage," "publicize" or "promote" animal or ecological terrorism. In addition to explicitly targeting First Amendment conduct, the bill had provisions pertaining to those who remain on the premises of an agricultural facility after they have been told to leave—in other words, people engaging in nonviolent civil disobedience. The bill, which failed, was introduced just shy of the fiftieth anniversary of a catalyzing moment in the civil rights movement, when four black students sat at a Woolworth's whites-only lunch counter and refused to move.

The attention and resources focused on eco-terrorism have clearly not been confined to one administration. These policies were initiated long before the Bush administration, and the Obama administration has continued that trend. Eco-terrorism has become institutionalized as an official priority of law enforcement. With this has come potentially dangerous consequences.

The addition of eco-terrorism to national security conversations has worked its way into ground-level issues of terrorism preparedness. The Homeland Infrastructure Threat and Risk Analysis Center is tasked with identifying dangers facing the country. In a 2007 presentation, sandwiched between slides on "Al-Qa'ida's Expanding Global Outreach" and biological weapons was a warning about animal rights and environmental extremists.

The Department of Homeland Security manages the Homeland

Security Exercise and Evaluation Program, which offers national guidance to local law enforcement in order to prevent terrorist attacks. A document from 2005 included sixty-four pages of detailed instructions on how to plan terrorism drills designed to keep us safer. One of the key steps in that planning process is choosing a universal adversary, which the document describes as a class of terrorist threat designed to provide trainees with "a realistic, capabilities-based opponent." Among the government's list of threats are antiglobalization activists and "Environmental/Animal rights groups."

In September 2009, Cherry Point Air Station in North Carolina held a terrorism training where environmentalists stormed the military base, took hostages, demanded money, and killed two Marines. The drill was used to practice the response of emergency workers. Environmentalists have never, in real life, taken hostages, stormed military bases or killed anyone. No matter how far-fetched, this was not an isolated drill. At Fort Lee in Virginia, a three-day antiterrorism drill pitted soldiers against protesters who chanted and held signs. At the University of California at Berkeley, the nation's largest homeland security drill involved animal rights activists holding hostages at gunpoint.

There is no doubt that these sites must prepare for potential terrorist attacks. Cherry Point is considered one of the best jet bases in the world; it trains Marines and also launches strike missions headed for Afghanistan. And tragedies like the Virginia Tech shooting have shown that universities must be prepared for grim scenarios in order to keep students safe. Mike Barton, deputy director of public affairs at Cherry Point, has said: "Essentially, our mission in life when we are not doing real-world operations is to train for real-world operations."

But these are not real-world operations. Training for a terrorist attack is not like shooting cans off a fence. Different groups have fundamentally different ideologies and cannot be approached the same way. Al Qaeda does not pose the same threat as environmentalists, who do not think the same way or use the same tactics, and preparing for one does not help prepare for the other. Preparing for terrorist attacks requires an understanding of the ideology and methodology of the terrorists, and these drills involving animal rights and environmental activists reflect an understanding of neither.

There are limited government resources, and an increase in attention in one area necessitates a reduction in another. In Minneapolis, Joint Terrorism Task Force agents approached a local activist in the lead-up to the Republic National Convention in 2008. They offered to pay him to become an informant and infiltrate vegan potlucks, with the hopes of learning about illegal activity planned for RNC demonstrations. While FBI agents are investigating vegan potlucks, they are not investigating more credible threats.

These concerns have been raised by government agencies, and gone unheeded. In 2003, the Justice Department's Office of the Inspector General audited the FBI and provided recommendations for improving its terrorism investigations. The audit raised multiple concerns with the bureau's treatment of animal rights and environmental activists as terrorists. Foremost among them were communications problems within the FBI, and the quality of terrorism intelligence sent by the bureau to state and local law enforcement. The audit revealed that the FBI's weekly Intelligence Bulletins and Quarterly Terrorist Threat Assessments often focused on political activists. The inspector general recommended that the FBI's intelligence updates focus on "domestic terrorist activities aimed at creating mass casualties or destroying critical infrastructure, rather than information on social protests and domestic radicals' criminal activities."

More important, the audit warned that the FBI's focus on animal rights and environmental activists placed public safety at risk. In one of its six recommendations, the inspector general's office advised the FBI to stop investigating animal rights and environmental activists as terrorists and to shift these cases to the FBI's criminal division. The FBI's definition of domestic terrorism has become too broad, the report said: "A more focused definition may allow the FBI to more effectively target its counterterrorism resources."

The FBI refused. Steven C. McGraw of the FBI's inspection division responded in a letter to the inspector general that these groups have "caused considerable damage to the U.S. economy" and that the Joint Terrorism Task Forces are the best way to investigate them. Although the inspector general's office does not have the power to override such refusals, the office wrote back and reiterated its concerns: "We believe that the FBI's priority mission to prevent high-consequence terrorist acts would be enhanced if the Counterterrorism Division did not have to spend time and resources on lower-threat activities by social protestors."

There have been some indications that federal law enforcement's focus on political activists has had consequences. An investigation by the *Seattle Post-Intelligencer*, relying on former FBI officials, revealed that the bureau knew of pervasive fraud in the mortgage industry and its potential for national and international economic crises. However, the bureau did not have the resources to investigate. After September 11th, about 2,400 FBI agents were reassigned and highly skilled white collar crime investigators were shifted to domestic terrorism investigations.

"We knew we had a broader problem, but you've got a Justice Department and the administration saying you need to concentrate on domestic intelligence and counterterrorism," a retired high-ranking FBI official told the paper. "It wasn't very popular to ask for resources for anything. It was dead on arrival."

Homeland security operations have been similarly criticized within Washington. In 2005, U.S. Representative Bennie G. Thompson, who is the ranking member on the House Committee on Homeland Security, issued a report with six other committee members criticizing the department for focusing on "eco-terrorism" while not addressing the threat of right-wing terrorists. "If DHS' long-term planning documents do not consider these and other risks posed by right-wing domestic terrorists," the report said, "then lower-level agents working to fight these groups may not be receiving enough budgetary, policy, or administrative support from their superiors. This means possible threats to our homeland could go undetected."

Thompson's warning proved astute. There has been a resurgence in right-wing violence. Joseph Stack flew a plane into an IRS building, killing himself and an IRS manager. Members of the self-proclaimed Christian militia Hutaree were arrested for allegedly plotting to assassinate federal, state and local police officers in hopes of sparking an antigovernment revolution. An anti-abortion activist murdered Dr. George Tiller. A white supremacist opened fire at the Holocaust museum, killing one person before killing himself. In government statements, legal proceedings and press reports, the word terrorism has been conspicuously absent from any discussion of these crimes.

When the Missouri Information Analysis Center (a homeland security fusion center) released a report on the "modern militia movement," it caused a national media frenzy. The credible intelligence in the report was overshadowed by the outrageous, such as a warning for police to look out for New World Order bumper stickers. The report was a national security anomaly, and the government treated it as such; government officials quickly issued an apology and vowed to reassess its homeland security operations.

A final impact of eco-terrorism rhetoric is that other criminals have caught on to the misplaced priorities. Animal rights and environmental activists have been used as scapegoats to steer law enforcement in the direction of leads they are all too eager to follow. In Boston, someone set fire to an exotic pet store, killing many of the animals inside, and scrawled "No more exploitation of animals" on the storefront. Investigators immediately attributed the crime to animal rights activists. The owner, who had attempted to frame activists, was sentenced to less than three years in prison.

In Maryland, a dozen luxury homes were burned. The fire caused at least $10 million in damage. The next day, an FBI official said environmentalists were suspected because of the homes' proximity to a nature preserve. The six men eventually convicted had a variety of motives, but defending the environment was not one of them. Investigators said two of the men made racist comments during their interrogations, and that the crimes were in part motivated by African American families moving into the predominantly white area. Patrick Walsh, the lead arsonist, seems to have learned a lesson from the FBI's willingness to blame activists; a search of his jail cell uncovered handwritten notes about financial schemes, including a letter soliciting money for a nonexistent environmental organization.

In Pennsylvania, someone released 2,800 mink from a fur farm and in the process killed the family's two dogs. The Fur Commission pushed the issue in the press, arguing that the crime had "all the earmarks" of the ALF (except for the murdering of animals). A week later, the *Pittsburgh Tribune* editorialized and conceded that the attack was atypical of animal rights terrorism, but maintained that activists should still be held responsible because, over time, vandalism has raised insurance premiums for fur farms. The rhetoric of terrorism has been institutionalized within law enforcement and large segments of the public to the point that even if activists clearly are not responsible, they are still considered guilty.

When I started down this path of investigating why animal rights and environmental activists have become the number one domestic terrorism threat, it seemed as though the impetus for that was the same one operative in so many aspects of American politics: money. The primary targets of this crackdown have been the ALF and ELF, which inflict economic damage through sabotage, and SHAC, which was formed solely to shut down a multinational corporation. When corporate interests have felt threatened, they have used their financial clout to lobby for eco-terrorism laws that target not only the ALF, ELF and SHAC, but anyone who causes a loss of corporate profits.

Government agencies have been quite open about this desire to protect financial interests. In a leaked Power Point presentation given to businesses with operations in Western Europe, the State Department outlined methods that corporations should use to deter animal rights protests. "Although incidents related to terrorism are most likely to make the front-page news, animal rights extremism is what's most likely to affect your day-to-day business operations," it said. The presentation also included a section on the national animal rights conference, a mainstream event with hundreds of attendees and appearances by celebrities. "Although many legitimate activists attend these events," the presentation notes, "the conference holds workshops on successful tactics used against your companies."

In their own words and their own documents, government agencies have made clear that eco-terrorists do not threaten people, they threaten profits. In a 2006 bulletin to federal, state and local law enforcement agencies, the Department of Homeland Security warned about eco-terrorism like "flyer [sic] distribution" and "tying up company phone lines." In addition to extremist tactics like "organizing protests" and "inundating computers with e-mails," the DHS notes, in passing, illegal actions like verbal harassment and vandalism. Nowhere is the word "violence" used, and the bulletin says there is no evidence of a pending attack on any corporation. Instead, explaining the need for vigilance, the DHS warned: "Attacks against corporations by animal rights extremists and eco-terrorists are costly to the targeted company and, over time, can undermine confidence in the economy."

Viewing this as a campaign to protect corporate profits also helps explain, to an extent, the surveillance and harassment of huge swaths of nonviolent activists. The mainstreaming of these movements, and the accompanying shift in public opinion, has potentially grave implications for industries that profit from the abuse of animals and the destruction of the environment. The animal rights and environmental movements, more than any other social movements, directly threaten corporate interests. They do so every time activists encourage people to go vegan, stop driving, consume fewer resources and live simply. They do not advocate boycotts so much as life-changes, and the changed lives they envision do not include some of the most powerful industries on the planet.

Yet this is only part of the explanation. It fits nicely into conventional political critiques, but it does not account for the true breadth and depth of these attacks and the fervor of their proponents. As I became immersed in the internal analyses of industry groups, think tanks and politicians, I realized that the perceived threat of these movements is much bigger than a threat to corporate pocketbooks. More than money is at stake.

During the Red Scare, communism was perceived as posing two distinct types of threats. The first were direct. Communist spies could infiltrate the ranks of the U.S. government, stealing state secrets and sabotaging military operations. Communist nation states could thereby position themselves to challenge U.S. global economic and military dominance. Much is still debated about the true nature of this threat, particularly in regard to individual agents of foreign powers operating within the U.S. government. Regardless of our judgments in hindsight, at that time communist spies and communist nation states were viewed as posing a direct, credible threat to national security, and this specter dominated U.S. policy.

The second threat was less concrete and more insidious. It was not a double agent stealing a briefcase of top-secret documents, it was a belief system that threatened core American values. Mitchell Palmer, attorney general under President Woodrow Wilson, along with his assistant, future FBI director J. Edgar Hoover, was an early and vocal leader against this menace. Palmer used the term "Reds" to encapsulate communists, anarchists and other subversives, and warned that they were working their values into the homes of everyday Americans. In his essay "The Case Against the Reds," Palmer justified raids and deportations, writing that the "tongues of revolutionary heat were licking the altars of the churches, leaping into the belfry of the school bell, crawling into the sacred corners of American homes, seeking to replace marriage vows with libertine laws, burning up the foundations of society." The government should not make distinctions between actual crimes and beliefs, Palmer argued—they are the same.

This cultural threat was perceived by many as an unholy war for the very heart of America, and often framed in biblical terms. "Our religious faith gives us the answer to the false beliefs of Communism," President Harry Truman said. "I have the feeling that God has created us and brought us to our present position of power and strength for some great purpose." For decades, the cultural threat of communism was perceived to be so perilous that it had to be confronted anywhere it surfaced.

In a 1947 FBI memo, the government warned that this might include the classic Christmas movie "It's a Wonderful Life." The film's archetypal villain was old man Potter, a banker. Its director, Frank Capra, was reported by the FBI to have "associated with left-wing groups and, on one other occasion to have made a picture which was decidedly socialist in nature—'Mr. Smith Goes to Washington.'" Government investigations of stars and films were endemic in Hollywood, rationalized by the belief that if communists could inject their message into popular media, they could poison the minds of millions of Americans.

Such priorities seem silly or hyperbolic now, because we, as a nation, have supposedly learned our lessons from the past. American history textbooks often divide the Red Scare into two distinct eras, each with a defined inception and conclusion. A dark period in the history of this country was only that—a period in which mistakes were made, but these were anomalies, promulgated through the zealotry and hubris of a few individuals.

The defining characteristics of the Red Scare, though, were not confined to one era; the mistakes of the past have evolved and adapted. Through those seeking to destroy new political and cultural threats, they endure.

In *The Clash of Civilizations*, Harvard political scientist Samuel P. Huntington argued that with the end of the Cold War, global conflict should not be viewed through the lens of nation states or economic systems. The primary clash, he warned in the early 1990s, would be along "cultural fault lines," particularly between the Christian West and Islam. Huntington's analysis is simplistic in that it parses out what he calls "major" civilizations and then treats them as unified masses, but his thesis generated enormous controversy because it bluntly hit upon what was, and is, at the heart of U.S. domestic and foreign policy, from the Red Scare to the War on Terrorism: culture war.

This is the context in which the current period of American history should be understood. In the minds of the industry groups, think tanks and politicians promoting war on the animal rights and environmental movements, they are engaged in a clash of civilizations. Like the Red Scare, with its hysteria against "godless communists" threatening the American capitalist way of life, this Green Scare is a culture war, a war of values. The animal rights and environmental movements are seen not as a competing civilization, but as threats to civilization itself.

At its most simplistic, this worldview is revealed in countless media interviews, websites and pamphlets in which activists are described as a threat to individual freedom and cultural traditions. It is the contemporary embodiment of what historian Richard Hofstadter famously called "the paranoid style in American politics": the eternal war of people in power to protect their power, and the eternal fear—dating to the inception of the republic—that the

American way of life is under attack. If animal rights and environmental activists have their way, the message goes, nobody will be able to eat meat, wear fur, take life-saving medications, enjoy circuses, cut trees, build homes, use electricity or drive cars.

This rhetoric has been a coordinated campaign, beginning at least in the 1980s when the American Medical Association released its "Animal Research Action Plan." It focused on ideology, claiming that animal rights activists must be shown to be "anti-science" and "a threat to the public's freedom of choice." The association said the public must be aware of the threats activists pose to human advancement, and advocated labeling them militants and terrorists.

Nearly twenty years later, Jonathan Blum, a senior vice president at Yum Brands, the parent company of KFC, testified before Congress that PETA members are "corporate terrorists." "Let's be clear," he said. "What PETA ultimately wants is a vegetarian or vegan world." A world that would put companies like KFC out of business. Bob Stallman, president of the American Farm Bureau, says that campaigns for improved animal welfare standards are "animal warfare" and threaten the agriculture industry to its core. Such fears are exaggerated, but there is truth to the claims.

The animal rights and environmental movements have multiple philosophical tributaries, as environmental scholar Bron Taylor calls them. The main currents flow from two sources, Australian philosopher Peter Singer and Norwegian philosopher Arne Næss. Singer's seminal work, *Animal Liberation*, outlined a moral framework defined not by species but by sentience. He popularized the idea of "speciesism" and is widely credited with inspiring the modern animal rights movement. In radical environmental circles, a comparable influence came from what Næss termed deep ecology, a philosophy that argues, sometimes in spiritual terms, that the natural world has value independent of human interest. There are countless streams of thought—Tom Regan's advocacy of legal rights for animals, Vandana Shiva's eco-feminism and many more.

Their confluence is the redefinition of what it means to be a human being. These movements are not content with creating another recycling campaign and they do not want animals to have bigger shackles and longer chains. At their core, they challenge fundamental beliefs that have guided humanity for thousands of years, and that have for the most part remained unquestioned by prior social justice movements: that human beings are the center of the universe and our interests are intrinsically superior to those of other species and the natural world.

"All of these beliefs stand in direct contrast to the notion of individualism as promoted by Western culture," according to a 2008 DHS report titled "Eco-terrorism: Environmental and Animal Rights Militants in the United States." Animal rights and environmental movements directly challenge civilization, modernity and capitalism, the report said. Their success "not only would fundamentally alter the nature of social norms regarding the planet's habitat and its living organisms, but ultimately would lead to a new system of governance and social relationships that is anarchist and antisystemic in nature."

In his influential position paper on the Animal Enterprise Protection Act, animal experimenter Edward J. Walsh advocated the law's expansion to respond not solely to threats of violence, but to threats to a way of life. He argued that even simple acts such as choosing to not wear fur, eat meat or attend rodeos "quietly, but effectively, promote the dissolution of our culture."

All civilized people believe in animal welfare and compassion, Walsh said, but animal rights activists go much further. "Be clear that here we are talking about redefining what it means to be an animal when we talk about animal rights," he said, "and when I suggest that animal rights terrorists should be treated harshly in our culture, understand that I am talking about those who have committed barbarous acts in their advocacy of an extreme philosophy that seeks ethical equality among all animals and harbors disdain for human beings as its organizing principle."

To some, the activists are a threat to the deeply held religious belief that humans were created by God to hold dominion over all other species and use them for whatever purposes we choose. To argue that animals and the environment deserve equal moral consideration as that given to humans is to argue that they are all equal before God, or that there is no god. Wesley J. Smith says those who embrace environmentalism have lost touch with Judeo-Christian values. Smith is a senior fellow at the Discovery Institute, which is best known for urging schools to teach creationism, and says the movements are a rebellion against "'human exceptionalism'—the view that ultimate moral value comes with being a member of the human species." The animal rights and environmental movements are not merely "pro-animal" or "pro-environment," they are "anti-human."

A good example of the breadth and depth of this culture war in practice occurred in California in the summer of 2008. In August, two incendiary devices exploded at the homes of two UC Santa Cruz scientists who experiment on animals. The FBI and the university rushed to attribute the crimes to animal rights activists, yet no animal rights group issued a communiqué or claim of responsibility.

The crimes came as the Humane Society of the United States was campaigning for Proposition 2, a historic animal welfare ballot initiative in California. Prop 2 regulates basic treatment of farm animals and mandates that pregnant pigs, veal calves and egg-laying hens have enough room to stand up, lie down and turn around. *Feedstuffs*, an agribusiness publication, said the measure represented the threat of a "vegetarian nation." It said that if this measure passed, others would follow, and it could signal a cultural shift against factory farming on a national and global scale. Fight them with everything you have, the industry warned, for the "dam must not be breached."

Humane Society leaders feared that the bombings would be used to tarnish their image. To preempt any allegations of supporting terrorism, the Humane Society offered a $2,500 reward for information leading to the conviction of the bombers. Industry groups were undeterred. The Center for Consumer Freedom responded, "Nobody should be fooled by HSUS's paltry gesture. While pretending to be part of the solution, the group continues to be a significant part of the *problem*—an over-zealous social movement bent on extending legal rights to animals." The group later published a full-page ad in the *New York Times* accusing HSUS of supporting terrorism because one of the group's executives spoke at a holiday party also attended by activists who once worked with another group called Hugs for Puppies, which had members who once worked with SHAC, which in turn had members who were convicted of animal enterprise terrorism.

Some leaders of the animal rights and environmental movements have argued that if it were not for the actions of radical activists, none of this would be happening. Underground groups give mainstream activists a bad name, they say, and their actions are "a gift to their critics." It is undeniable that opposition groups have exploited every opportunity to label activists as terrorists; when Dr. Jerry Vlasak testified before Congress and advocated physical violence, for example, savvy politicians issued a press release trumpeting the need for a new eco-terrorism bill. However, this says more about the opposition's tactics than the underlying cause.

Although there have been times when activists themselves have made this Green Scare easier, they have not created it: it exists not because of the nature of their words or their actions, but because these movements have grown increasingly effective and accepted. The only way to explain the conflation of mainstream and radical groups as terrorists is to assume that all of it—from ballot initiatives to sabotage—poses a threat.

As I became immersed in this issue, writing and speaking about it, I began to wonder if I might be doing more harm than good. The most dangerous consequence of this terrorism rhetoric is fear, so does raising public awareness just make more people afraid? The true threat of the Animal Enterprise Terrorism Act is the chilling effect on free speech, so would activists be better off not knowing? As a journalist, I have felt a responsibility to raise awareness about legal and legislative issues that have largely gone unnoticed. As someone who cares deeply about these issues, I've wondered if I'm just doing the job of the government and corporations for them by spreading fear.

It is clear, though, that ignoring these problems will not make them go away. The best way to cut through the fog of fear is to shine a light directly on the source. In Plato's allegory, the first step out of the cave was to turn around and recognize the fire. When we look closely at the court cases, legislation and public relations efforts, we see these campaigns in their true form. We can begin to understand that what is unfolding before us is not truth, it is shadow.

Drawing comparisons between this political climate and the Red Scare does not mean there is a direct correlation. The analogy is not meant to imply that the experiences of activists today are on par with those of the countless people whose lives were ruined by McCarthyism. Nor is it to imply that what animal rights and environmental activists are experiencing is more important than what others have endured for years; after September 11th, Arab, Muslim and South Asian people were rounded up and detained in the United States, and they continue to be racially profiled, none of which has happened to these overwhelmingly white movements. There is much to be gained by putting this in a historical context and recognizing patterns of government repression, yet there is a danger in trying to fit contemporary experiences into a historical mold—the analogy must end when change begins.

There is nothing inevitable about history repeating itself.

Fyodor Dostoyevsky wrote in *Notes from the Underground*, "The whole work of man really seems to consist in nothing but proving to himself every minute that he is a man and not a piano-key." The strategies, tactics and goals of many eras of government repression are similar, but when touched by them we do not need to play the same note. Naming names and pledging loyalty oaths did not protect anyone then, and it will not protect anyone now. Fear is not our only possible response. We are capable of more. We are not piano keys.

It will not be easy. There will be more media campaigns, eco-terror legislation and arrests. Through it all, one thing must be remembered about the activists labeled terrorists: they are in good company. Many of the radicals we revere today were feared and vilified in their time. Civil rights, American Indian and antiwar activists were constantly harassed and surveilled. Anarchists organizing for an eight-hour workday were set up in kangaroo courts for murder, then executed. Socialists have been sentenced for sedition and imprisoned for making speeches. This is not to say that all activists should pat each other on the back and compare themselves to Dr. King, but today's social justice movements must be placed in historical perspective.

We, as a culture, have created a mythology of repression and resistance. In history books, injustice is always so easily recognizable, social struggles are buffed to a Hollywood sheen so that the characters are either pure good or pure evil and the necessary response is equally straightforward. But at the time? At the time it's not always that easy to see.

The most disgraceful periods in history were arrived at slowly, methodically, with an infinite number of decisions being made, every day, by real people. There is no going to sleep one night in a democracy and waking up the next morning to police roundups. There is no "tipping point," there are many points, and at each of them we have a choice—do we continue down this path, because it has not yet affected us personally, or do we intervene? As Pastor Martin Niemoller said:

> They came first for the Communists, and I didn't speak up because I wasn't a Communist.
> Then they came for the Jews, and I didn't speak up because I wasn't a Jew.
> Then they came for the Catholics, and I didn't speak up because I was a Protestant.
> Then they came for me, and by that time there was no one left to speak up.

We have sacrificed too much in the name of fighting terrorism, and the enemy keeps growing. Since September 11th, the word has been stretched and pulled and hemmed and cuffed and torn and mended to fit a growing body of political whims. Ultimately, our response must be about the limits of the government's political tailoring. It is about reaching the point at which we have outgrown the rhetoric, and we decide to stop wearing the past.

BIBLIOGRAPHY

Chapter 1

Anonymous (2003, Summer). Diary of direct action. *Green Anarchist.*

Blackstock, N. (1988). *Cointelpro: The FBI's secret war on political freedom.* New York: Anchor Foundation.

Disclosure to the Accused, Illinois v. William Potter, No. 02-CM-5082 (2002, August 13).

Donnelly, M. (2006, May 24). Operation Backfire: Criminalizing dissent. *Counterpunch.* Retrieved March 1, 2009, from http://www.counterpunch.org/donnelly05242006.html.

Hays, T. (2004, May 4). Alleging abuse, detainees file lawsuit. *Associated Press.*

Kuipers, D. (2009). *Operation Bite Back: Rod Coronado's war to save American wilderness.* New York: Bloomsbury.

McGowan, D. (2008, April 15). Focus on: Civil Liberties Defense Center (CLDC). *Support for Daniel McGowan.* Retrieved May 1, 2010, from http://supportdaniel.org/blog/?p=33.

Potter, W. (2001, September 14). The new backlash: From the streets to the courthouse, the new activists find themselves under attack. *Texas Observer.*

Voluntary Statement by Al Cancel, Illinois v. William Potter, 02-7907 (2002, July 21).

Chapter 2

Alleyne, R. (2001, January 19). Terror tactics that brought a company to its knees. *Telegraph.* Retrieved March 10, 2010, from http://www.telegraph.co.uk/news/main.jhtml?xml=/news/2001/01/19/ncam119.xml.

Altman, L. K. (1995, March 21). Terror in Tokyo. *New York Times.* Retrieved March 10, 2010, from http://www.nytimes.com/1995/03/21/world/terror-tokyo-poison-nerve-gas-that-felled-tokyo-subway-riders-said-be-one-most.html.

Animal rights, activism vs. criminality: Hearing before the Committee on the Judiciary, United States Senate (Serial No. J-108-76), 108th Cong., 2nd Sess. (2004).

Associated Press (2007, February 15). Madrid bombing suspect denies guilt. *USA Today.* Retrieved May 1, 2008, from http://www.usatoday.com/news/world/2007-02-15-madrid-terror-trial_x.htm.

Balluch, M. (n.d.). Martin Balluch—the interview. *Abolitionist Online.* Retrieved July 20, 2008, from http://www.abolitionist-online.com/interview-issue04_bite.back-martin.balluch.shtml.

Blackwell, J. (n.d.). 1911: 'Trenton makes' history. *Trentonian.* Retrieved July 20, 2008, from http://www.capitalcentury.com/1911.html.

Broughton, Z. (2001). *The Argus.* Retrieved 2010, July 1, from http://www.theargus.co.uk.

Broughton, Z. (2001, March). Seeing is believing: Cruelty to dogs at Huntingdon Life Sciences. *Ecologist.*

Claiborne, W. (1998, August 8). Bombs explode at 2 U.S. embassies in Africa; scores dead. *Washington Post*, p. A1.

Close HLS (2006, December 12). News. Retrieved December 17, 2006, from http://www.closehls.net/archive/12_12_06.htm.

A controversial laboratory (2001, January 18). BBC. Retrieved July 19, 2008, from http://news.bbc.co.uk/2/hi/uk_news/1123837.stm.

Dawdy, P. (2004, June 9). A suspect roundup. *Seattle Weekly*, p. 11.

Delaware River Joint Toll Bridge Commission (2005, July 15). Commission rededicates, re-lights lower Trenton bridge, 'Trenton Makes, The World Takes' sign. Retrieved March 10, 2010, from http://www.drjtbc.org/default.aspx?pageid=270.

Epps, G. (2007, October 3). Vengeance is Brandon Mayfield's. *Salon*. Retrieved March 10, 2010, from http://www.salon.com/news/feature/2007/10/03/brandon_mayfield/.

Goodman, A. (2006, November 6). Madrid: 38,000-year jail terms sought. *CNN*. Retrieved March 10, 2010, from http://www.cnn.com/2006/WORLD/europe/11/06/spain.trial/.

Goodman, J. R., & Sanders, C. (forthcoming). In favor of tipping the balance: Animal rights activists in defense of residential picketing. *Society and Animals*.

Hamilos, P. (2007, October 31). The worst Islamist attack in European history. *Guardian*. Retrieved March 10, 2010, from http://www.guardian.co.uk/world/2007/oct/31/spain.

House of Lords Select Committee on Animals in Scientific Procedures (2001). Background memorandum by Huntingdon Life Sciences. Retrieved July 1, 2010, from http://www.parliament.the-stationery-office.com/pa/ld200102/ldselect/ldanimal/19/1071002.htm.

Ifill, G. (2004, May 26). Online NewsHour: Secretary of Homeland Security Tom Ridge. *NewsHour with Jim Lehrer*. Retrieved March 10, 2010, from http://www.pbs.org/newshour/bb/terrorism/jan-june04/ridge_05-26.html.

Kolata, G. (1998, April 16). Seeing is believing: Cruelty to dogs at Huntingdon Life Sciences. *New York Times*, p. A15.

Potter, W. (2004, September-October). The beagle brigade: A law that tells animal rights activists to heel. *Legal Affairs*, pp. 11–12.

Pressure builds on animal tests lab (2001, January 16). BBC. Retrieved July 19, 2008, from http://news.bbc.co.uk/2/hi/uk_news/1120259.stm.

Richman, J. (2004, May 27). Animal-rights activists charged; three living in East Bay could face prison time for enterprise terrorism. *Oakland Tribune*.

Rokke, M. (n.d.). *Diary of despair*. Philadelphia: Stop Huntingdon Animal Cruelty.

Rosebraugh, C. (2004). *Burning rage of a dying planet: speaking for the Earth Liberation Front*. New York: Lantern Books.

Schmidt, S. & Mintz, J. (2004, May 27). FBI seeks tips on 7 linked to Al Qaeda. *Washington Post*. Retrieved March 10, 2010, from http://www.washingtonpost.com/wp-dyn/articles/A58760-2004May26.html.

Serrano, K. (2007, November 4). Suit cites false-data desires, racial bias at lab. *Home News Tribune*.

Siegel, R. (2006, January 13). 'Trenton Makes, the World Takes': History of a slogan. *National Public Radio's All Things Considered*. Retrieved March 10, 2010, from http://www.npr.org/templates/story/story.php?storyId=5157037.

Stagno, B. (2000, November-December). Life science or living hell? *Satya*. Retrieved October 29, 2006.

Stop Huntingdon Animal Cruelty UK (n.d.). Who we are. Retrieved July 15, 2008, from http://www.shac.net/SHAC/who.html.

Superseding Indictment, United States v. Stop Huntingdon Animal Cruelty USA, Inc., No. 04-373 (n.d.), *available at* http://www.usdoj.gov/usao/nj/press/files/pdffiles/shacind2.pdf.

Townsend, M. (2003, April 20). Exposed: Secrets of the animal organ lab. *Guardian*. Retrieved July 1, 2010, from http://www.guardian.co.uk/uk/2003/apr/20/health.businessofresearch.

Transcript: Ashcroft, Mueller news conference (2004, May 26). CNN. Retrieved May 26, 2004, from http://www.cnn.com/2004/US/05/26/terror.threat.transcript.

United States Attorney's Office, District of New Jersey (2004, May 26). Militant animal rights group, seven members indicted for national campaign to terrorize company and its employees. Retrieved May 26, 2004, from http://www.usdoj.gov/usao/nj/press/files/shac0526_r.htm.

Walsh, D. (2007, September 12). Student's path to FBI informant; Using alias, woman tells of alleged terrorism plot. *Sacramento Bee*, p. B1.

Woolcock, N. (2005, August 25). Extremists seek fresh targets close to home. *Times (London)*, p. 27.

Chapter 3

Abbey, E. (1975). *The monkey wrench gang* (1st ed.). Philadelphia: Lippincott.

Abbey, E. (1990). *A voice crying in the wilderness*. New York: St. Martin's Press.

Acts of ecoterrorism by radical environmental organizations: Hearing before the Subcommittee on Crime of the Committee on the Judiciary, United States House of Representatives (Serial No. 142), 105th Cong., 2nd Sess. (1998).

American Civil Liberties Union (2002, December 6). How the USA Patriot Act redefines 'domestic terrorism'. Retrieved March 10, 2010, from http://www.aclu.org/national-security/how-usa-patriot-act-redefines-domestic-terrorism.

Animal Liberation Front Press Office (n.d.). Guidelines of the Animal Liberation Front. Retrieved August 1, 2009, from http://www.animalliberationpressoffice.org/Background.htm.

Anti-Defamation League (2008, May 2). Series of extremism training for NYPD. Retrieved June 1, 2009, from http://www.adl.org/learn.

Arnold, R. (1983, February). EcoTerrorism. *Reason*.

Arnold, R. (1997). *Ecoterror: The violent agenda to save nature, the world of the Unabomber*. Bellevue, Wash.: Free Enterprise Press.

Associated Press (1990, June 8). U.S. health chief stirs animal rights furor. *Chicago Tribune*, p. 5.

Axtman, K. (2003, December 29). The terror threat at home, often overlooked. *Christian Science Monitor*. Retrieved March 10, 2010, from http://www.csmonitor.com/2003/1229/p02s01-usju.html.

Barcott, B. (2000, October). Snoop: The secret life and prying times of Barry Clausen. *Outside*.

Bari, J. (1994). *Timber wars*. Common Courage Press.

Best, S. & Nocella, A. J. (2004). *Terrorists or freedom fighters?: Reflections on the liberation of animals*. New York: Lantern Books.

Bishop, B. (2006, April 15). Is it the Green Scare, eco-terrorism or none of the above? *Register-Guard*. Retrieved September 11, 2007, from http://www.registerguard.com.

Bush, G. W. (2001, September 20). Address to a joint session of Congress and the American people. Retrieved March 10, 2010, from http://georgewbush-whitehouse.archives.gov/news/releases/2001/09/20010920-8.html.

Case, D. (2002, March 12). The fringe: You too might be a terrorist! The war on the greens. *TomPaine*. Retrieved July 1, 2010, from http://web.archive.org/web/20040212183505/http://www.tompaine.com/feature.cfm/ID/5246.

Center for the Defense of Free Enterprise (2003). Ron Arnold named as ecoterrorism expert in major study. Retrieved April 1, 2010, from http://web.archive.org/web/20031109023619/http://cdfe.org/arnold_named_as_consultant.htm.

Chomsky, N. (2003). Terror and just response. *Terrorism and International Justice*, 69–87.

Chomsky, N. (2002). *Pirates and emperors, old and new: International terrorism in the real world*. Cambridge, MA: South End Press.

Clarkson, F. (2002, June 21). A radical antiabortionist backs down. *Salon*. Retrieved March 10, 2010, from http://dir.salon.com/story/news/feature/2002/06/21/abortion/index.html.

CNN (2001, November 6). 'You are either with us or against us.' *CNN*. Retrieved March 10, 2010, from http://archives.cnn.com/2001/US/11/06/gen.attack.on.terror/.

Compost, T. (2005, July-August). Victory in pepper spray torture trial. *Earth First Journal*, p. 3.

Conn, P. M. (2008, November 12). Terrorism in the name of animal rights. *Los Angeles Times*. Retrieved 2010, July 1, from http://www.latimes.com/news/printedition/opinion/la-oe-conn12-2008nov12,0,3327546.story.

Cookson, C. (2004, June 10). FBI warns biotech industry of animal extremists. *Financial Times*. Retrieved June 10, 2004, from http://www.ft.com.

Counterterrorism and infrastructure protection: Hearing before the Subcommittee of the Committee on Appropriations, United States Senate 106th Cong., 1st Sess. (1999).

Doyle, J. (1997, November 22). Sierra Club takes a swing at Riggs. *San Francisco Chronicle*, p. A19.

Dunn, E., Moore, M., & Nosek, B. (2005). The war of the words: How linguistic differences in reporting shape perceptions of terrorism. *Analyses of social issues and public policy*, 5(1), 67-86.

Earth Liberation Front Press Office (n.d.). Frequently asked questions. Retrieved August 1, 2009, from http://www.elfpressoffice.org/elffaqs.html.

Eco-terrorism and lawlessness on the national forests: Hearing before the Subcommittee on Forests and Forest Health of the Committee on Resources, United States House of Representatives (Serial No. 107-83), 107th Cong., 2nd Sess. (2002).

Eco-terrorism specifically examining Stop Huntingdon Animal Cruelty: Hearing before the Committee on Environment and Public Works, United States Senate (Serial No. 1005), 109th Cong., 1st Sess. (2005).

Eco-terrorism specifically examining the Earth Liberation Front and the Animal Liberation Front: Hearing before the Committee on Environment and Public Works, United States Senate (Serial No. 947), 109th Cong., 1st Sess. (2005).

Egan, T. (1991, December 19). Fund-raisers tap anti-environmentalism. *New York Times*, p. A18.

FBI agents tells farm group to be alert for growing eco-terrorism movement (2006, December 15). *Canadian Press*.

FBI: Eco-terrorism remains no.1 domestic terror threat. (2008, March 31). *Fox News*. Retrieved March 10, 2010, from http://www.foxnews.com/story/0,2933,343768,00.html.

Federal Bureau of Investigation (2005, May 23). When talk turns to terrors: Homegrown extremism in the U.S. Retrieved July 1, 2010, from http://www.fbi.gov/page2/may05/jlewis052305.htm.

Federal Bureau of Investigation (n.d.). *Counterterrorism analytical lexicon*.

Federal Bureau of Investigation (n.d.). *Terrorism in the United States 1996*.

Federal Bureau of Investigation (n.d.). *Terrorism in the United States 1997*.

Federal Bureau of Investigation (n.d.). *Terrorism in the United States 1998*.

Federal Bureau of Investigation (n.d.). *Terrorism in the United States 1999*.

Federal Bureau of Investigation (n.d.). *Terrorism in the United States 2000-2001*.

Federal Bureau of Investigation (n.d.). *Terrorism in the United States 2002-2005*.

Ficklin, J. & Andrew, P. (n.d.). *Fire in the eyes* [film].

Fire at UC Davis may be work of animal activists (1987, April 17). *Los Angeles Times*, p. 27.

Fletcher, H. (2008, April 21). Militant extremists in the United States. *Council on Foreign Relations*. Retrieved March 10, 2010, from http://www.cfr.org/publication/9236/american_militant_extremists_united_states_radicals.html.

Foreman, D. (1991). *Confessions of an eco-warrior*. New York: Harmony Books.

Foreman, D. (1993). *Ecodefense: A field guide to monkeywrenching*. Chico, Calif.: Abbzug Press.

Foundation for Biomedical Research (2006). *Illegal incidents report: A 25 year history of illegal activities by eco and animal extremists*. Washington, DC.

Foundation for Biomedical Research (2006). *Top 20 list of illegal actions by animal and eco-terrorists 1996–2006*. Washington, DC.

Goodman, A. (1997, November 19). Headwaters Forest. *Democracy Now*. Retrieved March 10, 2010, from http://www.democracynow.org/1997/11/19/headwaters_forest.

Goodman, A. (2004, September 8). Trial set to begin over use of pepper spray-soaked cotton swabs on non-violent protesters in 1997 Headwaters Forest. *Democracy Now*. Retrieved March 10, 2010, from http://www.democracynow.org/2004/9/8/trial_set_to_begin_over_use.

Greenwald, G. (2009, January 14). Tom Friedman offers a perfect definition of 'terrorism'. *Salon*. Retrieved March 10, 2010, from http://www.salon.com/opinion/greenwald/2009/01/14/friedman/.

Haines, C. (2005, May 19). FBI, ATF address domestic terrorism. *CNN*. Retrieved May 1, 2010, from http://www.cnn.com/2005/US/05/19/domestic.terrorism/.

Haines, C. (2008, October 6). Officials: Domestic terrorism biggest threat in Pa. *Herald Standard*. Retrieved October 8, 2008, from http://www.heraldstandard.com.

Hall, M. (2008, April 30). U.S. has Mandela on terrorist list. *USA Today*. Retrieved March 10, 2010, from http://www.usatoday.com/news/world/2008-04-30-watchlist_N.htm.

Haughney, C. (2001, March 27). Teenagers' activism takes a violent turn. *Washington Post*, p. A3.

Heller, J. (1961). *Catch-22*. New York: Simon and Schuster.

Herman, E. S. (1982). *The real terror network: Terrorism in fact and propaganda* (1st ed.). Boston: South End Press.

Hoffman, B. (2006). *Inside terrorism*. New York: Columbia University Press.

Hoffman, I. (2003, June 23). States, cities go own way in terror fight. *Oakland Tribune*.

Homeland Security Act of 2002, Pub. L. No. 107-296, 116 Stat. 2135 (2002).

Hsiao, A. (1998, November 10). The green menace. *Village Voice*, p. 26.

Information Network Associates (n.d.). 47th Society of Toxicology Annual Meeting Threat Assessment.

Inkerman Group (2007, September). The war on 'eco-terror': An analysis of the use of anti-terrorism legislation on activist movement in the UK & US. *The Inkerman Monitor*.

Irvin, D. (2007, September 22). Control debate, growers advised: Producers get tips on fighting PETA. *Arkansas Democrat-Gazette*.

Jacobellis v. Ohio, 378 U.S. 184 (1964).

Kenworthy, T. (2001, February 14). A green crusade erupts in flames; elusive 'Earth Liberation Front' claims responsibility for $30 million in damage, but law may be closing in. *USA Today*, p. A3.

King, M. L. (1964). *Why we can't wait*. New York: Signet books.

Kinsley, M. (2001, October 5). Defining terrorism: It's essential. It's also impossible. *Washington Post*, p. A37.

Koppelman, A. (2006, December 18). The terrorist you've never heard of. *Salon*. Retrieved March 10, 2010, from http://www.salon.com/news/feature/2006/12/18/tennessee_terrorist/index1.html.

Kornbluh, P. (2004). Chile and the United States: Declassified Documents Relating to the Military Coup, September 11, 1973. *National Security Archive Electronic Briefing Book No. 8*.

Krauthammer, C. (2003, May 16). Rebuilding Iraq. *Townhall*. Retrieved March 10, 2010, from http://www.townhall.com/columnists/CharlesKrauthammer/2003/05/16/rebuilding_iraq.

Laqueur, W. (1987). *The age of terrorism*. Boston: Little, Brown.

Levendosky, C. (1997, November 26). Public outraged over pepper-spray incident. *Venture County Star*, p. D7.

Levine, D. S. (2004, June 18). FBI says 1,100 biotechs face terror threat. *San Francisco Business Times*. Retrieved July 1, 2010, from http://sanfrancisco.bizjournals.com/sanfrancisco/stories/2004/06/21/story4.html.

Levitas, D. (2003, December 13). Our enemies at home. *New York Times*.

Long, J. & Denson, B. (1999, September 29). Can sabotage have a place in a democratic community? *Oregonian*, p. 1.

Man arrested, 10 rabbits confiscated in wake of break-in (1984, December 11). Associated Press.

Mandela, N. (1973). *No easy walk to freedom: Articles, speeches and trial addresses of Nelson Mandela*. London: Heinemann Educational.

Manes, C. (1990). *Green rage: Radical environmentalism and the unmaking of civilization*. Boston: Little, Brown.

McCarthy, R. M., & Sharp, G. (1997). *Nonviolent action: A research guide* (Garland reference library of social science ; v. 940). New York: Garland Pub.

Nack, J. (1991, September 4). Chlorine company targets Greenpeace. *Green Left*. Retrieved July 1, 2010, from http://www.greenleft.org.au/node/731.

NARAL Pro-Choice America Foundation (2009). *Anti-choice violence and intimidation*. Washington, DC.

National Abortion Federation (2009, April). NAF violence and disruption statistics. Retrieved March 10, 2010, from http://www.prochoice.org/pubs_research/publications/downloads/about_abortion/violence_stats.pdf.

New York Times (1996, October 5). Environmentalists say deal on redwoods is inadequate. *New York Times*, p. A9.

Philipkoski, K. (2004, June 16). Eco-terror cited as top threat. *Wired*. Retrieved March 10, 2010, from http://www.wired.com/medtech/health/news/2004/06/63812.

Phillips, B. (2008, April 3). Tourist or terrorist? Shelby County Sheriff's Office and the FBI teach people to spot potential terrorists. *Memphis Flyer*. Retrieved September 6, 2008, from http://www.memphisflyer.com/memphis/Content?oid=41348.

Platt, T. (1999, March). Engaging political will. *Fur Farm Letter*.

Portillo Jr., Ernesto (2007, December 19). Sheriff says terrorists abound in our midst. *Arizona Daily Star*. Retrieved September 6, 2008, from http://azstarnet.com/.

Potter, W. (2001, September 14). The new backlash: From the streets to the courthouse, the new activists find themselves under attack. *Texas Observer*.

Ridgeway, J. (2008, April 11). Cops and former Secret Service agents ran black ops on green groups. *Mother Jones*. Retrieved April 1, 2009, from http://www.motherjones.com.

Ridgeway, J., Schulman, D., & Corn, D. (2008, July 30). There's something about Mary: Unmasking a gun lobby mole. *Mother Jones*. Retrieved April 1, 2009, from http://www.motherjones.com.

Rogers, P. (2009, March 8). A decade after Headwaters deal, truce comes to Northern California redwood country. *San Jose Mercury News*.

Rood, J. Animal rights groups and ecology militants make DHS terrorist list, right-wing vigilantes omitted. *CQ Homeland Security*. Retrieved March 10, 2010, from http://www.cq.com/public/20050325_homeland.html.

Ryckman, Lisa L. (1986, January 26). Environmental 'warriors' use radical tactics to make point. *Los Angeles Times*, p. 3.

Scarce, R. (2006). *Eco-warriors: understanding the radical environmental movement*. Walnut Creek, Calif.: Left Coast Press.

Schmid, A. P. & Jongman, A. J. (1984). *Political terrorism: A research guide to concepts, theories, data bases, and literature*. New Brunswick, U.S.A.: North-Holland Distributors, Transaction Books.

Schoenmann, J. (1999, November 2). FBI examines threatening letters. *Las Vegas Review-Journal*. Retrieved April 1, 2009, from http://www.reviewjournal.com/lvrj_home/1999/Nov-02-Tue-1999/news /12270224.html.

Schuster, H. (2005, August 24). Domestic terror: Who's most dangerous? Eco-terrorists are now above ultra-right extremists on the FBI charts. *CNN*. Retrieved March 10, 2010, from http://www.cnn.com/2005/US/08/24/schuster.column/index.html.

Sharp, G. (2003). *There are realistic alternatives*. Boston: Albert Einstein Institution.

Sharp, G. (1959). The meanings of nonviolence: A typology. *Journal of Conflict Resolution*, 3(1), 41-66.

Sharp, G. (1970). *Exploring nonviolent alternatives*. Boston: P. Sargent.

Sharp, G. (1973). *The politics of nonviolent action*. Boston: P. Sargent.

Sharp, G. (1979). *Gandhi as a political strategist: With essays on ethics and politics*. Boston: P. Sargent.

Shishkin, P. (2008, September 13). American revolutionary: Quiet Boston scholar inspires rebels around the world. *Wall Street Journal*, p. 1.

Siegel, L. (1984, December 10). Animal rights' group, researchers argue over animal theft. *Associated Press*.

Slobodzian, J. (2003, December 4). 'Terrorist to abortionists' guilty. *Philadelphia Inquirer*, p. B1.

Smith, R. K. (2008). "Ecoterrorism"?: A critical analysis of the vilification of radical environmental activists as terrorists. *Environmental Law (Portland)*, 4(1), 537-576.

Southern Poverty Law Center (2002, Fall). Eco-violence: The record. *Intelligence Report, 107*.

Southern Poverty Law Center (2005, September). Decade of domestic terror documented by Center. *SPLC Report, 35*(3).

Stone, A. (1990, June 8). Under attack: Using animals for research; scientists test PR techniques. *USA Today*, p. A3.

Strassel, K. A. (2001, October 4). Left behind: These are lean times for fringe activists. *Wall Street Journal*. Retrieved 2010, July 1, from http://www.online.wsj.com.

Strausbaugh, J. A. (2006, April 15). Down on the farm, fears grow. *Lancaster Online*. Retrieved April 16, 2006, from http://www.lancasteronline.com/.

Target of Opportunity (2005). The hit list. Retrieved December 20, 2005, from http://www.targetofopportunity.com/enemy_targets.htm.

Taylor, B. (1998). Religion, violence and radical environmentalism: From Earth First! to the Unabomber to the Earth Liberation Front. *Terrorism and Political Violence*, 10(4), 1-42.

Tension high after pepper spray used on protesters (1997, October 31). *CNN*. Retrieved April 1, 2000, from http://www.cnn.com/EARTH/9710/31/pepper.spray.update/.

Tigar, M. E. (2007). *Thinking about terrorism: the threat to civil liberties in times of national emergency*. Chicago: American Bar Association.

Turse, N. (2007, May 24). The secret air war in Iraq. *Nation*. Retrieved March 10, 2010, from http://www.thenation.com/doc/20070611/turse.

UN seeks definition of terrorism (2005, July 26). BBC. Retrieved March 10, 2010, from http://news.bbc.co.uk/2/hi/americas/4716957.stm.

United States Department of Agriculture (2004, March). *APHIS facility security profile, form 271-R*.

United States Department of State (2002, May). *Patterns of global terrorism 2001*.

Usborne, D. (2005, May 20). Eco-militants are greatest terrorist threat, warns FBI. *Independent*, p. 29.

Wagner, T. (2008). Reframing ecotage as ecoterrorism: News and the discourse of fear. *Environmental Communication: A Journal of Nature and Culture*, 2(1), 25-39.

Walden: Earth Liberation Front a threat (2001, September 12). *National Journal's CongressDaily*.

Walzer, M. (1992). *Just and unjust wars: A moral argument with historical illustrations* (2nd ed.). New York: Basic Books.

War against eco-terrorists [editorial] (2001, October 7). *The Washington Times*, p. B2.

Weinstein, J. L. (2004, June 20). FBI accused of 'scare' tactics; An eco-terrorism warning prompted Portland police to put a local gathering under surveillance. *Portland Press Herald*, p. B1.

Wolke, H. (2006, April 6). Earth First! A founder's story. *Lowbagger*. http://www.lowbagger.org/foundersstory.html.

Zakin, S. (1993). *Coyotes and town dogs: Earth First! and the environmental movement*. New York: Viking.

Zamora, J. H. (2004, April 23). FBI to pay $2 million in Earth First suit. *San Francisco Chronicle*, p. B1.

Chapter 4

Abraham, K. (2006, September 7). Eye on ELF: Were eco-radicals illegally wire-tapped? *Eugene Weekly*. Retrieved March 15, 2010, from http://eugeneweekly.com/2006/09/07/news1.html.

ACLU sues Homeland Security for arresting, spying on vegans who protested ham. (2005, September 22). *Raw Story*. Retrieved March 15, 2010, from http://www.rawstory.com/news/2005/ACLU_sues_Homeland_Security_for_arresting_spying_on_vegans_who_protested_0922.html.

American Civil Liberties Union (2006, March 14). ACLU releases first concrete evidence of FBI spying based solely on groups' anti-war views. Retrieved March 15, 2010, from http://www.aclu.org/safefree/spying/24528prs20060314.html.

Anti-Defamation League (n.d.). Ku Klux Klan—History. Retrieved March 15, 2010, from

http://www.adl.org/learn/ext_us/kkk/history.asp?LEARN_Cat=Extremism&LEARN_
SubCat=Extremism_in_America&xpicked=4&item=kkk.

Asthana, A., & DeYoung, K. (2006, September 8). Bush calls for greater wiretap authority. *Washington Post*, p. A1.

Babington, C., & Eggen, D. (2006, March 1). Gonzales seeks to clarify testimony on spying; extent of eavesdropping may go beyond NSA work. *Washington Post*, p. A8.

Bamford, J. (1983). *The puzzle palace: A report on America's most secret agency.* New York: Penguin Books.

Bamford, J. (2009). *The shadow factory: The ultra-secret NSA from 9/11 to the eavesdropping on America.* New York: Doubleday.

Barnard, J. (2006, November 10). 4 plead in ecoterror case; 5- to 8-year sentences recommended. *Associated Press.*

Barnard, J. (2007, May 26). Arsonist fell under spell of ecoterror guru. *Associated Press.*

Bernton, H. (2006, November 10). 4 more plead guilty in ecosabotage cases; trial may be avoided;

Bishop, B. (2006, September 8). Wiretap possibility raised in eco-sabotage case. *Register-Guard.* Retrieved September 29, 2006, from http://www.registerguard.com.

Block, R. (2006, April 27). Pentagon steps up intelligence efforts inside US borders. *Wall Street Journal*, p. A1.

Bridis, T. (2005, December 20). ACLU says FBI misuses terror powers. *Associated Press.*

Bridis, T. (2005, January 18). FBI stops using Carnivore wiretap software. *Associated Press.*

Burress, C. (1998, November 24). UC finalizes pioneering research deal with biotech firm; pie tossers leave taste of protest. *San Francisco Chronicle*, p. A17.

Cato, J. (2006, July 31). Beating a federal rap not easy. *Pittsburgh Tribune-Review.* Retrieved August 16, 2010.

Cauley, L. (2006, May 11). NSA has massive database of Americans' phone calls; 3 telecoms help government collect billions of domestic records. *USA Today*, p. A1.

Churchill, W. & Vander, W., Jim (2002). *The COINTELPRO papers: Documents from the FBI's secret wars against dissent in the United States* (2nd ed.). Cambridge, MA: South End Press.

Cox, A. M. (1999, March-April). The medium is the meringue. *Mother Jones.*

Davis, A. (2003, May 22). Use of data collection systems is up sharply following 9/11. *Wall Street Journal.* Retrieved June 1, 2003, from http://www.wsj.com.

Davis, J. K. (1992). *Spying on America: The FBI's domestic counterintelligence program.* New York: Praeger.

Defense in ecoterrorism case drops wiretap motion in Oregon (2006, November 3). Associated Press.

Department of Homeland Security (2007, January 5). Overview: FY 2007 Homeland Security Grant Program. Retrieved July 1, 2010, from http://www.dhs.gov/xlibrary/assets/grants-2007-program-overview-010507.pdf.

Department of Justice Office of the Inspector General (2010, September). A review of the FBI's investigations of certain domestic advocacy groups.

Donner, F. J. (1990). *Protectors of privilege: Red squads and police repression in urban America.* Berkeley: University of California Press.

Drogin, B. (2008, December 7). Spying on pacifists, greens and nuns: A Maryland trooper who went undercover to infiltrate nonviolent groups labeled dozens of people as terrorists. *Los Angeles Times*, p. A18.

Eco-terrorism specifically examining the Earth Liberation Front and the Animal Liberation Front: Hearing before the Committee on Environment and Public Works, United States Senate (Serial No. 947), 109th Cong., 1st Sess. (2005).

Edds, K. (2004, June 14). Radical environmentalists take aim at suburbia. *Washington Post,* p. A3.

Egan, T. (2005, December 9). 6 arrests years after ecoterrorist acts. *New York Times,* p. A18.

Egelko, B. (2006, August 18). Judge's rejection of Bush wiretaps just first round. *San Francisco Chronicle,* p. A1.

Eggen, D. (2005, September 13). FBI agents often break informant rules. *Washington Post,* p. A15.

Eggen, D. (2006, July 19). Bush thwarted probe into NSA wiretapping. *Washington Post,* p. A4.

Eggen, D. (2007, August 14). Lawsuits may illuminate methods of spy program. *Washington Post,* p. A1.

Electronic Privacy Information Center. Foreign Intelligence Surveillance Act Orders 1979–2007. Retrieved 2010, July 1, from http://epic.org/privacy/wiretap/stats/fisa_stats.html.

Fattah, H. M. (2006, January 20). Bin Laden warns of attacks in U.S. but offers truce. *New York Times,* p. A1.

Federal Bureau of Investigation (2003, October 15). *FBI Intelligence Bulletin no. 89.*

Federal Bureau of Investigation (n.d.). *Terrorism in the United States 2000-2001.*

Fireant Collective (2001, May). *Setting fires with electrical timers: An Earth Liberation Front Guide.*

Galvan, L. (2044, April 24). Peace Fresno files complaint: Now-deceased deputy is accused of infiltrating group. *Fresno Bee,* p. B1.

Gangi, M. (2007, March-April). "Some sort of anti-snitch." *Earth First Journal,* p. 40.

Glick, D. (2003). *Powder burn: Arson, money, and mystery on Vail Mountain.* New York: PublicAffairs.

Goodman, A. (2007, June 11). Facing seven years in jail, environmental activist Daniel McGowan speaks out about the Earth Liberation Front, the Green Scare and the government's treatment of activists as "terrorists". *Democracy Now.* Retrieved March 10, 2010, from http://www.democracynow.org/2007/6/11/exclusive_facing_seven_years_in_jail.

Gordon, A. (2009, October 9). Vegan protesters prevail over cops in court. *Atlanta Progressive News.* Retrieved March 15, 2010, from http://www.atlantaprogressivenews.com/news/0527.html.

Gregory, G. (1998, January 22). Investors buy Redmond slaughterhouse. *Oregonian,* p. D2.

Harper, M. C. (1984). The Consumer's Emerging Right to Boycott: NAACP v. Claiborne Hardware and Its Implications for American Labor Law. *Yale LJ, 93,* 409.

Harvey, A. (2008, March 8). Yacht racer to arsonist: ELF member, turned U.S. witness, describes her double life as high-tech worker and key figure. *Rocky Mountain News,* p. 4.

Hersh, S. M. (2006, May 29). Listening in: Seymour Hersh on the NSA's domestic surveillance program. *New Yorker,* p. 24.

Hoffman, I., & Holstege, S. (2003, July 15). State's terror analysts reined in. *Oakland Tribune.*

Hsu, Spencer S. (2005, December 20). FBI papers show terror inquiries into PETA; other groups tracked. *Washington Post,* p. A11.

Isikoff, M. (2005, November 21). Profiling: How the FBI tracks eco-terror suspects. *Newsweek,* p. 6.

Janofsky, M. (2006, January 21). 11 indicted in 17 cases of sabotage in West. *New York Times,* p. A9.

Japenga, A. (1993, May 10). When the Feds locked up Jonathan Paul for refusing to testify, the animal rights movement gained an accidental hero. *Los Angeles Times*, p. E1.

Jezzabell (2009, July-August). Checking in with family and friends of Daniel McGowan. *Earth First Journal*, p. 16.

Kaplan, D. E., Ekman, M. M., & Marek, A. C. (2006, May 8). Spies among us. *U.S. News & World Report*, pp. 40–49.

Kesich, G. (2006, October 26). Activists fear they've become FBI targets. *Portland Press Herlad*, p. B1.

Klein, M. (2006, May 17). AT&T whistle-blower's evidence. *Wired*. Retrieved March 15, 2010, from http://www.wired.com/science/discoveries/news/2006/05/70908.

Knickerbocker, B. (2006, January 30). Eco-vigilantes: All in 'The Family?' *Christian Science Monitor*, p. 20.

Kristiansen, L. J. (2010). *Screaming for change: Articulating a unifying philosophy of punk rock.* Lanham, Md.: Lexington Books.

LaFranchi, H. & Bowers, F. (2006, January 20). Bin Laden message: 'I'm still here.' *Christian Science Monitor*, p. A1.

Lee, J. (2007, September 17). Enemy of the state: The story of Daniel McGowan. *The Indypendent.*

Leonnig, C. D. (2007, April 3). Police log confirms FBI role in arrests. *Washington Post*, p. B1.

Leonnig, C. D. & Sheridan, M. B. (2006, March 2). Saudi group alleges wiretapping by U.S.; defunct charity's suit details eavesdropping. *Washington Post*, p. A1.

Lichtblau, E. (2003, November 23). F.B.I. scrutinizes antiwar rallies. *New York Times*, p. A1.

Lichtblau, E. (2005, December 19). F.B.I. watched activist groups, new files show. *New York Times*, p. A1.

Lichtblau, E. (2008, July 3). Judge rejects Bush's view on wiretaps. *New York Times*, p. A17.

Lichtblau, E., & Risen, J. (2005, December 18). Eavesdropping effort began soon after Sept. 11 attacks. *New York Times*, p. A44.

McCall, W. (2008, June 4). Radical 'snitch' in Western arsons gets probation. *Associated Press.*

McCullagh, D. (2007, January 30). FBI turns to broad new wiretap method. *ZDNet*. Retrieved March 11, 2010, from http://news.zdnet.com/2100-9595_22-151059.html.

McGlone, T. (2005, December 22). FBI tried to link PETA to terror groups. *Virginian-Pilot*, p. B1.

McGowan, D. (2007, November-December). "And the rest is history." an interview with Daniel McGowan. *Earth First Journal*, p. 22.

McGowan, D. (2007, August 8). My friend Jonathan Paul. *Support for Daniel McGowan.* Retrieved March 10, 2010, from http://supportdaniel.org.

McGowan, D. (2007, November 24). A lack of honesty and integrity—On Darren Thurston. *Support for Daniel McGowan.* Retrieved November 25, 2008, from http://supportdaniel.org.

McGowan, D. (2008, January-February). An interview with Daniel McGowan: Part two. *Earth First Journal*, p. 23.

McGowan, D. (2008, March 19). Free to be freed (sooner than later). Retrieved April 16, 2008, from http://supportdaniel.org/blog/?p=30.

McLure, J. (2006, September 4). DOJ losing ground in wiretap fight. *Legal Times*. http://www.legaltimes.com.

Memorandum in Support of Request for Production of Surveillance Data and Material, United States v. McGowan, No. CR 06-60124-AA (2006, August 17).

Mendoza, M. (1997, January 4). Program to protect horses sends them to slaughter. *Associated Press.*

Miller, G. (2006, January 20). U.S. verifies Bin Laden tape, calls his offer of a truce a ploy. *Los Angeles Times*, p. A1.

Office of the Inspector General (2005, September). *The Federal Bureau of Investigation's Compliance with the Attorney General's Investigative Guidelines.*

Ortega, B. (1999, March 10). The woods are full of eco-terrorists. *Wall Street Journal.*

Paul, C. (2007, May 24). My brother, the 'terrorist'. *Los Angeles Times*, p. A25.

Plea Agreement, United States v. Block, No. CR 06-60126-AA (2006, October 17).

Plea Agreement, United States v. Gerlach, No. CR 06-60079-AA (2006, July 19).

Plea Agreement, United States v. McGowan, No. CR 06-60124-AA (2006, October 17).

Plea Agreement, United States v. Meyerhoff, No. CR 06-60078-1-AA (2006, July 19).

Plea Agreement, United States v. Paul, No. CR 06-60125-AA (2006, October 17).

Plea Agreement, United States v. Savoie, No. CR 06-60080-AA (2006, July 19).

Plea Agreement, United States v. Tankersley, No. CR 06-60071-AA (2006, July 19).

Plea Agreement, United States v. Thurston, No. CR 06-60069-1-AA (2006, July 19).

Plea Agreement, United States v. Tubbs, No. CR 06-60070-1-AA (2006, July 19).

Plea Agreement, United States v. Zacher, No. CR 06-60126-AA (2006, October 17).

Potter, W. (2009). Making an animal rights "terrorist." *Bite Back Magazine*, 14.

Prosecution declares victory: Defendants acknowledged crimes. *Seattle Times*, p. B1.

Rankin, B. (2009, September 26). Vegans' rights violated, jury finds. *Atlanta Journal-Constitution*, p. B1.

Rein, L. (2008, October 8). Md. police put activists' names on terror lists. *Washington Post*, p. A1.

Riccardi, N. (2006, March 27). FBI keeps watch on activists. *Los Angeles Times*, p. A1.

Risen, J. & Lichtblau, E. (2005, December 16). Bush lets U.S. spy on callers without courts. *New York Times*, p. A1.

Roberts, C. (2007, August 22). Transcript: Debate on the Foreign Intelligence Surveillance Act. *El Paso Times.*

Rosebraugh, C. (2004). *Burning rage of a dying planet: Speaking for the Earth Liberation Front.* New York: Lantern Books.

Rothschild, M. (2009, May 26). FBI infiltrates Iowa City protest group. *The Progressive.* Retrieved March 5, 2010, from http://www.progressive.org/mc052609.html.

Select Committee to Study Governmental Operations (1976, April 23). *Supplementary detailed staff reports on intelligence activities and the rights of Americans: Book III.*

Shane, S. (2006, February 6). For some, spying controversy recalls a past drama. *New York Times*, p. A18.

Shapiro, A. (2006, January 20). Eleven activists charged with domestic terrorism. *National Public Radio's All Things Considered.* Retrieved January 20, 2006, from http://www.npr.org/templates/story/story.php?storyId=5165548.

Shorrock, T. (2008, May 19). Blacklisted by the Bush government. *Salon.* Retrieved September 1, 2009, from http://www.salon.com/news/feature/2008/05/19/al-haramain/index.html.

Solomon, J. (2007, June 14). FBI finds it frequently overstepped in collecting data. *Washington Post*, p. A1.

Southern Poverty Law Center (2007, Spring). Patriot groups active in the year 2006. *Intelligence Report, 125.*

Spielman, F. (2009, June 8). Court cancels limits on city's 'Red Squad.' *Chicago Sun-Times.* Retrieved June 10, 2010, from http://www.suntimes.com/news/cityhall/1612567,chicago-police-red-squad-060809.article.

Superseding Indictment, United States v. Christianson, No. CR 08-CR-107-C (2008, July 17).

Thurston, D. (2007, December 21). Fired back: Some words in response to Operation Backfire. *Free Darren.* Retrieved December 22, 2007, from http://freedarren.org.

Transcript: 11 indicted in ecoterrorism plots (2006, January 20). CNN. Retrieved September 1, 2009, from http://transcripts.cnn.com/TRANSCRIPTS/0601/20/ywt.01.html.

United States Department of Justice (2006, January 20). Eleven defendants indicted on domestic terrorism charges. Retrieved September 8, 2007, from http://www.usdoj.gov/opa/pr/2006/January/06_crm_030.html.

United States Sentencing Commission (2006). *Sourcebook of federal sentencing statistics.*

Valdez, A. (2006, August 30). Terror-fying the greens: Did investigators use post-9/11 warrantless wiretaps to bust accused eco-saboteurs. *Willamette Week.* Retrieved September 29, 2006, from http://www.wweek.com/editorial/3243/7938.

Virginia Fusion Center (2006, July 1). State tracked protesters in the name of security; officials say they have stopped monitoring antiwar and political rallies. *Los Angeles Times,* p. A1.

Virginia Fusion Center (2009, March). *2009 Virginia terrorism threat assessment.*

Warner, J. & White, P. (2003, July 17). Big brother under the bumper: Boulder residents find mysterious tracking systems on their cars. *Boulder Weekly.* Retrieved August 8, 2003, from http://www.boulderweekly.com/archive/071703/coverstory.html.

Chapter 5

Albert, J. G. (2008, December 25). What were those 1960s terrorists thinking, anyway? *Counterpunch.* Retrieved March 10, 2009.

Animal Enterprise Protection Act, Pub. L. No. 102-346 (1992).

Animal rights, activism vs. criminality: Hearing before the Committee on the Judiciary, United States Senate (Serial No. J-108-76), 108th Cong., 2nd Sess. (2004).

Brief from Appellant, United States v. Harper, No. CR 06-4436 (2007, October 22).

Burton, F. (2006, March 16). SHAC convictions: The martyrdom effect. *STRATFOR.* Retrieved March 17, 2006, from http://www.stratfor.com/shac_convictions_martyrdom_effect.

Cherry, E. (2006). Veganism as a cultural movement: A relational approach. *Social Movement Studies,* 5(2), 155-170.

Cook, J. (2006, February 7). Thugs for puppies. *Salon.* Retrieved February 7, 2006, from http://www.salon.com/life/feature/2006/02/07/thugs_puppies.

Crane, Paul T. (2006). True threats and the issue of intent. *Virginia Law Review, 92,* 1225.

Eco-terrorism specifically examining the Earth Liberation Front and the Animal Liberation Front: Hearing before the Committee on Environment and Public Works, United States Senate (Serial No. 947), 109th Cong., 1st Sess. (2005).

Freking, K. (2002, September 22). Congress comes to Stephens' aid. *Arkansas Democrat-Gazette,* p. A1.

Greer v. Spock, 424 U.S. 828 (1976).

Haenfler, R. (2004). Rethinking subcultural resistance: Core values of the straight edge movement. *Journal of Contemporary Ethnography,* 33(4), 406.

Hawken, P. (2007). *Blessed unrest: How the largest movement in the world came into being, and why no one saw it coming.* New York: Viking.

Hentoff, N. (1992). *Free speech for me—but not for thee: How the American left and right relentlessly censor each other.* New York: HarperCollins Publishers.

Kopel, D. (1999, August 1). The day they came to sue the book; lawsuit against Paladin Press. *Reason*, p. 59.

Lahickey, B. (1998). *All ages: Reflections on straight edge.* Revelation Books.

Love, J. (1985). *The U.S. anti-apartheid movement: Local activism in global politics.* New York: Praeger.

Mozingo, J. (2006, September 5). A thin line on animal rights; Dr. Jerry Vlasak stays carefully in the world of medicine while serving as a spokesman for extremists who threaten laboratory researchers. *Los Angeles Times*, p. B1.

National Association for Biomedical Research (2006, February 6). SHAC trial gets underway in New Jersey today. Retrieved July 15, 2007, from http://www.nabr.org/members/ Events/SHAC/Trial2006.

No Master's Voice (1988). The ALF is watching and there's no place to hide [vinyl LP].

O'Hara, C. (1999). *The philosophy of punk: More than noise.* San Francisco: AK Press.

Pogash, C. (2003, December 5). $50,000 reward offered after 2 blasts. *Los Angeles Times*, p. B6.

Ray, P. K. (1990). *Down memory lane: Reminiscences of a Bengali revolutionary.* New Delhi: Gian.

Rodriguez, M. (2003, August 30). Animal rights group claims it bombed biotech firm. *Los Angeles Times*, p. B8.

Rosebraugh, C. (2004). *Burning rage of a dying planet: Speaking for the Earth Liberation Front.* New York: Lantern Books.

Schabner, D. (2003, May 5). 'Terror' group web site a puzzle for Feds. *ABC News.* Retrieved April 1, 2009.

Stone, G. R. (2004). *Perilous times: Free speech in wartime from the Sedition Act of 1798 to the war on terrorism* (1st ed.). New York: W. W. Norton & Co.

Sunstein, C. R., Seidman, L. M., Karlan, P. S., Stone, G. R., & Tushnet, M. V. (2008, January 18). *The First Amendment, Third Edition.* Aspen Publishers, Inc.

Susman, T. (2005, August 7). Feds turn up the heat on 'ecoterrorists.' *Newsday*, p. A6.

Tao, A. (2005, November 22). Animal rights activists create PR crisis. *PharmExec.* Retrieved 2005, November 30, from http://www.pharmexec.com.

Target of Opportunity (2005). The hit list. Retrieved December 20, 2005, from http://www. targetofopportunity.com/enemy_targets.htm.

United States v. Fullmer, et al., No. CR 06-4211 (2006).

Volokh, E. (2004). Speech as conduct: Generally applicable laws, illegal courses of conduct, situation-altering utterances, and the uncharted zones. *Cornell Law Review*, 90, 1277.

Volokh, E. (2005). Crime-Facilitating Speech. *Stanford Law Review*, 57, 1095.

Volokh, E. (2005). Deterring speech: When is it "McCarthyism"? When is it proper? *California Law Review*, 93(5), 1413-1454.

Walkom, T. (2006, March 13). U.S. terror hunt targets animal activists. *The Toronto Star*, p. A6.

Woods, R. & Ungoes-Thomas, J. (2006, February 26). Focus: A campaigning hero. *Sunday Times.* Retrieved March 1, 2010, from http://www.timesonline.co.uk/tol/news/uk/article735136.ece.

Chapter 6

18 Pa. C.S. §3311.

2 Okla Stat. §5-104 et seq.

42 Pa. C.S. §8319.

A.C.A. §5-62-201, et seq. Farm Animal and Research Facilities.

A.R.S. §11-1023. Unauthorized release of animals; classification; damages.

Agricultural Terrorism Prevention and Response Act of 2001, H.R. 3198, 107th Cong., 1st Sess. (2001).

Agriculture Facilities Protection Act of 2005, S. 1532, 109th Cong., 1st Sess. (2005).

Agroterrorism Reduction Act, S. 1775, 107th Cong., 1st Sess. (2001).

Ala. Code §13A-11-150 et seq. Offenses Against Animal Research and Animal Production Facilities.

American Legislative Exchange Council (2003). *Animal & ecological terrorism in America.*

American Legislative Exchange Council (2009, July). Spring task force summit. *Inside ALEC,* p. 6.

American Medical Association (1989, June). Animal research action plan.

Animal Enterprise Protection Act, Pub. L. No. 102-346 (1992).

Animal Research Facilities Act of 1989, S. 727, 101st Cong., 1st Sess. (1989).

Animal rights activist enters guilty pleas in arson, theft (1995, March 7). *Oregonian,* p. B5.

Animal rights raiders destroy years of work (1992, March 8). *New York Times,* p. 51.

Associated Press (1988, March 24). Man sentenced in break-in. *Oregonian,* p. B5.

Beltran, X. (2002). Applying RICO to eco-activism: Fanning the radical flames of eco-terror. *Boston College Environmental Affairs Law Review,* 29(281).

Best, S., & Nocella, A. J. (2006). *Igniting a revolution: Voices in defense of the Earth.* Oakland, CA: AK Press.

Blum, D. (1994). *The monkey wars.* New York: Oxford University Press.

Brotman, B. (1990, November 2). Building a resistance: Tired of animal rights groups' threat and accusations, biomedical researchers are standing up for their work. *Chicago Tribune,* p. Tempo 1.

C.R.S.A. §18-9-206. Unauthorized release of an animal—penalty—restitution.

California Penal Code §602. Animal Enterprise Protection Act.

Center for Consumer Freedom (2006, December 12). Charlotte's tangled web. Retrieved December 13, 2006, from http://www.consumerfreedom.com/news_detail.cfm/head-line/3194.

Chynoweth, A. (n.d.). *No gravy for the cat* [film].

Commonhorsesense.com (n.d.). Advertisement: Animal rights groups will stop at nothing. Retrieved September 1, 2006, from http://www.commonhorsesense.com.

Darling, J. (2007, September 28). Son of executed 'atomic spies' speaks on civil liberties. *Mail Tribune.* Retrieved September 29, 2007, from http://www.mailtribune.com.

Defenders of Wildlife, & Natural Resources Defense Council (n.d.). *Corporate America's trojan horse in the states: The untold story behind the American Legislative Exchange Council.*

Denial of Entry to Federal Lands, H.R. 1185, 102d Cong., 1st Sess. (1991).

Deegan, D. (2001). *Managing activism.* London: Kogan Page Limited.

Denson, B. & Long, J. (1999, October 3). Environment-motivated sabotage spreading throughout the west. *Seattle Times,* p. B7.

Department of Justice & Department of Agriculture (1993). *Report to Congress on the extent and effects of domestic and international terrorism on animal enterprises.*

Ecoterrorism Prevention Act of 2004, H.R. 4454, 108th Cong., 2d Sess. (2004).

Environmental Terrorism Reducation Act, H.R. 2583, 107th Cong., 1st Sess. (2001).

Fariello, G. (1995). *Red scare: Memories of the American Inquisition*. New York: Norton.

Farm Animal and Research Facilities Protection Act of 1991, H.R. 2407, 102d Cong., 2d Sess. (1991).

Farm Animal and Research Facilities Protection Act of 1991, H.R. 3270, 101st Cong., 1st Sess. (1989).

Farm Animal Facilities Protection Act of 1989, S.1330, 101st Cong., 1st Sess. (1989).

FL ST §828.40 through 43. Florida Animal Enterprise Protection Act.

Ford, R., Woolcock, N., & Irving, R. (2005, October 25). Terror laws will apply to animal rights lobby. *Times* (London). Retrieved March 1, 2009, from http://www.timesonline.co.uk/tol/news/uk/article582382.ece.

Forest Users' Protection Act, H.R. 2711, 101st Cong., 1st Sess. (1987).

Ga. Code Ann. §4-11-30 through 35. Georgia Farm Animal and Research Facilities Protection Act.

Gen.Laws 1956, §4-1-29.

Girgen, J. (2008). *Constructing animal rights activism as a social threat: Claims-making in the New York Times and in congressional hearings*. Diss. Florida State University.

Goodman, J. S. (2007). Shielding corporate interests from public dissent: An examination of the undesirability and unconstitutionality of eco-terrorism legislation. *JL & Pol'y, 16*, 823.

Guillermo, K. S. (1993). *Monkey business: The disturbing case that launched the animal rights movement*. Washington, D.C.: National Press Books.

Guither, H. D. (1998). *Animal rights: History and scope of a radical social movement*. Carbondale: Southern Illinois University Press.

Haag, J. (1987, April 16). Untitled. *United Press International*.

Hands Off Our Kids Act of 2001, H.R. 1847, 107th Cong., 1st Sess. (2001).

Hearing before the House Judiciary Committee of the Tennessee General Assembly 104th Cong., 2nd Sess. (2006, April 25).

Heartland Institute (n.d.). Personnel details: Mrs. Alexandra (Sandy) Liddy Bourne. Retrieved July 1, 2010, from http://www.heartland.org/.

Humane Society of the United States (2006, January 11). The Comments of the Humane Society of the United States on the Animal Enterprise Terrorism Act, S. 1926.

Humphrey, T. (2006, May 1). GOP claims Dem abuse; Senate Republicans say they'll boycott 'local bills' of House Democrats. *Knoxville News-Sentinel*, p. B1.

I.C. §18-7037, 18-7040-41.

I.C.A. §717A.1 through 3.

IC 35-43-1-2.

IL ST CH 720 §215/3, et seq. Animal Research and Production Facilities Protection Act.

Johnson, D. (2007). Cages, clinics, and consequences: The chilling problems of controlling special interest extremism. *Oregon Law Review, 86*, 249-294.

Join ALEC. (n.d.). Retrieved 2009, September 9, from http://www.alec.org/AM/Template.cfm?Section=Join_ALEC.

K.S.A. 47-1825 through 1828. Farm Animal and Field Crop and Research Facilities Protection Act.

Hummell, K. A. (2004, January). The American Legislative Exchange Council's attack on civil liberties. *Defenders of Wildlife*.

Parker, A. (n.d.). Beyond AETA: How corporate-crafted legislation brands activists as terrorists. *National Lawyers Guild.*

Peterson, K. (2001, July 9). Eco-terrorists targeted by get tough state laws. *Stateline.* Retrieved September 1, 2009, from http://www.stateline.org/live/ViewPage.action?siteNodeId=13 6&languageId=1&contentId=14386.

Knickerbocker, B. (2003, November 26). New laws target increase in acts of ecoterrorism. *Christian Science Monitor.* Retrieved September 15, 2009, from http://www.csmonitor. com.

Knight-Ridder Newspapers (1989, April 9). Senator rips animal rights raids. *Chicago Tribune,* p. 22.

KRS §437.410, et seq. Protection of Animal Facilities.

Lamont v. Postmaster General, 381 U.S. 301 (1965), *available at* http://www.heartland.org/.

LSA-R.S. 9:2799.4.

M.G.L.A. 266 §104B.

M.S.A. §346.56, 604.13.

McCoy, K. E. (2007). Subverting justice: An indictment of the Animal Enterprise Terrorism Act. *Animal L, 14,* 53.

MD Code, C. L., §6-208.

MO.St.Ann.578.407.

Mont. Code Ann., §81-30-101, et seq.

Mont. Code Ann., §87-3-142.

Moran, K. (2003, January 10). Sportsmen's group targets anti-hunters. *New York Post,* p. 86.

Morano, M. (2006, May 1). New movie called 'soft core eco-terrorism' for kids. *CNSNews.* Retrieved May 1, 2006, from http://www.cnsnews.com.

Morris, A. D. (1984). *The origins of the civil rights movement: Black communities organizing for change.* New York, London: Free Press/Collier Macmillan.

MS ST §69-29-301, et seq.

N.C.G.S.A. §14-159.2.

N.D. Cent. Code §12.1-21.1-01, et seq.

N.H. Rev. Stat. Ann. §644:8-e.

N.J.S.A. 2C:17-3.

N.Y. Agric. & Mkts. Law §378.

National Association for Biomedical Research (2003, February 21). 2002 year-end summary of state legislation. Retrieved September 9, 2009, from http://www.nabr.org/ NABRMembersOnly/.

National Association for Biomedical Research (n.d.). State law book. Retrieved September 9, 2009, from http://www.nabr.org/NABRMembersOnly/.

Neb.Rev.St. §25-21, 236.

Ohio R.C. §2923.31.

Olsson, K. (2002, September-October). Ghostwriting the law: A little-known corporate lobby is drafting business-friendly bills for state legislators across the country. *Mother Jones,* p. 17.

ORS §164.887, 164.889, 167.312.

Otis, G. A. (2003, November 18). Terrorist tactics: A state law would pin the T-word on animal-rights and eco protesters. *Village Voice,* p. 40.

Panton, J. (2006, April 18). Animal rights protesters: Don't ban them, beat them. *Spiked.* Retrieved April 19, 2006, from http://www.spiked-online.com/index.php/site/article/281/.

Patoski, J. N. (1989, October). Animal fights. *Texas Monthly*, pp. 102–104.

Pluta, R. (1992, February 28). University suspects animal rights activists in fire. *United Press International*.

Powers, W. (2006, December 9). The secret warriors. *National Journal*.

Price, J. (1990, March 1). Crimes by animal activists prompt call for federal law. *Washington Times*, p. A5.

Researchers and Farmers Freedom From Terrorism Act of 2000, H.R. 5429, 106th Cong., 2d Sess. (2000).

Ruskin, L. (2001, September 12). Stevens, Murkowski and Young vow retribution. *Anchorage Daily News*, p. A9.

S.C. Code Ann. §47-21-10, et seq.

S.D. Code §40-38, et seq.

Sabin, A. J. (1993). *Red Scare in court: New York versus the International Workers Order.* Philadelphia: University of Pennsylvania Press.

Schmickle, S. (1992, November 10). Firebombing is investigated as act of terrorism. *Minneapolis Star Tribune*, p. B1.

Smurthwaite, D. (1988, July 17). With moral certainty. *Northwest Magazine*, p. 5.

Stone, G. R. (2004). *Perilous times: Free speech in wartime from the Sedition Act of 1798 to the war on terrorism* (1st ed.). New York: W. W. Norton & Co.

Stop Terrorism of Property Act of 2003, H.R. 3307, 108th Cong., 1st Sess. (2003).

Swan, J. A. (2003, October 17). Time to terminate ecoterrorism. *National Review*. Retrieved October 20, 2003, from http://www.nationalreview.com/swan/swanstory200310170957. asp.

Tenn. Code Ann. §39-14-801, et seq.

Terrorism Against Animal-Use Entities Prohibition Improvement Act, H.R. 4883, 108th Cong., 2d Sess. (2004).

The Animal Enterprise Terrorism Act: Hearing before the Subcommittee on Crime, Terrorism, and Homeland Security, of the Committee on the Judiciary, House of Representatives (Serial No. 109-125), 109th Cong., 2nd Sess. (2006).

U.S. Sportsmen's Alliance (2003, February 14). Legislators' association gives nod to model terrorism bill.

United Press International (1989, April 3). Protesters say they set fires.

Utah Code Ann. §76-6-110, et seq.

Va. Code Ann. §18.2-403.4, 18.2-421, 18.2-499.

Violent and Repeat Juvenile Offender Accountability and Rehabilitation Act of 1999, H.R. 1501, 106th Cong., 1st Sess. (1999).

W. Va. St. §19-19-6.

Walsh, E. J. (2000, February). The Animal Enterprise Protection Act: A scientist's perspective. *Lab Animal*, 29(2), 24-29.

Warchol, G. (2007, February 12). Corporate group sets new lobbying standard. *Salt Lake Tribune*.

Wash. Rev. Code. §§4.23.580, 4.24.570, 4.24.575, 9.08.080.

Watson, P. (1994). *Ocean warrior: My battle to end the illegal slaughter on the high seas.* St. Leonards, NSW, Australia: Allen & Unwin.

Watson, P., Rogers, W., & Newman, J. (1982). *Sea Shepherd: My fight for whales and seals.* New York: Norton.

Western Wildlife Unit of the Animal Liberation Front (2006). *Memories of Freedom.* Wis.St.895.57, 943.75.

Wolf, N. (2007, October 14). Talk by Naomi Wolf. Retrieved July 1, 2010, from http://www.youtube.com/watch?v=RjALf12PAWc.

Chapter 7

Anonymous (2006, September 20). *Bite Back Magazine.* Retrieved June 18, 2007, from http://www.directaction.info./news_sep20_06.htm.

Capralogics (n.d.). FAQ. http://www.capralogics.com/faq.htm.

Conn, P. M. & Parker, J. V. (2008). *The animal research war.* New York: Palgrave Macmillan.

Eckelbecker, L. (2006, October 1). Rules of engagement: Activists upping ante in bid to disrupt animal-based research. *Worcester Telegram & Gazette.* Retrieved September 20, 2009, from http://www.telegraph.com.

Goodman, A. (2006, October 3). First member of SHAC 7 heads to jail for three year sentence. *Democracy Now.* Retrieved October 4, 2006, from http://www.democracynow.org/article.pl?sid=06/10/03/142235.

Harper, J. (2004, Summer). Seven HLS campaign volunteers arrested by FBI, charged with terrorism. *No Compromise.*

Heffernan, N. (1985, June 4). Panel stiffens law on lab animal thefts. *Los Angeles Times,* p. 3.

Lahickey, B. (1998). *All ages: Reflections on straight edge.* Revelation Books.

Maag, C. (2006, January-February). America's #1 threat. *Mother Jones,* p. 19.

Morley, H. R. (2006, May 5). 'Terrorist' ad sparks mystery on Street. *Knight-Ridder Tribune Business News.*

Munro, L. (2005). Strategies, action repertoires and DIY activism in the animal rights movement. *Social Movement Studies,* 4(1), 75-94.

National Association for Biomedical Research (n.d.). NABR ad. Retrieved August 13, 2009, from http://www.nabr.org/Portals/8/NABR_new_Final_ad.pdf.

Parry, W. (2006, September 19). Activist: Prison terms could drive others to stealthy violence. Associated Press.

People for the Ethical Treatment of Animals (1985, April 20). 260 animals including a primate was rescued by ALF. [Press release]. Retrieved May 1, 2010, from http://w3.nexis.com

People for the Ethical Treatment of Animals (1986). *Britches* [film].

Rapattoni, L. (1985, April 20). United Press International.

Siegel, L. (1985, April 25). NIH director denounces lab animals thefts as acts of terrorism. Associated Press.

Support Jake (n.d.). Retrieved May 1, 2010, from http://www.myspace.com/veganjedi.

The problem of conspiracy (1971, February 15). *Time.* Retrieved July 1, 2010, from http://www.time.com/time/magazine/article/0,9171,904723,00.html.

Trial (1999). Reflections. On *Are these our lives?* [CD]. Albany: Equal Vision Records.

United States Attorney's Office, District of New Jersey (2006, March 2). Militant animal rights group, six members convicted in campaign to terrorize company, employees and others. Retrieved March 2, 2006, from http://www.justice.gov/usao/nj/press/files/shac0302_r.htm.

United States Attorney's Office, District of New Jersey (2006, September 12). Three militant animal rights activists sentenced to between four and six years in prison. Retrieved September 12, 2006, from http://www.usdoj.gov/usao/nj/press/files/pdffiles/shac0912rel.pdf.

United States Sentencing Commission (2006). *Sourcebook of federal sentencing statistics.*

Whitman, J. (2006, April 29). Mystery surrounding ad that slams the Big Board. *New York Post,* p. 21.

Chapter 8

About Dennis (n.d.). Retrieved April 1, 2009, from http://kucinich.house.gov/Biography/.

Albainy-Jenei, S. (2007, May 10). Security tight at BIO 2007. *BIO Voice.* http://biovoice. blogspot.com/2007/05/security-tight-at-bio2007.html.

Animal Agriculture Alliance (2007, March 12). Leading prosecutor to keynote stakeholders summit. Retrieved April 13, 2008, from http://www.animalagalliance.org/.

Animal Agriculture Alliance (2007, March 21). AETA sends a clear signal says leading prosecutor. Retrieved April 13, 2008, from http://www.animalagalliance.org/.

Animal Enterprise Protection Coalition (n.d.). Animal Enterprise Terrorism Act talking points. Retrieved September 30, 2006, from https://secure5.webfirst.com/nabr.org/ members/AEPC/.

Animal Enterprise Protection Coalition (n.d.). Coalition members. Retrieved September 30, 2006, from https://secure5.webfirst.com/nabr.org/members/AEPC/.

Animal Enterprise Protection Coalition (n.d.). House scorecard. Retrieved September 30, 2006, from https://secure5.webfirst.com/nabr.org/members/AEPC/.

Animal Enterprise Protection Coalition (n.d.). Introduction. Retrieved September 30, 2006, from https://secure5.webfirst.com/nabr.org/members/AEPC/.

Animal Enterprise Protection Coalition (n.d.). Sample letters to Congress. Retrieved September 30, 2006, from https://secure5.webfirst.com/nabr.org/members/AEPC/.

Animal Enterprise Protection Coalition (n.d.). Sample news release. Retrieved September 30, 2006, from https://secure5.webfirst.com/nabr.org/members/AEPC/.

Animal Enterprise Protection Coalition (n.d.). Senate scorecard. Retrieved September 30, 2006, from https://secure5.webfirst.com/nabr.org/members/AEPC/.

Animal Enterprise Protection Act, Pub. L. No. 102-346 (1992).

Anonymous (2006, December 17). *Bite Back Magazine.* Retrieved July 15, 2009, from http://www.directaction.info/news_dec17_06.htm.

Anonymous (2006, December 18). *Bite Back Magazine.* Retrieved July 15, 2009, from http://www.directaction.info/news_dec18_06.htm.

Anonymous (2006, December 20). *Bite Back Magazine.* Retrieved July 15, 2009, from http://www.directaction.info/news_dec20_06.htm.

Anonymous (2006, December 7). Durban, South Africa: Action in solidarity with greenscare indictees. *Portland Independent Media Center.* Retrieved December 10, 2006, from http://portland.indymedia.org.

Anonymous (2006, November 29). *Bite Back Magazine.* Retrieved July 15, 2009, from http://www.directaction.info/news_nov29_06.htm.

Anonymous (2006, November 4). *Bite Back Magazine.* Retrieved July 15, 2009, from http://www.directaction.info/news_nov04_06.htm.

Anonymous (2006, September 20). *Bite Back Magazine.* Retrieved July 15, 2009, from http://www.directaction.info./news_sep20_06.htm.

Barson, M. (1992). *"Better dead than red!": A nostalgic look at the golden years of Russiaphobia, red-baiting, and other commie madness.* New York: Hyperion.

Bite Back Magazine (2004). *2004 Direct Action Report.* Retrieved 2005, April 1, from http://www.directaction.info.

Blankstein, A. & Krikorian, G. (2008, February 6). Terror unit probes fire at home: An incendiary device ignites at the house of UCLA researcher who does animal research. *Los Angeles Times*, p. B4.

Branigin, W. (2006, November 8). Democrats take majority in house; Pelosi poised to become speaker; Senate still up for grabs. *Washington Post*. Retrieved March 22, 2007, from http://www.washingtonpost.com.

Brenneman, K. (2006, April 5). Fur store owner wants PDX police protection. *KGW-TV*. Retrieved April 6, 2006, from http://www.kgw.com.

Bush remarks on "mission accomplished" banner embarrass White House (2003, October 30). Agence France Press.

Castle, Rep. (2006, November 13). Speaking on Route 1 bridge. *Congressional Record*, p. H8589.

Citizen's Commission on Civil Rights (2007). The erosion of rights: Declining civil rights enforcement under the Bush administration. Retrieved April 13, 2007, from http://www.cccr.org/publications/index.cfm.

Denson, B. (2008, January 26). Furrier ordered to pay protesters' legal fees. *Oregonian*, p. A1.

Dorey, E. (2005, February 7). Tough new UK animal rights laws. *Chemistry and Industry*, p. 4.

Epstein, D. (2006, August 22). Throwing in the towel. *Inside Higher Ed*. Retrieved August 23, 2006, from http://www.insidehighered.com/news/2006/08/22/animal.

Extremists attacks on global food chain increase (2009, February 25). *Drovers*. Retrieved March 1, 2009, from http://www.drovers.com/printFriendly.asp?ed_id=5270.

Foxx, Rep. (2006, November 15). Speaking on baseball. *Congressional Record*, p. H8651.

Fredrickson, C. & Graves, L. (2006, March 6). Animal Enterprise Terrorism Act, S. 1926 and H.R. 4239. Retrieved October 30, 2006, from http://www.aclu.org/free-speech/aclu-letter-congress-urging-opposition-animal-enterprise-act-s-1926-and-hr-4239.

Fredrickson, C. & Johnson, M. (2006, October 30). ACLU urges needed minor changes to AETA, but does not oppose bill. Retrieved October 30, 2006, from http://www.aclu.org/images/general/asset_upload_file809_27356.pdf.

Fur Commission USA (2006, November 14). Mission accomplished! AETA passes both houses! http://furcommission.com/.

Gckas, Rep. (1993, September 15). Extension of remarks on Animal Enterprise Protection Act. *Congressional Record*, p. E2175.

Gill, J. (2008, April 24). US animal rights attacks on rise. *Times Higher Education*. Retrieved May 1, 2009, from http://www.timeshighereducation.co.uk.

Heuser, S. (2007, May 9). Taking no chances. *Boston Globe*. Retrieved May 9, 2007, from http://www.bostonglobe.com.

Jackson Lee, Rep. (2006, November 13). Speaking on soccer. *Congressional Record*, p. H8582.

Keim, B. (2007, May 16). Animal rights, civil liberties and human suffering: Q&A with Frankie Trull. *Wired*. Retrieved May 16, 2007, from http://blog.wired.com/wiredscience/2007/05/animal_rights_c.html.

Keim, B. (2007, May 8). What do we have to fear from animal rights extremists? *Wired*. Retrieved May 8, 2007, from http://blog.wired.com/wiredscience/2007/05/what_do_we_have.html.

King, M. L. Jr. (1967, April 4). Beyond Vietnam. *The Martin Luther King Jr. Research and Education Institute*. Retrieved April 1, 2007, from http://mlk-kpp01.stanford.edu/.

Kock, W. (2006, November 13). Memorial groundbreaking honors MLK's legacy. *USA Today*.

Kucinich, Rep. (2006, November 13). Speaking on Animal Enterprise Terrorism Act. *Congressional Record*, p. H8594.

Millar, M. (2006, July 27). Animal rights attacks on pharmaceutical staff in sharp decline. *Personnel Today*. Retrieved April 1, 2007, from http://www.personneltoday.com/articles/2006/07/27/36624/animal-rights-attacks-on-pharmaceutical-staff-in-sharp.html.

Miller, G. (2007, December 21). Animal extremists get personal. *Science*, pp. 1856-1858.

Mitchell, S. (2007, May 7). Extremists may target biotech. *UPI*.

MLK Memorial Foundation (n.d.). Quick facts about the memorial. Retrieved April 12, 2007, from http://www.mlkmemorial.org.

Monastersky, R. (2008, February 6). UCLA professor's house is firebombed. *Chronicle of Higher Education*. Retrieved February 8, 2008, from http://chronicle.com/article/UCLA-Professor-s-House-Is/40396.

N.A.A.C.P. decries stand of Dr. King on Vietnam (1967, April 11). *New York Times*, p. 1.

National Association for Biomedical Research (n.d.). Advertisement: Your home is next. Retrieved November 20, 2006, from http://www.nabr.org/Portals/8/NABR_new_Final_ad.pdf.

National Lawyers Guild opposes Animal Enterprise Terrorism Act (2006, October 30). Retrieved November 1, 2006, from http://www.nlg.org/news/statements/AETA_Act.htm.

North American Animal Liberation Press Office (2006, December 20). Activists shrug off new Animal Enterprise Terrorism Act. Retrieved July 15, 2009, from http://www.animalliberationpressoffice.org/press_releases/2006/pr_06_12_20_aeta.htm.

North American Animal Liberation Press Office (2006, September 19). 23 rabbits liberated from Massachusetts laboratory: Action claimed in solidarity with recently sentenced activists in anti-HLS campaign. Retrieved August 19, 2009, from http://www.animalliberationpressoffice.org/press_releases/2006/pr_06_09_19_capralogics.htm.

North American Animal Liberation Press Office (2008, February 6). UCLA vivisector gets return visit from animal liberationists. Retrieved August 19, 2009, from http://www.animalliberationpressoffice.org/press_releases/pr_08_02_06_londonburns.htm.

North American Animal Liberation Press Office (2008, October 6). Animal liberationists mock California law AB 2296. Retrieved August 19, 2009, from http://www.animalliberationpressoffice.org/.

North American Animal Liberation Press Office (2008, October 9). New California law leads to increased underground actions. Retrieved October 10, 2008, from http://www.animalliberationpressoffice.org.

North American Animal Liberation Press Office (2009). 2008 year-end report on animal liberation activities in North America. Retrieved July 15, 2009, from http://www.animalliberationpressoffice.org.

Norwood, Rep. (2006, December 5). Speaking on baseball. *Congressional Record*, p. E2073.

Osborne, J. (2009, June 3). Animal rights terrorism on the rise in U.S. *Fox News*. Retrieved March 15, 2009, from http://www.foxnews.com/story/0,2933,525039,00.html.

Paddock, R. C. & LaGanga, M. L. (2008, August 5). Officials decry attacks on UC staff. *Los Angeles Times*, p. B1.

Patton, V. (2006, November 29). Fur store owner: Terror charges for activists. *KGW-TV*. Retrieved December 1, 2006, from http://www.kgw.com.

Pershing, B. (2008, June 11). Kucinich forces votes on Bush's impeachment. *Washington Post*, p. A2.

Phillips, P. (2007). *Censored 2008: The Top 25 Censored Stories of 2006–07*. Seven Stories Press.

Potter, W. (2006, November 13). House passes Animal Enterprise Terrorism Act with little discussion or debate: Notes from the House floor. *Green Is the New Red*. Retrieved August 13, 2009, from http://www.greenisthenewred.com/blog/aeta-passes-house-recap/142/.

Prince, S. & Heinz, S. (2006, November 30). Activist looks beyond fur shop's move. *Oregonian*, p. B2.

Quotes from leaders of the animal rights movement (n.d.). *National Animal Interest Alliance*. Retrieved March 1, 2008, from http://www.naiaonline.org/articles/archives/animalrightsquote.htm.

Richardson, V. (2007, June 1). Ecoterror waning despite SUV bombings: Specialist says heyday has ended, credits better law enforcement. *Washington Times*, p. A6.

Rose, J. (2008, June 7). Animal-rights group turns attention to Nicholas Ungar Furs in Portland. *Oregonian*. Retrieved May 1, 2010, from http://www.oregonlive.com/news/oregonian/index.ssf?/base/news/121280912130720.xml&coll=7.

Rybicki, E. (2006, December 8). Suspension of the rules in the House: Principal features. *Congressional Research Service*.

Schneider, J. (2003, May 12). House and Senate rules of procedure: A comparison. *Report for Congress (Order Code RL30945)*.

Schrecker, E. (1998). *Many are the crimes: McCarthyism in America*. Boston: Little, Brown.

Schrecker, E. (2002). *The age of McCarthyism: A brief history with documents*. New York: Palgrave.

Scorecard for 111th Congress: U.S. House (n.d.). *American Civil Liberties Union*. Retrieved March 20, 2009, from http://action.aclu.org/site/VoteCenter?page=congScorecard.

Sending a clear signal to animal activists (2007, March 29). *Dairy Herd Management*. Retrieved April 14, 2007, from http://www.dairyherd.com.

Sensenbrenner speaks with Jay Weber on climategate (2009, December 7). Retrieved December 10, 2009, from http://sensenbrenner.house.gov/News/DocumentSingle.aspx?DocumentID=159311.

Sensenbrenner to tell Copenhagen: No climate laws until 'scientific fascism' ends (2009, December 9). *Fox News*. Retrieved December 10, 2009, from http://www.foxnews.com/politics/2009/12/09/sensenbrenner-climate-fascism/.

Sensenbrenner, Rep. (2006, November 13). Speaking on Animal Enterprise Terrorism Act. *Congressional Record*, p. H8594.

Smith, K. L. & Zepp, I. G. (1998). *Search for the beloved community: The thinking of Martin Luther King, Jr.* Valley Forge, Pa.: Judson Press.

Sutner, S. (2006, November 30). Animal protesters get results: McGovern pledges to help overturn animal terrorism law. *Telegram & Gazette*, p. B4.

Tady, M. (2006, November 13). New 'terrorism' laws to protect animal abusers' profits. *New Standard*. Retrieved November 14, 2006, from http://newstandardnews.net/content/index.cfm/items/3883.

Terrorism statistics flawed (2006, April 12). *Center for Defense Information*. Retrieved April 17, 2008, from http://www.cdi.org.

Thousands attend groundbreaking for MLK memorial (2006, November 13). *PBS Newshour*. Retrieved November 14, 2006, from http://www.pbs.org/newshour/bb/social_issues/july-dec06/mlk_11-13.html.

Top 100 contributors Congressman F. James Sensenbrenner Jr. 2005–2006 (n.d.). *Center for Responsive Politics*. Retrieved March 20, 2009, from http://www.opensecrets.org/.

Trounson, R. & Mozingo, J. (2006, August 26). UCLA to protect animal research: The acting chancellor says the university will defend against 'domestic terrorism' directed at faculty engaged in scientific studies. *Los Angeles Times*, p. A1.

U.S. judge refuses to restrict protesters at Portland fur shop (2007, May 23). *Oregonian*. Retrieved May 25, 2007, from http://www.oregonlive.com.

Walker, S. (1999). *In defense of American liberties: A history of the ACLU*. Carbondale: Southern Illinois University Press.

Chapter 9

Acts of Terrorism Transcending National Boundaries, Pub. L. No. 110-326, 122 Stat. 3560 (2006).

Abraham, K. (2006, November 22). Flames of dissent: Part 3, eco-anarchy imploding. *Eugene Weekly*, p. 12.

Affidavit for Search Warrants by John L. Ferreira, Special Agent, Federal Bureau of Investigation (2005, December).

Barnard, J. (2007, June 5). McGowan sentenced to seven years for ecoterrorism fires. *Associated Press*.

Barnard, J. (2007, May 15). Federal prosecutors compare ELF arsonists to KKK. *Associated Press*.

Barnard, J. (2007, May 24). Earth Liberation Front arsonist sentenced to 13 years. *Associated Press*.

Barnard, J. (2007, May 27). Animal Liberation Front arsonist sentenced to 12 years. *Associated Press*.

Bishop, B. (2007, June 2). Pair to do federal time for arsons. *Register-Guard*, Eugene, OR. Retrieved September 11, 2007, from http://www.registerguard.com.

Bishop, B. (2007, May 24). Arson attacks ruled terrorism: A judge sentences an environmental activist to 13 years for a string of crimes, but gives him credit for cooperating. *Register-Guard*, p. A1.

Bishop, B. (2007, May 26). Third arsonist sentenced to 9 years. *Register-Guard*, p. A1.

Block, N. & Zacher, J. (2007, July 11). First epistle: Phoenix from the flames. Retrieved July 15, 2007, from http://www.ecoprisoners.org/nathanjoyanna.htm.

Carter, D. (2006, August 14). New federal courthouse in downtown Eugene, Oregon, is a courthouse. *Daily Journal of Commerce*.

Defendant Kevin Tubbs' Memorandum on the Application of U.S.S.G. 3A1.4, United States v. Tubbs, No. CR 06-60070-AA (2007, May 4).

Defendant's Memorandum of Law in Opposition to Application of the Terrorism Enhancement, United States v. Meyerhoff, No. CR 06-60078-AA (2007, May 4).

Eco-terrorism and lawlessness on the national forests: Hearing before the Subcommittee on Forests and Forest Health of the Committee on Resources, United States House of Representatives (Serial No. 107-83), 107th Cong., 2nd Sess. (2002).

Eggen, D. (2007, September 27). Patriot Act provisions voided. *Washington Post*, p. A2.

Fattig, P. (2007, August 2). Eco-arson sends Paul to prison for 4 years. *Mail Tribune*. Retrieved August 3, 2007, from http://www.mailtribune.com/apps/pbcs.dll/article?AID=/20070802/NEWS/708020325.

Fattig, P. (2007, June 6). 'Good intentions gone bad'. *Mail Tribune*. Retrieved August 3,

2007, from http://www.mailtribune.com/apps/pbcs.dll/article?AID=/20070606/NEWS/706060308.

Federal Domestic Terrorism Sentencing Enhancement, U.S.S.G. §3A1.4, 186 A.L.R Fed. 147 (2003).

Gjelten, T. (2009, December 14). Pentagon, CIA eye new threat: Climate change. *National Public Radio's Morning Edition*. Retrieved December 15, 2009, from http://www.npr.org.

Government's Sentencing Memorandum, United States v. Thurston, No. CR 06-60069-AA (2007, May 4).

Grigoriadis, V. (2006, August 10). The rise and fall of the eco-radical underground. *Rolling Stone*, pp. 73-107.

Harris, S. (2007, July 13). The terrorism enhancement: An obscure law stretches the definition of terrorism, and metes out severe punishments. *National Journal*, pp. 34-40.

Hoffman, H. (2002, June 10). Green Scare: Activists targeted as 'terrorists'. *In These Times*, p. 3.

Kristof, N. (2007, August 16). The big melt. *New York Times*, p. 21.

McCall, W. (2007, May 23). Federal prosecutor: Oregon man was a leader of radical cell. *Associated Press*.

Memorandum in Opposition to Application of the Terrorism Enhancement, United States v. McGowan, No. CR 06-60124-AA (2007, May 4).

Memorandum of Law Opposing Imposition of Terrorism Enhancement, United States v. Gerlach, No. CR 06-60079-AA (2007, May 4).

Memorandum on Terrorism Enhancement, United States v. Zacher and Block, No. CR 06-60124-AA (2007, April 26).

Memorandum Opinion, United States v. Thurston, No. CR 06-60069-AA (2007, May 21).

Memorandum Opposing Application of the Terrorism Enhancement, United States v. Thurston, No. CR 06-60069-AA (2007, May 4).

Meyerhoff statement (2007, May 23). *Register-Guard*. Retrieved May 25, 2007, from http://www.registerguard.com/rgn/index.php/rgup/meyerhoff_statement/.

Oko, D. (2002, February 8). Ecoterrorists under fire. *Mother Jones*. Retrieved February 5, 2010, from http://motherjones.com/politics/2002/02/ecoterrororists-under-fire.

Patton, V. (2006, November 29). Fur store owner: Terror charges for activists. *KGW-TV*. Retrieved December 1, 2006, from http://www.kgw.com.

Paul, C. (2007, May 24). My brother, the 'terrorist'. *Los Angeles Times*, p. A25.

Peeples, M. (2003, September 13). 16th street Baptist church bombing: Forty years later, Birmingham still struggles with violent past. *National Public Radio's All Things Considered*. Retrieved March 1, 2005, from http://www.npr.org/templates/story/story.php?storyId=1431932.

Rampton, S. Fools rush in: The militia movement and Klamath Falls. *PR Watch*. Retrieved September 30, 2009, from http://www.prwatch.org/prwissues/2003Q2/fools.html.

Roselle, M. & Mahan, J. (2009). *Tree spiker: From Earth First! to lowbagging: My struggles in radical environmental action*. New York: St. Martin's Press.

Schuster, H. (2005, August 24). Domestic terror: Who's most dangerous? Eco-terrorists are now above ultra-right extremists on the FBI charts. *CNN*. Retrieved March 10, 2010, from http://www.cnn.com/2005/US/08/24/schuster.column/index.html.

Southern Poverty Law Center (2001, Winter). Conflict in Klamath. *Intelligence Report, 104*.

Southern Poverty Law Center (2007, Spring). Patriot groups active in the year 2006. *Intelligence Report, 125*.

Sowell, J. (2004, August 27). Convicted firefighter loses appeal in Tiller forest arson case. *News-Review*. Retrieved May 1, 2005, from http://www.nrtoday.com/article/20040827/NEWS/108270018&SearchID=7321977519589.

Supplemental Memorandum Regarding Application of Terrorism Guideline, United States v. Paul, No. CR 06-60125-AA (2007, May 11).

Tolme, P. (2001, November 26). Terrorizing the environmental movement. *Salon*. Retrieved April 1, 2006, from http://www.salon.com/politics/feature/2001/11/26/ecoterror/print.html.

Top Ten Green Projects (2007, April 23). Retrieved January 1, 2008, from http://www.aiatopten.org/hpb/overview.cfm?ProjectID=776.

Townsend, M. & Harris, P. (2004, February 22). Now the Pentagon tells Bush: Climate change will destroy us. *Guardian*. Retrieved July 1, 2009, from http://www.guardian.co.uk.

Tullis, T. (2008, March 27). Is Briana Waters a terrorist? *Salon*. Retrieved April 1, 2008, from http://www.salon.com/news/feature/2008/03/27/briana_waters.

United States Department of Justice (2006, January 20). Eleven defendants indicted on domestic terrorism charges. Retrieved September 8, 2007, from http://www.usdoj.gov/opa/pr/2006/January/06_crm_030.html.

Wright, J. (2007, May 30). Arson defendant spared 'terrorist' label. *Register-Guard*, p. F1.

Chapter 10

Aref, et al. v. Holder, et al., D.C.

Ayres Jr., B. D. (1988, June 8). Prisoner charges poor conditions are U.S. 'psychiatric experiment'. *New York Times*, p. A18.

Baldwin, B. (2008, January 31). Former eco-terrorist organized environmental film festival. *Style Weekly*. Retrieved July 1, 2010, from http://styleweekly.com.

Bales, W. D. & Mears, D. P. (2008). Inmate social ties and the transition to society: Does visitation reduce recidivism? *Journal of Research in Crime and Delinquency*, 45(3), 287.

Benkahla v. Federal Bureau of Prisons, et al., 2:09-cv-00025-WTL-DML (S.D. Indiana 2009).

Churchill, W. & Vander, W., Jim (1992). *Cages of steel: The politics of imprisonment in the United States*. Washington, D.C.: Maisonneuve Press.

Churchill, W. & Vander, W., Jim (2002). *The COINTELPRO papers: Documents from the FBI's secret wars against dissent in the United States* (2nd ed.). Cambridge, MA: South End Press.

Commerce, Justice, Science, and related agencies appropriations for 2009: Hearing before a subcommittee of the Committee on Appropriations, United States House of Representatives (Serial No. 42-792), 110th Cong., 2nd Sess. (2008).

"Communication Management Units" Federal Register 75:65 (6 April 2010) p. 17324.

Conley, J. K. (2008, March 5). Memorandum for all regional directors: Referrals for the Communications Management Units.

Department of Justice Office of the Inspector General. (2003, December). The Federal Bureau of Investigation's efforts to improve the sharing of intelligence and other information. *Audit Report 04-10*.

Department of Justice Office of the Inspector General. (2006, September). The Federal Bureau of Prisons' monitoring of mail for high-risk inmates. *Report Number I-2006-009*.

Dhafir, R. (2007, February 7). A letter from Dr. Dhafir about his transfer and new prison situation. Retrieved March 1, 2009, from http://www.dhafirtrial.net/2007/02/07/a-letter-from-dr-dhafir-about-his-transfer-and-new-prison-situation/.

Eggen, D. (2007, February 27). Facility holding terrorism inmates limits communication. *Washington Post*, p. A7.

Eisler, P. (2009, March 11). Terrorist watch list hits 1 million. *USA Today*, p. A1.

Exhibit F, Comments of Civil Liberties Groups. Federal Register 71:63 (3 April 2006) p. 16520.

Federal Bureau of Prisons (1999, January 29). Program statement on non-discrimination toward inmates. Retrieved May 1, 2010, from http://www.bop.gov/policy/progstat/1040_004.pdf.

Federal Bureau of Prisons (2006, November 30). *Institution Supplement, THX-5270.07A*.

Federal Bureau of Prisons (2007, July 3). *Institution Supplement, THX-5267.08B*.

Federal Bureau of Prisons (2008, March 20). *Institution Supplement, MAR-5270.07A*.

Federal Bureau of Prisons (2008, March 5). *Institution Supplement, FLM 5267.08A*.

Federal Bureau of Prisons (2008, November 13). *Institution Supplement, MAR-5321.07A*.

Federal Bureau of Prisons (2008, September 3). Notice to inmate of transfer to Communications Management Unit; Register number: 63794-053.

Federal Bureau of Prisons (n.d.). Federal prison facility locator. Retrieved May 1, 2010, from http://www.bop.gov/DataSource/execute/dsFacilityLoc.

Gonzales, L. (1989). *The still point*. Fayetteville: University of Arkansas Press.

Hughes, K. (2007, May-June). Dr. Rafil A. Dhafir at Terre Haute Prison's new Communications Management Unit. *Washington Report on Middle East Affairs*, pp. 12–13.

Johnson, C. (2009, March 18). Prison officials are loosening restrictions on Taliban supporter. *Washington Post*, p. A6.

Katz, B. (2010, March 30). Locked up with militants, freed American talks. *Reuters*.

Katz, B. (2010, March 30). Special U.S. prisons unconstitutional: lawsuit. *Reuters*.

Kogan, R. (1990, June 26). Cruel punishment: A rough, raw look at 3 women in prison. *Chicago Tribune*, p. 5.

Korn, R. (1988). Follow-up report on the effects of confinement in the High Security Unit at Lexington. *Social Justice*, 15(1), 20-29.

Lassiter, C. (1990, September-October). Robo prison. *Mother Jones*, p. 54.

"Limited Communication for Terrorist Inmates." Federal Register 71:63 (3 April 2006) p. 16520.

Luers, J. (2006, September 15). Dispatches. Retrieved July 1, 2010, from http://www.freefreenow.org/jw_dispatches.html.

McGowan, D. (2009, June 8). Tales from inside the U.S. Gitmo. *Huffington Post*. Retrieved July 1, 2010, from http://www.huffingtonpost.com.

Miller, J. G. (1996). *Search and destroy: African-American males in the criminal justice system*. New York: Cambridge University Press.

Mortensen, C. (2008, December 4). Terrorist prison. *Eugene Weekly*. Retrieved May 1, 2010, from http://www.eugeneweekly.com/2008/12/04/news1.html.

Myers, L. (2005, March 1). Imprisoned terrorists still advocating terror. *MSNBC*. Retrieved July 1, 2010, from http://www.msnbc.com.

O'Connor, S. (2007, April 5). Chains of love. *Good*. Retrieved 2010, March 1, from http://www.good.is.

Pizarro, J. & Stenius, V. M. K. (2004). Supermax prisons: Their rise, current practices, and effect on inmates. *The Prison Journal*, 84(2), 248.

Reeves, J. (2007, May 15). Extremist taunts his victims from prison. *Associated Press.*

Rosenblatt, E. (1996). *Criminal injustice: Confronting the prison crisis.* Boston, MA: South End Press.

Rosenblum, N. (1990). POV: *Through the Wire* [film]. PBS.

Rudolph, E. (2008, April 23). Supermax prison issues. *Army of God.* Retrieved July 1, 2010, from http://www.armyofgod.com/EricRudolphSuperMaxPrisonIssues.html.

Stepanian, A. (2010, May 11). Isolated in federal communication management units, silenced voices need ours. *Huffington Post.* Retrieved July 1, 2010, from http://www.huffington-post.com.

Terrorist recruitment and infiltration in the United States: Hearing before the Subcommittee on Terrorism, Technology, and Homeland Security of the Committee on the Judiciary, United States Senate 108th Cong., 1st Sess. (2003).

Theoharis, J. (2009, April 2). Guantanamo at home. *Nation.* Retrieved April 5, 2009, from http://www.thenation.com/doc/20090420/theoharis.

Van Bergen, J. (2007, February 16). Documents show new secretive US prison program isolating Muslim, Middle Eastern prisoners. *Raw Story.* Retrieved February 17, 2008, from http://www.rawstory.com/news/2007/Documents_show_new_secretive_new_US_0216.html.

Chapter 11

American Medical Association (1989, June). Animal research action plan.

An act of distinction [editorial] (2010, July 22). *Nature,* 466.

Anonymous. (2008, October 21). *Bite Back Magazine.* Retrieved July 15, 2009, from http://directaction.info/news_oct21c_08.htm.

Are vegetarian diets worse than terrorists? (n.d.). *Bible Life.* Retrieved September 14, 2008, from http://www.biblelife.org/animal_rights.htm.

Ballou, B. R. & Mishra, R. (2006, October 7). Pet store manager charged with willful burning of shop. *Boston Globe,* p. B2.

Beal, T. (2005, December 13). 2 animal activists convicted of disrupting mountain lion hunt in Sabino Canyon. *Arizona Daily Star.* Retrieved December 15, 2005, from http://www.azstarnet.com/sn/hourlyupdate/106800.php.

Berman, P. T. & O'Hara-Forster, B. (1989, August 28). Road to war: Every time a Hitler threat ended in compromise, Hitler won. *Time,* p. 40.

Bernick Jr., B. (2009, February 6). Legislator takes aim at feds and 'eco-terrorists'. *Deseret Morning News.*

Branigin, William & Hsu, Spencer S.). Pilot slams into IRS office in Texas. *Washington Post,* p. A3.

California dam must not be breached (2008, June 8). *Feedstuffs.* Retrieved September 6, 2008, from http://www.feedstuffs.com.

Cole, D. (2003). *Enemy aliens: Double standards and constitutional freedoms in the war on terrorism.* New York: New Press : Distributed by W.W. Norton & Co.

Colson, C. (2007, November 13). Speciesism and rights for animals. *Christian Post.* Retrieved September 14, 2008, from http://www.christianpost.com.

Communist party membership no longer a fireable offence in California (2008, May 16). *Guardian.* Retrieved May 21, 2008, from http://www.guardian.co.uk/world/2008/may/16/usa1.

Copeland, L. (2004, November 15). Domestic terrorism: New trouble at home. *USA Today*, p. A1.

Cote, J. (2008, August 5). Firebombs suggest new tactics for animal activists. *San Francisco Chronicle*, p. B1.

Covil, W. (2009, September 1). Fort Lee training to protect soldiers and families. Retrieved July 1, 2010, from http://www.wtvr.com/wtvr-fort-lee-training-exercise,0,2674495. story.

Coyle, M. (2008, January 28). DOJ upbraided over stalled DNA program. *National Law Journal*.

Criminal Complaint, United States v. Buddenberg, Khajavi, Pope, Stumpo, No. 5 09 70175 (2009, February 19).

Defendant's Motion to Dismiss, United States v. Stumpo, No. CR 09-263 RMW (2009, June 8).

Department of Homeland Security, Universal Adversary Dynamic Threat Assessment (2008, May 7). *Ecoterrorism: Environmental and animal-rights militants in the United States.*

Department of Homeland Security, Office of Grants & Training (2005, December). *Homeland security exercise and evaluation program, Volume V: Prevention exercises.*

Department of Homeland Security, Office of Intelligence and Analysis (2006, April 13). *Preventing attacks by animal rights extremists and eco-terrorists: Fundamentals of corporate security.*

Department of Justice Office of the Inspector General (2006, September). The Federal Bureau of Prisons' monitoring of mail for high-risk inmates. *Report Number I-2006-009.*

Dostoyevsky, F. (1992). *Notes from the underground.* New York: Dover Publications.

Doyle, M. (2009, February 10). FOIA terror. *McClatchy.* Retrieved May 1, 2010, from http://washingtonbureau.typepad.com/law/2009/02/why-are-you-hassling-me.html.

Dramatic anti terrorism drill. (2009, September 16). WITN. Retrieved October 1, 2009, from http://www.witn.com/home/headlines/59564022.html.

Farrell, J. & Martin, J. P. (2010, September 30). Rendell's office releases content of all bulletins on planned protests. *Philadelphia Inquirer.* Retrieved September 30, 2010, from http://www.philly.com.

Federal Bureau of Investigation (2009, February 26). Ohio man sentenced to 20 years for terrorism conspiracy to bomb targets in Europe and the United States. Retrieved February 27, 2009, from http://cincinnati.fbi.gov/doj/pressrel/2009/ci022609.htm.

Federal Bureau of Investigation (2004, April 15). *Tactics used by eco-terrorists to detect and thwart law enforcement operations.* Retrieved March 4, 2009, from http://wikileaks.org.

Food industry must coalesce or lose war (2007, April 2). *Feedstuffs.* Retrieved September 6, 2008, from http://www.feedstuffs.com.

Fox News (2008, March 31). FBI: Eco-terrorism remains no.1 domestic terror threat. *Fox News.* Retrieved March 10, 2010, from http://www.foxnews.com/story/0,2933,343768,00. html.

Fur Commission USA. Hit lists of resource providers and others. Retrieved May 1, 2010, from http://www.furcommission.com/news/newsF05n.htm.

Gehrke, S. (2009, March 5). May trial set for two men accused of releasing mink at South Jordan farm. *Salt Lake Tribune.*

Ghate, O. (2006, February 26). Who will defend industry from eco-terrorism? *Capitalism Magazine.* Retrieved September 21, 2008, from http://www.CapMag.com/article. asp?ID=4584.

Goldstein, B. (2007, November 27). Terrorism: The slide show—a Power Point demonstration by the Department of Homeland Security. *Slate.* Retrieved September 6, 2008, from http://www.slate.com.

Golimowski, J. (2007, July 31). Pro-animal groups push agenda on Capitol Hill. *Cybercast News Service.* Retrieved August 2, 2007, from http://www.cnsnews.com.

Heflin, C. (2008, September 27). Investigators waited four years for break in Washtenaw County ecoterrorism case. *MLive.com.* Retrieved September 30, 2009, from http://www.mlive.com/news/ann-arbor/index.ssf/2008/09/investigators_waited_four_year.html.

Hofstadter, R. (1965). *The paranoid style in American politics, and other essays* (1st ed.). New York: Knopf.

Homeland Infrastructure Threat and Risk Analysis Center (n.d.). Homeland security threat overview [Power Point presentation].

Indictment, United States v. Buddenberg, Khajavi, Pope, Stumpo, No. CR 09-263-RMW (2009, March 12).

Johnson, C. (2010, March 30). 9 members of militia group charged in plot against U.S. *Washington Post,* p. A4.

Kempner, J. (2008). The chilling effect: How do researchers react to controversy. *Public Library of Science Medicine,* 5(11), e222.

Knoll, C. & Bookwalter, G. (2008, August 2). Firebombs target UC researchers. *Contra Costa Times.* Retrieved May 9, 2010, from http://w3.nexis.com.

Kocieniewski, D. (2008, February 13). Usually on attack, U.S. attorney in Newark finds himself on the defensive. *New York Times.* Retrieved April 1, 2010, from http://www.nytimes.com.

Lamont v. Postmaster General, 381 U.S. 301 (1965), *available at* http://www.heartland.org/.

Luce, E. & Ward, A. (2008, June 24). McCain aide hits nerve with terror remark. *Financial Times.* Retrieved July 14, 2008, from http://www.ft.com/cms/s/0/9d80f892-4177-11dd-9661-0000779fd2ac.html?nclick_check=1.

Lustgarten, A. (2010, September 8). Do 'environmental extremists' pose a criminal threat to gas drilling? *Pro Publica.* Retrieved 2010, September 20, from http://www.propublica.org.

Manning, S. (2004, December 6). Eco-terrorism suspected in Md. fires. *Associated Press.*

Marris, E. (2010, July 22). Animal rights 'terror' law challenged. *Nature,* 466.

Martosko, D. (2008, August 12). 'Humane' charities contribute to violence [letter to the editor]. *Las Vegas Review-Journal,* p. B8.

Miller, G. (2009, February 1). CIA retains power to abduct. *Los Angeles Times,* p. A1.

Missouri Information Analysis Center (2009, February 20). *The modern militia movement.* Retrieved March 15, 2009, from http://wikileaks.org.

Moran, G. (2008, March 27). Activist Coronado gets year in prison for arson talk. *San Diego Union-Tribune.* Retrieved 2008, September 6, http://www.signonsandiego.com/news/metro/20080327-1257-bn27rod.html.

Morgan, E. (2010, February 5). Layton man sentenced to 2 years in prison for mink-farm raid. *Deseret Morning News.* Retrieved February 5, 2010, from http://deseretnews.com.

Noakes, J. A. (1998). Bankers and common men in Bedford Falls: How the FBI determined that" It's a Wonderful Life" was a subversive movie. *Film History,* 10(3), 311-319.

North American Animal Liberation Press Office (2008, August 22). 300 captive mink released from South Jordan, Utah fur farm. Retrieved August 23, 2008, from http://www.animalliberationpressoffice.org.

North American Earth Liberation Front Press Office (2008, November 11). Earth Liberation Front press office to new Obama administration: Protect the environment or the ELF will. Retrieved November 12, 2008, from http://www.elfpressoffice.org/naelfpo111108.pdf.

Order Dismissing Indictment Without Prejudice and Denying as Moot Other Pending Motions, United States v. Joseph Buddenburg, Maryam Khajavi, Nathan Pope, Adriana Stumpo, No. CR 09-00263 RMW (2010, July 12).

Overseas Security Advisory Council (2006, November 15). Animal rights extremists: Targets, tactics, business response & countermeasures [Power Point presentation].

Peet, J. (2010, June 12). NJIT homeland security center studies groundbreaking anti-terrorism technology. *NJ.com*. Retrieved July 1, 2010, from http://www.nj.com/news/index.ssf/2010/06/njit_scientists_homeland_secur.html.

Police on high alert over radical protestors (2009, February 5). *WLNS TV 6*. Retrieved February 6, 2009, from http://www.wlns.com/Global/story.asp?S=9793261&nav=menu25_2.

Robin, C. (2004). *Fear: The history of a political idea.* Oxford; New York: Oxford University Press.

Rucker, P. (2010, March 25). Former militiaman unapologetic for calls to vandalize offices over health care. *Washington Post.* Retrieved May 1, 2010, from http://www.washingtonpost.com.

Sanger, D. E. (2009, May 16). Obama after Bush: Leading by second thought. *New York Times*, p. A3.

Sherman, J. & Cogan, M. (2010, March 24). The backlash: Reform turns personal. *Politico.* Retrieved May 1, 2010, from http://www.politico.com.

Shukovsky, P. (2009, January 28). FBI saw mortgage fraud early, agents say they lacked resources to pursue it. *Seattle Post-Intelligencer*, p. A1.

Shukovsky, P., Johnson, T., & Lathrop, D. (2007, April 11). The FBI's terrorism trade-off: Focus on national security after 9/11 means that the agency has turned its back on thousands of white-collar crimes. *Seattle Post-Intelligencer.* Retrieved 2010, January 1, from http://www.seattlepi.com/national/311046_fbiterror11.html.

Smith, W. J. (2009, April 22). Homo Sapiens, get lost. *National Review.*

Snyders, M. (2008, May 21). Moles wanted: In preparation for the Republican National Convention, the FBI is soliciting informants to keep tabs on local protest groups. *City Pages* (Minneapolis/St. Paul). Retrieved May 1, 2010 from http://w3.nexis/com.

Squires, J. & Brown, J. M. (2009, February 21). Four arrested in string of animal rights attacks on UC scientists. *Santa Cruz Sentinel.* Retrieved February 21, 2009, from http://www.santacruzsentinel.com.

Stallman, B. (2007, March). Animal warfare: coming to your state soon. *American Farm Bureau.* Retrieved September 6, 2008, from http://www.fb.org.

Statement of Senator Barack Obama to the U.S. Senate Committee on Environment & Public Works (2005, May 18). Retrieved May 1, 2010, from http://epw.senate.gov/hearing_statements.cfm?id=237833.

SUV Owners of America delivers 'cease and desist' petition to Arianna Huffington zealots (2003, August 27). *PR Newswire.*

Taylor, B. (2008). The Tributaries of Radical Environmentalism. *Journal for the Study of Radicalism*, 2(1), 27-61.

The Humane Society of the United States (2008, August 4). The HSUS offers reward in UC Santa Cruz arsons. Retrieved May 1, 2010, from http://www.hsus.org/press_and_publications/press_releases/hsus_offers_reward_in_ca_arsons_080408.html.

The mink slaughter [editorial] (2007, June 12). *Pittsburgh Tribune Review*. Retrieved June 12, 2007, from http://www.pittsburghlive.com/x/pittsburghtrib/opinion/archive/s_512094.html.

The Ayers connection; Obama erred in associating with the ex-Weatherman. But he's not hanging out with 'terrorists.' [Editorial] (2008, October 7). *Los Angeles Times*, p. A18.

Thompson, B. G. (2005, April 19). 10 years after the Oklahoma City bombing, the Department of Homeland Security must do more to fight right-wing domestic terrorism. *House Committee on Homeland Security*. Retrieved 2010, July 1, from http://www.globalsecurity.org.

Thompson, H. S. (2003). *The kingdom of fear: Loathsome secrets of a star-crossed child in the final days of the American century*. New York: Simon & Schuster.

Trask, D. F. (1969). *World War I at home: Readings on American life, 1914-1920*. New York: Wiley.

Trujillo, H. R. (2005). The radical environmentalist movement. In *Aptitude for destruction volume 2: Case studies of organizational learning in five terrorist groups*. RAND.

Truman, H. S. (1951, April 3). Address at the cornerstone laying of the New York Avenue Presbyterian church. Retrieved May 1, 2009, from http://www.trumanlibrary.org/publicpapers/index.php?pid=280.

United States Department of Justice (2005, December 5). Three Charles County subdivision arson defendants sentenced. Retrieved May 1, 2010, from http://www.justice.gov/usao/md/.

United States Department of Justice (2009, February 2). Final defendant pleads guilty to anti-Obama assaults. Retrieved May 1, 2010, from http://newyork.fbi.gov/dojpressrel/pressrel09/nyfo020209.htm.

Van Putten, M. (2001, November 14). Environmental activism [letter to the editor]. *New York Times*, p. A26.

Walsh, E. J. (2000, February). The Animal Enterprise Protection Act: A scientist's perspective. *Lab Animal*, 29(2), 24-29.

White, E. (2008, October 10). Feds acknowledge Mich. arsonist was key informant. *Associated Press*.

Widdowson, A. (2008, September 14). Urban Shield tests police ability. *The Daily Californian*. Retrieved September 15, 2008, from http://www.dailycal.org.

Wilber, D. Q. (2009, September 3). Museum shooting planned, officials say. *Washington Post*, p. B1.

Wilson, D. C. (2009, September 16). Marines hold training drill for real life situations. Retrieved July 1, 2010, from http://www.jdnews.com/news/real-67694-drill-situations.html.

Wolf, N. (2007). *The end of America: Letter of warning to a young patriot*. White River Junction, Vt.: Chelsea Green.

Zakin, S. (2006, August 10). The caged lion: Environmentalist Rod Coronado returns to prison a decade after his radical heyday. *LA Weekly*. Retrieved April 1, 2008, from http://w3.nexis.com.

ACKNOWLEDGMENTS

It is an honor to become part of the rich history that is City Lights, and to work with an editor as talented as Elaine Katzenberger. To me the people at City Lights represent everything that is good about the craft, and I appreciate how lucky I am to work with Elaine, who has managed to improve these pages without inserting her own voice. Any faults that remain in this work are truly my own.

This could not have been written without the many people who allowed me into their lives during difficult times. I am grateful to those profiled in these pages, and especially to their family members. Tami Drake, Andrea Lindsay, Jenny Synan, and many others inspired me with their loyalty and strength.

It is a rare breed who are not only committed to their own writing, but willing to tirelessly support others. Ed Perlman, Cathy Alter, and David Everett at Johns Hopkins were there every step of the way, and made me aspire to a higher standard. Jessie Duquette, Joe Callahan, Oliver Uberti and Monica Hesse were gracious in their editing, as were Ryan Shapiro and many others with their research. And to Aubrey Edwards, Will Mangum, and Adam Gnade: the beautiful things you create constantly inspire me to work harder.

In some ways, this path would never have been opened without the confidence of Tsoghig Hekimian and Lisa Graves. Meanwhile, the exhaustive and brilliant legal guidance of Lauren Regan, of the Civil Liberties Defense Center, and Matthew Strugar, of the Center for Constitutional Rights, has made me feel guilty for any lawyer jokes I have ever told.

The thought of this book competing with countless others for people's attention is daunting, to say the last. Casey Suchan, Denis Hennelly, and Hal Weiss were generous with their time and talent in creating a beautiful promotional trailer. And I am indebted to Alyson Sinclair of City Lights for her publicity efforts and wisdom.

No matter how solitary a process this book has been, I have always known that waiting outside of my cave are dear friends. The fact that they still speak to me after the last four years is a testament to their character. Justin Goodman, Andy Stepanian, Danielle Thompson and Blair Parsons cannot be thanked enough for always being there. Robert Jensen has truly been a mentor, both personally and politically; I am fortunate to also count him as a friend. And to Ashley Byrne, for your love and partnership, I am without words.

Above all else, I am thankful to my family, who have been relentless and unwavering in their support. Every day I am more appreciative of the power of that gift.

Will Potter is an award-winning independent journalist based in Washington, D.C., who focuses on "eco-terrorism," the environmental and animal rights movements and civil liberties post-9/11. He has written for publications including the *Chicago Tribune*, the *Dallas Morning News* and *Legal Affairs*, and has testified before the U.S. Congress about his reporting. Potter has also worked at the American Civil Liberties Union on policy issues including the Patriot Act. He is the creator of GreenIsTheNewRed.com, where he blogs about the Green Scare.